Kaplan Publishing are constantly finding new ways to support students looking for exam success and our online resources really do add an extra dimension to your studies.

This book comes with free MyKaplan online resources so that you can study anytime, anywhere. **This free online resource is not sold separately and is included in the price of the book.**

Having purchased this book, you have access to the following online study materials:

CONTENT	AAT	
	Text	Kit
Electronic version of the book	✓	✓
Knowledge Check tests with instant answers		✓
Mock assessments online	✓	✓
Material updates	✓	✓

How to access your online resources

Received this book as part of your Kaplan course?
If you have a MyKaplan account, your full online resources will be added automatically, in line with the information in your course confirmation email. If you've not used MyKaplan before, you'll be sent an activation email once your resources are ready.

Bought your book from Kaplan?
We'll automatically add your online resources to your MyKaplan account. If you've not used MyKaplan before, you'll be sent an activation email.

Bought your book from elsewhere?
Go to **www.mykaplan.co.uk/add-online-resources**
Enter the ISBN number found on the title page and back cover of this book.
Add the unique pass key number contained in the scratch panel below.
You may be required to enter additional information during this process to set up or confirm your account details.

This code can only be used once for the registration of this book online. This registration and your online content will expire when the examinations covered by this book have taken place. Please allow one hour from the time you submit your book details for us to process your request.

Please scratch the film to access your unique code.

Please be aware that this code is case-sensitive and you will need to include the dashes within the passcode, but not when entering the ISBN.

AUDIT AND ASSURANCE

STUDY TEXT

Qualifications and Credit Framework

Q2022

This Study Text supports study for the following AAT qualifications:

AAT Level 4 Diploma in Professional Accounting

AAT Diploma in Professional Accounting at SCQF Level 8

AUDIT AND ASSURANCE

KAPLAN PUBLISHING'S STATEMENT OF PRINCIPLES

LINGUISTIC DIVERSITY, EQUALITY AND INCLUSION

We are committed to diversity, equality and inclusion and strive to deliver content that all users can relate to.

We are here to make a difference to the success of every learner.

Clarity, accessibility and ease of use for our learners are key to our approach.

We will use contemporary examples that are rich, engaging and representative of a diverse workplace.

We will include a representative mix of race and gender at the various levels of seniority within the businesses in our examples to support all our learners in aspiring to achieve their potential within their chosen careers.

Roles played by characters in our examples will demonstrate richness and diversity by the use of different names, backgrounds, ethnicity and gender, with a mix of sexuality, relationships and beliefs where these are relevant to the syllabus.

It must always be obvious who is being referred to in each stage of any example so that we do not detract from clarity and ease of use for each of our learners.

We will actively seek feedback from our learners on our approach and keep our policy under continuous review. If you would like to provide any feedback on our linguistic approach, please use this form (you will need to enter the link below into your browser).

https://forms.gle/U8oR3abiPpGRDY158

We will seek to devise simple measures that can be used by independent assessors to randomly check our success in the implementation of our Linguistic Equality, Diversity and Inclusion Policy.

AUDIT AND ASSURANCE

Published by:

Kaplan Publishing UK
Unit 2 The Business Centre
Molly Millar's Lane
Wokingham
Berkshire
RG41 2QZ

ISBN 978-1-83996-882-2

© Kaplan Financial Limited, 2024

The text in this material and any others made available by any Kaplan Group company does not amount to advice on a particular matter and should not be taken as such. No reliance should be placed on the content as the basis for any investment or other decision or in connection with any advice given to third parties. Please consult your appropriate professional adviser as necessary. Kaplan Publishing Limited, all other Kaplan group companies, the International Accounting Standards Board, and the IFRS Foundation expressly disclaim all liability to any person in respect of any losses or other claims, whether direct, indirect, incidental, consequential or otherwise arising in relation to the use of such materials.

Printed and bound in Great Britain.

Acknowledgements

This product contains copyright material and trademarks of the IFRS Foundation®. All rights reserved. Used under licence from the IFRS Foundation®. Reproduction and use rights are strictly limited. For more information about the IFRS Foundation and rights to use its material please visit www.ifrs.org.

Disclaimer: To the extent permitted by applicable law the Board and the IFRS Foundation expressly disclaims all liability howsoever arising from this publication or any translation thereof whether in contract, tort or otherwise (including, but not limited to, liability for any negligent act or omission) to any person in respect of any claims or losses of any nature including direct, indirect, incidental or consequential loss, punitive damages, penalties or costs.

Information contained in this publication does not constitute advice and should not be substituted for the services of an appropriately qualified professional.

IFRS

The IFRS Foundation logo, the IASB logo, the IFRS for SMEs logo, the 'Hexagon Device', 'IFRS Foundation', 'eIFRS', 'IAS', 'IASB', 'IFRS for SMEs', 'IASs', 'IFRS', 'IFRSs', 'International Accounting Standards' and 'International Financial Reporting Standards', 'IFRIC', NIIF® and 'SIC' are **Trade Marks** of the IFRS Foundation.

IFRS

Trade Marks

The Foundation has trade marks registered around the world (**'Trade Marks'**) including 'IAS®', 'IASB®', 'IFRIC®', 'IFRS®', the IFRS® logo, 'IFRS for SMEs®', IFRS for SMEs® logo, the 'Hexagon Device', 'International Financial Reporting Standards®', NIIF® and 'SIC®'.

Further details of the Foundation's Trade Marks are available from the Licensor on request.

AUDIT AND ASSURANCE

CONTENTS

	Page number
Introduction	P.7
Unit guide	P.11
The assessment	P.27
Study skills	P.28

STUDY TEXT

Chapter		
1	Principles of auditing	1
2	Accounting systems and internal controls	15
3	Planning, controlling and recording	47
4	Audit evidence, techniques and procedures	91
5	Audit verification work 1 – General principles	121
6	Audit verification work 2 – Inventory	129
7	Audit verification work 3 – Non-current assets	153
8	Audit verification work 4 – Receivables, cash and bank	169
9	Audit verification work 5 – Liabilities, shareholders' funds and statutory books	203
10	Audit verification work 6 – Statement of profit or loss	227

AUDIT AND ASSURANCE

STUDY TEXT

Chapter

11	Completion stages of an audit	233
12	The reporting function	253
13	The legal and professional framework	271
14	Professional ethics	291
15	Responsibilities and liabilities of the auditor	307
16	Internal audit	321
17	Financial reporting topics	335
Mock Assessment Questions		345
Mock Assessment Answers		363
References		379
Index		I.1

This document references IFRS® Standards and IAS® Standards, which are authored by the International Accounting Standards Board (the Board), and published in the 2023 IFRS Standards Red Book.

AUDIT AND ASSURANCE

INTRODUCTION

HOW TO USE THESE MATERIALS

These Kaplan Publishing learning materials have been carefully designed to make your learning experience as easy as possible and to give you the best chance of success in your AAT assessments.

They contain a number of features to help you in the study process.

The sections on the Unit Guide, the Assessment and Study Skills should be read before you commence your studies.

They are designed to familiarise you with the nature and content of the assessment and to give you tips on how best to approach your studies.

STUDY TEXT

This study text has been specially prepared for the revised AAT qualification introduced in February 2022.

It is written in a practical and interactive style:

- key terms and concepts are clearly defined
- all topics are illustrated with practical examples with clearly worked solutions based on sample tasks provided by the AAT in their examining style
- frequent practice activities at the end of the chapters ensure that what you have learnt is regularly reinforced
- 'pitfalls' and 'examination tips' help you avoid commonly made mistakes and help you focus on what is required to perform well in your examination
- 'Test your understanding' activities are included within each chapter to apply your learning and develop your understanding.

ICONS

The chapters include the following icons throughout.

They are designed to assist you in your studies by identifying key definitions and the points at which you can test yourself on the knowledge gained.

Definition

These sections explain important areas of Knowledge which must be understood and reproduced in an assessment.

Example

The illustrative examples can be used to help develop an understanding of topics before attempting the activity exercises.

Test your understanding

These are exercises which give the opportunity to assess your understanding of all the assessment areas.

Foundation activities

These are questions to help ground your knowledge and consolidate your understanding on areas you're finding tricky.

Extension activities

These questions are for if you're feeling confident or wish to develop your higher level skills.

Quality and accuracy are of the utmost importance to us so if you spot an error in any of our products, please send an email to mykaplanreporting@kaplan.com with full details.

Our Quality Co-ordinator will work with our technical team to verify the error and take action to ensure it is corrected in future editions.

AUDIT AND ASSURANCE

Progression

There are two elements of progression that we can measure: first how quickly learners move through individual topics within a subject; and second how quickly they move from one course to the next. We know that there is an optimum for both, but it can vary from subject to subject and from learner to learner. However, using data and our experience of learner performance over many years, we can make some generalisations.

A fixed period of study set out at the start of a course with key milestones is important. This can be within a subject, for example 'I will finish this topic by 30 June', or for overall achievement, such as 'I want to be qualified by the end of next year'.

Your qualification is cumulative, as earlier papers provide a foundation for your subsequent studies, so do not allow there to be too big a gap between one subject and another.

We know that exams encourage techniques that lead to some degree of short term retention, the result being that you will simply forget much of what you have already learned unless it is refreshed (look up Ebbinghaus Forgetting Curve for more details on this). This makes it more difficult as you move from one subject to another: not only will you have to learn the new subject, you will also have to relearn all the underpinning knowledge as well. This is very inefficient and slows down your overall progression which makes it more likely you may not succeed at all.

In addition, delaying your studies slows your path to qualification which can have negative impacts on your career, postponing the opportunity to apply for higher level positions and therefore higher pay.

You can use the following diagram showing the whole structure of your qualification to help you keep track of your progress.

AUDIT AND ASSURANCE

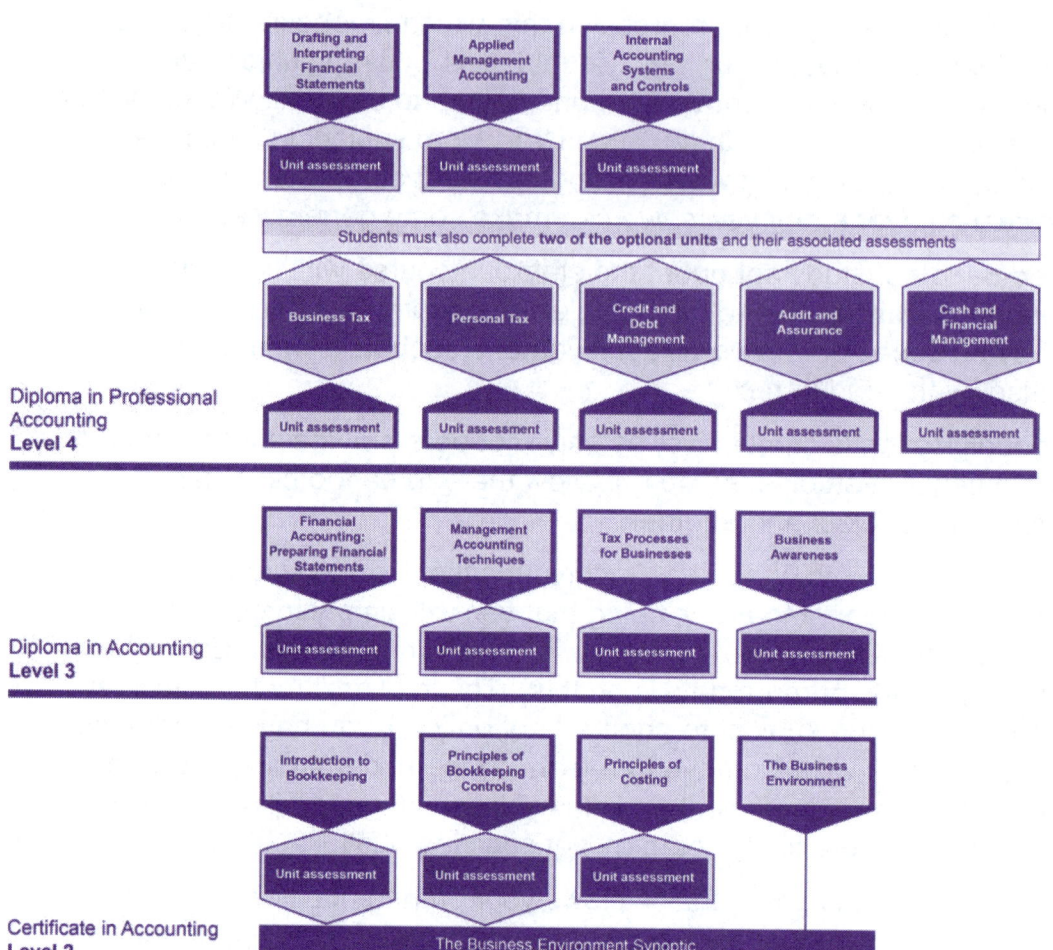

UNIT GUIDE

Introduction

This unit aims to develop a wider understanding of the principles and concepts, including the legal and professional rules of audit and assurance services.

The unit will provide learners with an awareness of the audit process from planning and risk assessment to the final completion and production of the auditor's report.

The unit also aims to provide a practical perspective on audit and assurance, with an emphasis on the application of audit and assurance techniques to current systems. Learners will be equipped with the skills required to undertake an audit under supervision and will gain an understanding of relevant regulatory frameworks and ethical requirements.

Learners will explore issues such as independence as well as the audit process, from the initial planning process, including risk assessments and gathering evidence, through to completion and reporting findings.

The unit places an emphasis upon the application of techniques to current situations and as such, offers a practical as well as a theoretical perspective. Throughout the unit, the concept of professional scepticism is explored and challenged.

Learners will require an understanding of financial accounting, as this knowledge will be used during the practical application of audit techniques.

Audit and Assurance is an **optional** unit in the Professional Diploma in Accounting.

AUDIT AND ASSURANCE

Learning outcomes

On completion of these units the learner will be able to:

- demonstrate an understanding of the audit and assurance framework
- demonstrate the importance of professional ethics
- evaluate the planning process for audit and assurance
- evaluate procedures for obtaining sufficient and appropriate evidence
- review and report findings.

AUDIT AND ASSURANCE

Scope of content

To perform this unit effectively you will need to know and understand the following:

Chapter

1 **Demonstrate an understanding of the audit and assurance framework**

1.1 **The concepts and principles** — 1

Learners need to understand:

- the meaning of the term 'audit'
- the meaning of the term 'assurance'
- the general principles of audit and assurance
- the audit expectation gap
- the difference between reasonable and limited assurance
- the difference between positive and negative expression of assurance
- the benefits gained from assurance
- the meaning of:
    - true and fair view
    - presents fairly
    - faithful representation as applied to the external audit
- the importance of professional scepticism and professional judgement.

Learners need to be able to:

- apply a questioning attitude to all audit activities.

1.2 **The regulatory environment** — 1, 12, 15

Learners need to understand:

- the approach to the regulation of audit in the UK
- the use of audit standards in the UK

AUDIT AND ASSURANCE

Chapter

- the role of the:
  - accountancy profession in the regulation of audits
  - International Auditing and Assurance Standards Board (IAASB)
- the role of law (detail contained in the Companies Act in relation to the requirement for a statutory audit, directors' responsibilities and auditors' responsibilities).

1.3 The role of corporate governance in the audit and assurance process   13, 15

Learners need to understand:

- the principles of good corporate governance
- the comply or explain principle
- the respective responsibilities of management, internal auditors and external auditors in relation to the financial statements
- the importance of an effective audit committee.

1.4 The role of internal audit   13, 16

Learners need to understand:

- the difference between internal and external audit
- the requirement for internal audit
- the roles of internal auditing including:
  - reviewing accounting and systems of internal control
  - examining financial operating information
  - special investigations e.g. fraud
  - reviewing compliance with external regulation
  - reviewing value for money (VFM)

- The different types of internal audit work including:
  - financial
  - operation
  - project
  - VFM
  - social and environmental
  - management
- the risks associated with a lack of independence.

2 Demonstrate the importance of professional ethics

2.1 The principles and characteristics of ethical codes and the implications for the auditor — 14

Learners need to understand:

- the importance of a code of ethics for the profession, including the AAT Code of Professional Ethics
- the consequences of failing to comply with the AAT Code of Professional Ethics, including damages, and legal and professional penalties
- the auditor's liability to the company and shareholders under contract, and liability to third parties under tort of negligence
- the requirement for professional indemnity insurance
- the supervisory requirements for accounting technicians when carrying out an audit.

Learners need to be able to:

- apply the AAT Code of Professional Ethics to audit activities.

AUDIT AND ASSURANCE

Chapter

2.2 Threats to the independence of auditors 14

Learners need to understand:

- how audit and assurance work may compromise the fundamental principles of:
  - integrity
  - objectivity
  - professional competence and due care
  - confidentiality
  - professional behaviour
- the significance of independence and its relationship with objectivity
- the threats of:
  - self-interest
  - self-review
  - advocacy
  - familiarity
  - intimidation.

Learners need to be able to:

- evaluate circumstances that may threaten the application of the fundamental principles.

2.3 Safeguards to eliminate or reduce threats to independence of auditors 14

Leaners need to be able to:

- evaluate firm-wide safeguards:
  - use of different personnel with different reporting lines for the provision of non-assurance services to an audited entity
  - procedures for monitoring and managing the reliance on revenue received from a single client

- procedures that will enable the identification of interests or relationships between the firm or members of the engagement team and clients
- disciplinary mechanisms to promote compliance with policies and procedures

- evaluate audit safeguards:
    - independent review of audit working papers
    - consultation with an independent third party
    - disclosure and discussion of ethical issues with those charged with governance
    - rotation of senior personnel
    - evaluate matters that should be referred to senior members of audit staff.

2.4 The fundamental ethical principles in relation to internal and external audit   14

Learners need to be able to:

- recognise:
    - when to disclose information with or without clients' permission
    - when to take precautions if acting for competing clients
    - the importance of data security.

AUDIT AND ASSURANCE

Chapter

3   Evaluate the planning process for audit and assurance

| 3.1 | The concept of risk | 2, 3, 4 |

Leaners need to understand:

- components of the audit risk model
    - inherent risk
    - control risk
    - detection risk:
        - sampling
        - non-sampling risk
- relationship between the components, particularly how auditors manage detection risk in order to keep audit risk at an acceptably low level
- how factors such as the entity's operating environment and its system of internal control affect the assessment of inherent and control risk
- the risk assessment process:
    - risk matrix
    - low, medium or high
    - numerical grade
- how analytical procedures can be used to identify potential understatement or overstatement of items in the financial statements.

Learners need to be able to:

- identify audit risks
- identify analytical procedures that could expose understatement or overstatement of items in the financial statements.

AUDIT AND ASSURANCE

3.2 The concept of materiality

Learners need to understand:

- the difference between 'performance materiality' and materiality for the financial statements as a 'whole'
- the role of materiality in planning an audit and evaluating misstatements
- methods used to calculate materiality thresholds
- the difference between 'material' and 'material and pervasive'.

Learners need to be able to:

- calculate materiality levels.

3.3 Audit procedures

Learners need to be able to:

- develop procedures to obtain sufficient appropriate evidence in respect of the relevant assertions for key figures in the financial statements, particularly:
    - non-current assets
    - inventory
    - receivables
    - cash and bank
    - borrowings
    - payables
    - provisions
    - revenue
    - purchases
    - payroll and other expenses
    - other payables and other receivables.

AUDIT AND ASSURANCE

Chapter

3.4 **The role of audit working papers**   2, 3, 11

Learners need to understand:

- the role of audit documentation in providing evidence as a basis for the auditor's opinion
- the form and content of working papers and supporting documentation
- the importance of retaining working papers for future reference
- recording techniques (flow charts, internal control questions and checklists)
- the impact of technology on auditing.

Learners need to be able to:

- evaluate systems of internal control using system records:
  - flow charts
  - internal control questions
  - checklists
- identify the merits and limitations of using standardised questionnaires and checklists.

4 **Evaluate procedures for obtaining sufficient appropriate evidence**

4.1 **Methods used to obtain audit evidence**   4, 5, 6, 7, 8, 9, 10

Learners need to understand:

- types of verification techniques
  - inspection
  - observation
  - external confirmation
  - recalculation
  - reperformance
  - analytical procedures
  - enquiry

- the characteristics of good evidence
- the reliability and relevance of different sources of audit evidence
- the differences between tests of controls and substantive procedures.

Learners need to be able to:

- identify when it is appropriate to use each type of verification technique
- evaluate methods used to test:
  - controls
  - transactions
  - balances.

4.2 Audit techniques in an IT environment

Learners need to know:

- types of automated tools and techniques:
  - test data
  - integrated test facilities
  - audit software
  - data analytic tools
- how automated tools and techniques are used to test controls and interrogate the audited entity's files
- the benefits and drawbacks of using automated tools and techniques.

AUDIT AND ASSURANCE

Chapter 4

4.3 Different sampling techniques

Learners need to understand:

- statistical and non-statistical sampling methods
- the advantages and disadvantages of different sampling methods:
  - block
  - haphazard
  - judgmental
  - random
  - stratified
  - systematic.

Learners need to be able to:

- distinguish between statistical and non-statistical sampling
- determine when it is more appropriate to examine 100% or a selection of items
- distinguish between selection methods and when they should be used
- identify factors affecting sample sizes
- identify appropriate populations from which to select samples.

4.4 Audit approach

2, 3, 4, 5, 6, 7, 8, 9, 10, 16

Learners been to understand:

- the definition of internal control and each of its components' control activities including:
  - performance reviews
  - information processing
  - physical controls
  - segregation of duties
  - monitoring of controls by management
  - monitoring of controls by an internal audit function

- preventative controls
- detective controls
- the role of internal audit as part of the internal control environment
- limitations of internal controls
- factors relating to the operating environment that influence control risk
- factors relating to systems of internal control that influence control risk.
- establish why auditors need to understand the audited entity's internal controls
- determine when to use a mixture of tests of controls and substantive procedures or substantive procedures only
- identify why it is appropriate to use a mixture of tests of controls and substantive procedures or substantive procedures only
- identify how errors and irregularities can be mitigated by control procedures.

4.5 Audit assertions

5, 6, 7, 8, 9, 10

Learners need to know:

- assertions contained in the financial statements:
  - payables
  - receivables
  - inventories
  - bank and cash
  - non-current assets
  - non-current liabilities

Learners need to be able to:

- identify audit procedures to test financial statement assertions.

AUDIT AND ASSURANCE

		Chapter
5	**Review and report findings**	
5.1	**Matters to be referred to senior colleagues**	4

Learners need to be able to:

- evaluate misstatements for materiality
- identify deviations from an audited entity's prescribed procedures
- identify matters including:
  - unauthorised transactions
  - non-routine transactions
  - related party transactions
  - transactions above or below market rates
  - suspected fraud.

5.2	**External audit opinion**	11, 12

Learners need to understand:

- elements of an audit opinion
- elements of an external audit report

Learners need to be able to:

- identify a suitable audit opinion arising from
  - significant uncertainties
  - material misstatements
  - inability to obtain sufficient and appropriate evidence (limitation on scope).

		Chapter
5.3	**Report audit findings to management**	11, 12

Learners need to understand:

- elements of a report on deficiencies in internal control
- how deficiencies in internal control are reported to management
- how deficiencies in internal control are reported to the audit committee.

Learners need to be able to:

- identify the consequences of deficiencies in internal controls and how the deficiencies can be remedied
- report findings to management.

Delivering this unit

This unit links with:

- Level 4 Drafting and Interpreting Financial Statements
- Level 4 Internal Accounting Systems and Controls

AUDIT AND ASSURANCE

THE ASSESSMENT

Test specification for this unit assessment

Assessment type
Computer based unit assessment

Marking type
Partially computer/ partially human marked

Duration of exam
2 hours 30 minutes

The assessment for this unit consists of six compulsory, independent tasks.

Included in the assessment are a number of extended writing requirements.

The competency level for AAT assessment is 70%.

Learning outcomes		Weighting
1	Demonstrate an understanding of the audit and assurance framework	10%
2	Demonstrate the importance of professional ethics	15%
3	Evaluate the planning process for audit and assurance	25%
4	Evaluate procedures for obtaining sufficient and appropriate evidence	35%
5	Review and report findings	15%
Total		100%

STUDY SKILLS

Preparing to study

Devise a study plan

Determine which times of the week you will study.

Split these times into sessions of at least one hour for study of new material. Any shorter periods could be used for revision or practice.

Put the times you plan to study onto a study plan for the weeks from now until the assessment and set yourself targets for each period of study – in your sessions make sure you cover the whole course, activities and the associated questions in the workbook at the back of the manual.

If you are studying more than one unit at a time, try to vary your subjects as this can help to keep you interested and see subjects as part of wider knowledge.

When working through your course, compare your progress with your plan and, if necessary, re-plan your work (perhaps including extra sessions) or, if you are ahead, do some extra revision/practice questions.

Effective studying

Active reading

You are not expected to learn the text by rote, rather, you must understand what you are reading and be able to use it to pass the assessment and develop good practice.

A good technique is to use SQ3Rs – Survey, Question, Read, Recall, Review:

1 **Survey the chapter**

   Look at the headings and read the introduction, knowledge, skills and content, so as to get an overview of what the chapter deals with.

2 **Question**

   Whilst undertaking the survey ask yourself the questions you hope the chapter will answer for you.

AUDIT AND ASSURANCE

3 Read

Read through the chapter thoroughly working through the activities and, at the end, making sure that you can meet the learning objectives highlighted on the first page.

4 Recall

At the end of each section and at the end of the chapter, try to recall the main ideas of the section/chapter without referring to the text. This is best done after short break of a couple of minutes after the reading stage.

5 Review

Check that your recall notes are correct.

You may also find it helpful to re-read the chapter to try and see the topic(s) it deals with as a whole.

Note taking

Taking notes is a useful way of learning, but do not simply copy out the text.

The notes must:

- be in your own words
- be concise
- cover the key points
- well organised
- be modified as you study further chapters in this text or in related ones.

Trying to summarise a chapter without referring to the text can be a useful way of determining which areas you know and which you don't.

Three ways of taking notes

1 Summarise the key points of a chapter

2 Make linear notes

A list of headings, subdivided with sub-headings listing the key points.

If you use linear notes, you can use different colours to highlight key points and keep topic areas together.

Use plenty of space to make your notes easy to use.

3   Try a diagrammatic form

The most common of which is a mind map.

To make a mind map, put the main heading in the centre of the paper and put a circle around it.

Draw lines radiating from this to the main sub-headings which again have circles around them.

Continue the process from the sub-headings to sub-sub-headings.

Annotating the text

You may find it useful to underline or highlight key points in your study text – but do be selective.

You may also wish to make notes in the margins.

Revision phase

Kaplan has produced material specifically designed for your final examination preparation for this unit.

These include pocket revision notes and an exam kit that includes a bank of revision questions specifically in the style of the new syllabus.

Further guidance on how to approach the final stage of your studies is given in these materials.

Further reading

In addition to this text, you should also read the 'Accounting Technician' magazine every month to keep abreast of any guidance from the examiners.

AUDIT AND ASSURANCE

Principles of auditing

Introduction

This chapter demonstrates the features of an audit and introduces the fundamental principles within audit work. This is the basis for the whole Audit and Assurance assessment and introduces some important concepts for the rest of the syllabus.

ASSESSMENT CRITERIA
The concepts and principles (1.1)
The regulatory environment (1.2)

CONTENTS	
1	What is an audit?
2	Important principles in audit work
3	Auditing standards
4	Features of an audit

1 What is an audit?

1.1 The purpose of an external audit

The need for an audit arises from the separation between the management and the ownership of companies – directors are responsible for running the company on behalf of the shareholders. Financial statements are prepared by the directors in order to account for their stewardship to the shareholders, and an examination by an independent person (i.e. the external auditor) gives them credibility.

Once the external auditor has conducted their examination, the auditor expresses an opinion in an auditors' report attached to the financial statements.

1.2 Definition of Assurance and Audit

Definition

Assurance – an assurance engagement is one in which a practitioner expresses a conclusion designed to enhance the degree of confidence of the intended users, other than the responsible party, about the outcome of the evaluation or measurement of a subject matter against criteria.

Definition

Audit of financial statements – an audit is a type of assurance engagement and is a process which results in expression of an opinion as to whether the financial statements give a true and fair view of the entity's affairs at the period end, and as to whether they have been properly prepared in accordance with the applicable accounting standards.

The Companies Act 2006 identifies that an external audit is a legal requirement for all UK companies, except those which meet two of the following three criteria: (1) annual turnover not exceeding £10.2m, (2) total assets value not exceeding £5.1m and (3) 50 or fewer employees (this is for companies with an accounting period starting on or after 1 January 2016).

There are a number of benefits of an audit that mean a company might choose to be audited even if it does not legally need to be, such as:

- Adds credibility.
- It is an independent verification.
- There are a number of by-products, such as the fact that an audit can act as a fraud deterrent and the auditor will provide recommendations on internal controls.

Throughout the study materials, we shall be referring to International Standards on Auditing (ISAs) which are produced by the International Auditing and Assurance Standards Board (IAASB) and which, after approval by the UK Financial Reporting Council (FRC), must be followed when carrying out audits in the UK and Ireland.

Note: The government has announced the abolition of the FRC. It will be replaced with a new regulator, the Audit, Reporting and Governance Authority (ARGA). At the time the Study Text went to print, the exact details of this change were not known, so references will still be made to the FRC as the regulator of the accountancy profession.

1.3 Expression of opinion – the audit report

ISA 700 (Revised) *Forming an opinion and reporting on financial statements* indicates the required content of an auditor's report. This includes the audit opinion, which is usually expressed in 'true and fair' terms. The idea of 'true and fair' is developed later in this chapter.

An extract from a standard audit report is shown below.

 Example

INDEPENDENT AUDITOR'S REPORT TO THE MEMBERS OF XYZ CO (EXTRACT)

Opinion

In our opinion, the financial statements:

- give a true and fair view of the state of the company's affairs as at……..and its profit (or loss) for the year then ended
- have been properly prepared in accordance with United Kingdom Generally Accepted Accounting Practice; and
- have been prepared in accordance with the requirements of the Companies Act 2006.

Registered Auditors

Date   Address

1.4 Financial statements

The 'financial statements' comprise:

- Statement of financial position
- Statement of profit or loss
- Statements of cash flows
- Statement of changes in equity
- notes to all of the above, including the accounting policies note.

1.5 Misconceptions about the financial statements

There are a number of common misconceptions about the financial statements. The main ones are as follows.

- The statement of financial position is a statement of the value of the business. Wrong – the amounts at which assets and liabilities are stated do not reflect the amount that the business could be sold for.

- The auditors are responsible for preparing the financial statements on which they report. Wrong – the directors are responsible for selecting suitable accounting policies and preparing the financial statements.

- The amounts in financial statements are stated precisely. Wrong – the majority of figures involve some degree of estimation and auditors work with the concept of materiality (see section 2.2).

ISA 700 (Revised) seeks to address these misconceptions in the following ways.

1.6 Directors' and auditors' responsibilities

The auditor's report contains a clear statement of the respective responsibilities of directors and auditors as follows:

The company's directors are responsible for the preparation and fair presentation of the financial statements in accordance with applicable law as well as relevant accounting and auditing standards (whether they are UK or international standards).

Readers are made aware that the financial statements have been prepared by the company's management (whose interests may be affected by the resulting figures). The auditor expresses an opinion on those figures.

1.7 Basis of opinion

'We conducted our audit in accordance with International Standards on Auditing (ISAs). Our responsibilities under those standards are further described in the Auditor's Responsibilities for the Audit of the Financial Statements section of our report. We are independent of the Company in accordance with the International Ethics Standards Board for Accountants' Code of Ethics for Professional Accountants (IESBA Code) together with the ethical requirements that are relevant to our audit of the financial statements in [jurisdiction], and we have fulfilled our other ethical responsibilities in accordance with these requirements and the IESBA Code. We believe that the audit evidence we have obtained is sufficient and appropriate to provide a basis for our opinion.' [ISA 700 (Revised)]

Auditors aim to provide reasonable assurance. It would be impractical and unduly expensive to provide a guarantee that all errors and irregularities have been uncovered during the audit.

1.8 True and fair view

The use of the word 'view' indicates that a professional judgement has been reached.

The meaning of 'true and fair' has been much debated. It is not defined in the Companies Act or International Standards on Auditing. This is deliberate and any 'definitions' cited in textbooks or elsewhere should be regarded with caution.

A starting point for discussion could be that a true and fair view means that the financial statements are free from material misstatements and faithfully represent the financial performance and position of the entity.

Truth relates to factual accuracy (bearing in mind materiality – see section 2.2) and correctness, whilst fairness relates to the presentation of information and the view conveyed to the reader.

The word 'fair' in particular is difficult because it is subjective – one person's idea of what is fair may not be another's. The auditor must consider the overall impression created by the financial statements as a whole.

Faithful representation is the concept that financial statements be produced that accurately reflect the condition of a business i.e. financial statements should be complete, error-free and unbiased.

1.9 Accounting standards

The courts will treat compliance with accepted accounting principles as evidence that financial statements are true and fair.

The Companies Act 2006 requires the notes to the financial statements to state:

- whether the financial statements are prepared in accordance with applicable accounting standards, and
- particulars of and reasons for material departures from accounting standards.

> **Test your understanding 1**
>
> 1 What are the respective responsibilities of the directors and the external auditors regarding the financial statements of a company?
> 2 Explain what is meant by a true and fair view.

2 Important principles in audit work

2.1 Introduction

Audit work is a detailed and meticulous process which we shall examine in this text. There are, however, some basic principles which apply to audit work and it will be useful to go through these first.

2.2 Materiality

The auditor does not perform tests aimed at detecting all errors. As part of the planning process, the auditor will determine the maximum amount of error that the auditor is prepared to accept and still be satisfied that the financial statements show a true and fair view. An error over and above this maximum amount is referred to as a material error.

A material error may be:

- qualitative (e.g. transactions relating to directors are considered material by nature regardless of their value), or
- quantitative (e.g. the monetary value of the disclosed figure is incorrect).

The concept of materiality is developed in Chapter 3.

2.3 Selective testing and audit sampling

The auditor will carry out tests to ascertain whether the financial statements are free from material misstatement. These tests must be sufficient to provide evidence of material errors, if such errors exist.

The auditor does not usually test every transaction or item within an account balance, but will limit tests to a selection of items ('selective testing'). However, if the population is small, the auditor may test all of the items.

Where the auditor tests a representative sample of items in order to draw conclusions about an entire set of data, the selective testing is termed 'audit sampling'.

Audit sampling is detailed in Chapter 4.

2.4 Risk

To apply selective testing procedures, the auditor will wish to target the areas of the financial statements which are most prone to material error ('risky').

In some companies there may be many risk areas. This may be due, in part, to the type of industry in which the company operates, e.g. there may be a greater risk of material misstatement occurring in the financial statements of a high technology company than there is in a stable industry.

Also, some areas or account headings may be more prone to material error than others, e.g. inventory is usually subject to more material errors than cash at bank, because its valuation is more subjective.

As part of the planning process, the auditor will analyse risk in order to:

- direct audit tests to those areas most prone to material error
- determine the overall assurance required from a test or combination of tests (and therefore what will constitute 'sufficient' audit evidence).

Audit risk and planning are considered in greater detail in Chapter 3.

2.5 Reasonable assurance

The auditor's opinion on the financial statements is based on the concept of reasonable assurance; their report does not constitute a guarantee that the financial statements are free of misstatement.

As the auditor does not examine every single piece of available audit information and because professional judgement is required when drawing conclusions from the evidence, there is a risk that the auditor will draw an incorrect conclusion: absolute confidence, certainty or assurance is not possible.

There are two levels of assurance you need to be aware of:

	Limited	Reasonable
Level	Moderate – conclusion expressed negatively.	High – conclusion expressed positively.
Example of engagement	Report on effectiveness of internal controls. Review of business plan or forecasts.	Statutory audit.
Example of report wording	'Nothing has come to our attention that indicates the system of internal control is not operating effectively.'	'Financial Statements show a true and fair view.'

A conclusion expressed negatively is less certain than a positively expressed opinion. It implies that matters could exist which cause the statement to be unreasonable, but that the practitioner has not uncovered any such matters. A practitioner gives this type of opinion when a limited assurance engagement is being carried out and a lower level of evidence is sought.

Note: Auditors will never give absolute assurance for a number of reasons:

- Audit evidence is persuasive, not conclusive.
- Auditors do not test everything.
- There are areas of judgement in the financial statements.
- There are inherent limitations of internal controls and accounting systems (see Chapter 2).
- Auditors test according to materiality (see later in this session).

2.6 The expectation gap

There is a common misconception that an unmodified audit report provides assurance that no frauds or other irregularities have occurred in the period. Wrong – the auditor is concerned with material misstatements in the financial statements; fraud is one possible cause of such a misstatement, but it is the misstatement which concerns the auditor, rather than the fraud itself. This is considered in more detail in Chapter 15.

This misconception, together with a lack of comprehension of the auditing principles discussed earlier (selective testing, materiality, etc.), have been referred to as part of the 'expectation gap'.

The 'expectation gap' has become a jargon phrase used to describe the difference between:

- public perceptions of the responsibilities of auditors
- the legal and professional reality.

3 Auditing standards

3.1 Introduction

The International Auditing and Assurance Standards Board (IAASB) works to improve the uniformity of auditing practices worldwide by issuing pronouncements, particularly ISAs and promoting their acceptance. Their aim is to set standards which facilitate the convergence of national and international auditing standards.

ISAs are to be applied in every audit of historical financial information. Failure to apply ISAs could leave the auditor open to accusations of negligence, which could lead to claims for compensation as well as disciplinary action.

The IAASB's Standards contain basic principles and essential procedures, together with related guidance, in the form of explanatory and other material, including appendices.

From an assessment point of view, it is important to be aware of the broad principles laid down by those standards that are relevant to the syllabus. However, there is no need to memorise the detailed content or formal definitions that they contain.

4 Features of an audit

4.1 Who is the external auditor?

The law defines who can be the statutory auditor and this is considered in Chapter 13. In this context, 'the auditor' can be a person or firm.

Practically, 'the auditor' includes all members of the audit team on a particular assignment.

The person who takes overall responsibility for the performance of the assignment and who signs the auditor's report is known as the engagement partner. The auditor may delegate certain aspects of the audit work to other persons but the overall responsibility for the performance of the audit is the engagement partner's alone.

4.2 Audit team

A typical audit team for a large company audit might be made up as follows:

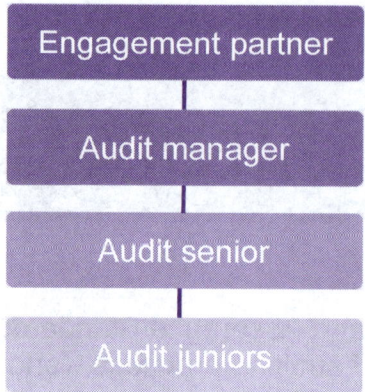

4.3 The process of auditing

An audit consists of a cycle of activities which can be broken down into a number of distinct phases as shown below. Review the phases illustrated and discussed below to gain an overview. This will all be developed in later chapters.

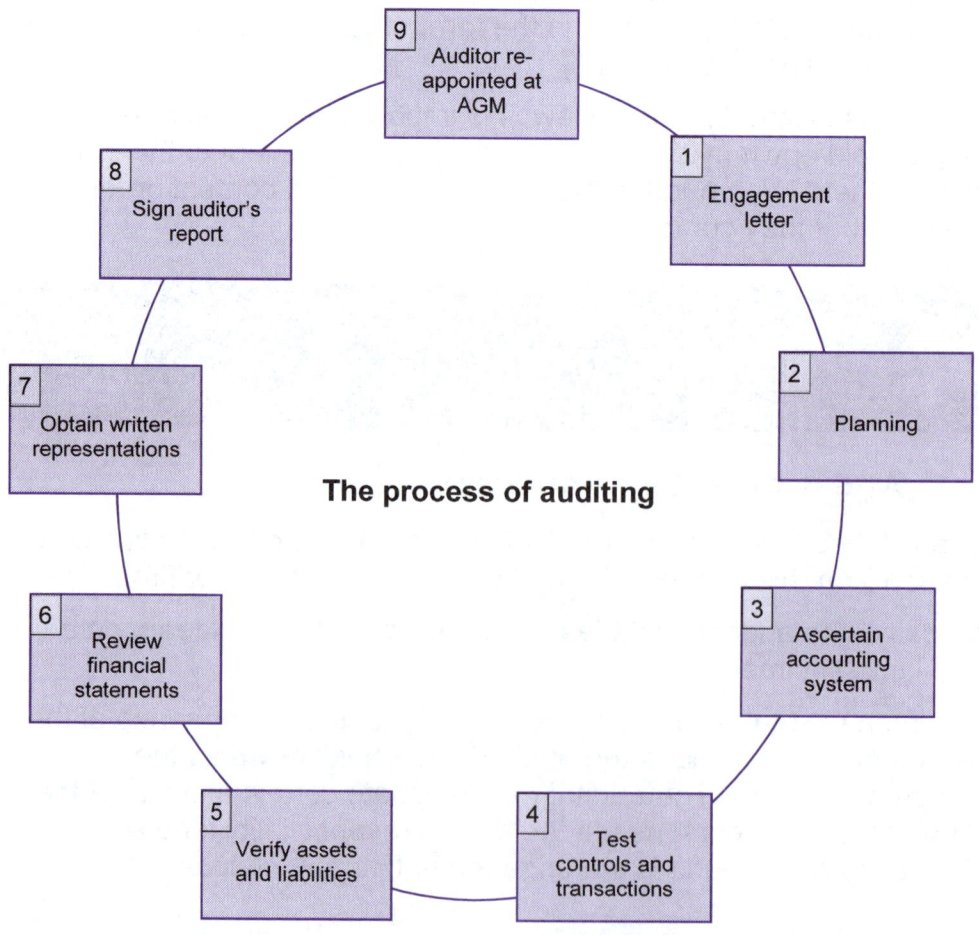

AUDIT AND ASSURANCE

1. **Engagement letter.** Every auditor should send their client an engagement letter which sets out the auditor's duties and responsibilities. (See Chapter 3)

2. **Planning.** The auditor must plan and control the audit work if the work is to be done to a high standard of skill and care. (See Chapter 3)

3. **Ascertain accounting systems.** An auditor must enquire into and ascertain the client's system of accounting and internal control in order to understand how accounting data is prepared and to gain an impression as to whether systems are reliable. It is the information generated from these systems which is summarised in the financial statements. (See Chapter 2)

4. **Test controls and transactions.** The auditor should test the controls if the auditor intends to rely on them and the auditor must test the records in order to obtain evidence that they are a reliable basis for the preparation of accounts. If systems are weak or unreliable, a high level of detailed work is needed. (See Chapter 4)

5. **Verify assets and liabilities.** The auditor must verify the figures appearing in the financial statements. (See Chapters 5 to 10)

6. **Review financial statements.** The auditor reviews the financial statements to see if overall they appear sensible and are consistent with the auditor's knowledge of the entity. (See Chapter 11)

7. **Obtain written representations.** The auditor asks management to confirm formally the truth and fairness of certain aspects of the financial statements, usually subjective areas. (See Chapter 11)

8. **Sign auditor's report.** The auditor signs the auditor's report once the directors have approved the accounts. Audited accounts are laid before the members at the company's Annual General Meeting (AGM). (See Chapter 12)

9. **Re-appointment.** The end of the AGM signifies the end of the auditor's term of office. The members of the company may decide by a majority to re-appoint the auditor if the auditor wishes to continue to act for the company. (See Chapter 13)

Test your understanding 2

1. What do the financial statements comprise of?
2. Who is responsible for the preparation of the financial statements?

5 Summary

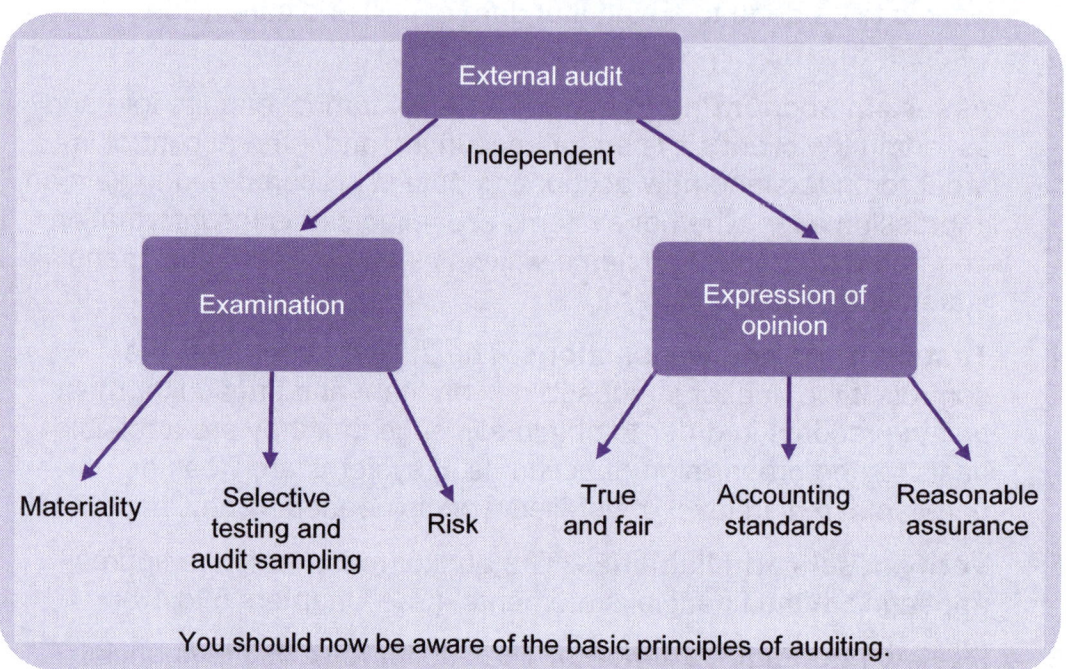

You should now be aware of the basic principles of auditing.

Test your understanding answers

Test your understanding 1

1 The directors are responsible for the preparation of the financial statements of a company. The external auditor's responsibility is to report to the shareholders on whether the financial statements show a true and fair view.

2 A true and fair view has no legal or formal definition. However, 'true' indicates that the figures are based upon fact and correctness while 'fair' indicates that the figures in the financial statements are presented so as to give an accurate impression of the position of the company.

Test your understanding 2

1 Statement of financial position.

Statement of profit or loss.

Cash flow statement.

Statement of changes in equity.

Notes to the financial statements.

2 The directors.

AUDIT AND ASSURANCE

Accounting systems and internal controls

Introduction

This chapter introduces the accounting systems and the methods used to gain an understanding of how these systems work. The chapter will start with a discussion of flowcharting and its use within an audit and will then go on to discuss internal controls in further detail.

ASSESSMENT CRITERIA	CONTENTS
The concept of risk (3.1)	1 Accounting systems
The role of audit working papers (3.4)	2 Flowcharting
Audit approach (4.4)	3 Internal controls
Evaluate audit techniques used in an IT environment (4.2)	4 Preliminary evaluation of internal controls
	5 Reliance on internal controls
	6 Management and supervision

1 Accounting systems

1.1 Overview of the audit approach

The audit approach will usually depend on the perceived strength of internal controls and has four main stages.

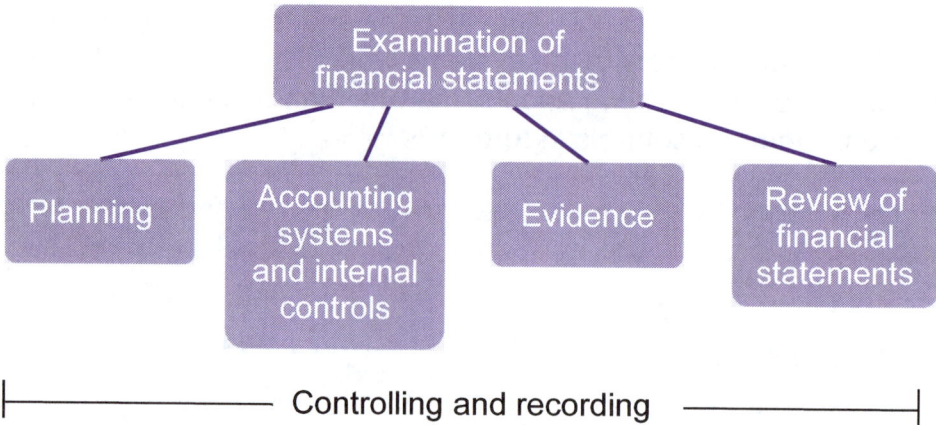

Ascertaining the accounting systems and control environment is one aspect of planning necessary to determining the audit approach.

If auditors, after obtaining an understanding of the accounting system and control environment, expect to be able to rely on their assessment of control risk to reduce the extent of their substantive procedures, they should make a preliminary assessment of control risk, and should plan and perform tests of control to support that assessment.

Note that tests of control are optional because a wholly substantive audit (where no reliance is placed on internal controls) can be performed if the auditor regards it as a more cost-effective approach.

1.2 External auditor's responsibility

To assess the adequacy of the accounting system as a basis for the preparation of financial statements (Companies Act 2006).

1.3 Management's responsibility

To maintain an accounting system adequate to provide proper accounting records (Companies Act 2006).

AUDIT AND ASSURANCE

1.4 What is an 'adequate' accounting system?

An adequate accounting system provides assurance that:

- all transactions have been recorded
- errors in processing become apparent, and
- assets and liabilities exist and are recorded at the correct amounts.

The adequacy of the system will be assessed with reference to the size, nature and complexity of the enterprise.

1.5 Examples of 'adequacy'

Type of business	Adequate accounting system
Small mainly cash sales, small number of suppliers.	Analysed bank ledger account and list of unpaid invoices.
Large manufacturing company with several products and a number of separate locations.	Complex accounting system, in order to collate and process information from numerous sources.

1.6 Recording the systems

If the auditor is to be able to assess the accounting system effectively, it must be recorded (including any internal controls). This could be done using either:

- narrative notes
- flowcharts (see below)
- internal control questionnaires/evaluations (see later in this chapter)
- a combination of these methods.

2 Flowcharting

2.1 The purpose of flowcharting

The purpose of flowcharting is to reduce a procedure to its basic components and to emphasise logical relationships, so that a connected pattern of activity can be traced from the beginning to the end.

The technique is simple but unfortunately flowcharting in practice lacks a uniform terminology, both in the descriptions of types of flowchart and in the symbols to be used.

The flowcharts dealt with in this chapter are called 'system flowcharts' or 'document flowcharts'. System flowcharts or document flowcharts depict, in outline, the sequence of events in a system showing document flow and the department or function responsible for each event.

AUDIT AND ASSURANCE

2.2 Flowcharting conventions

Example

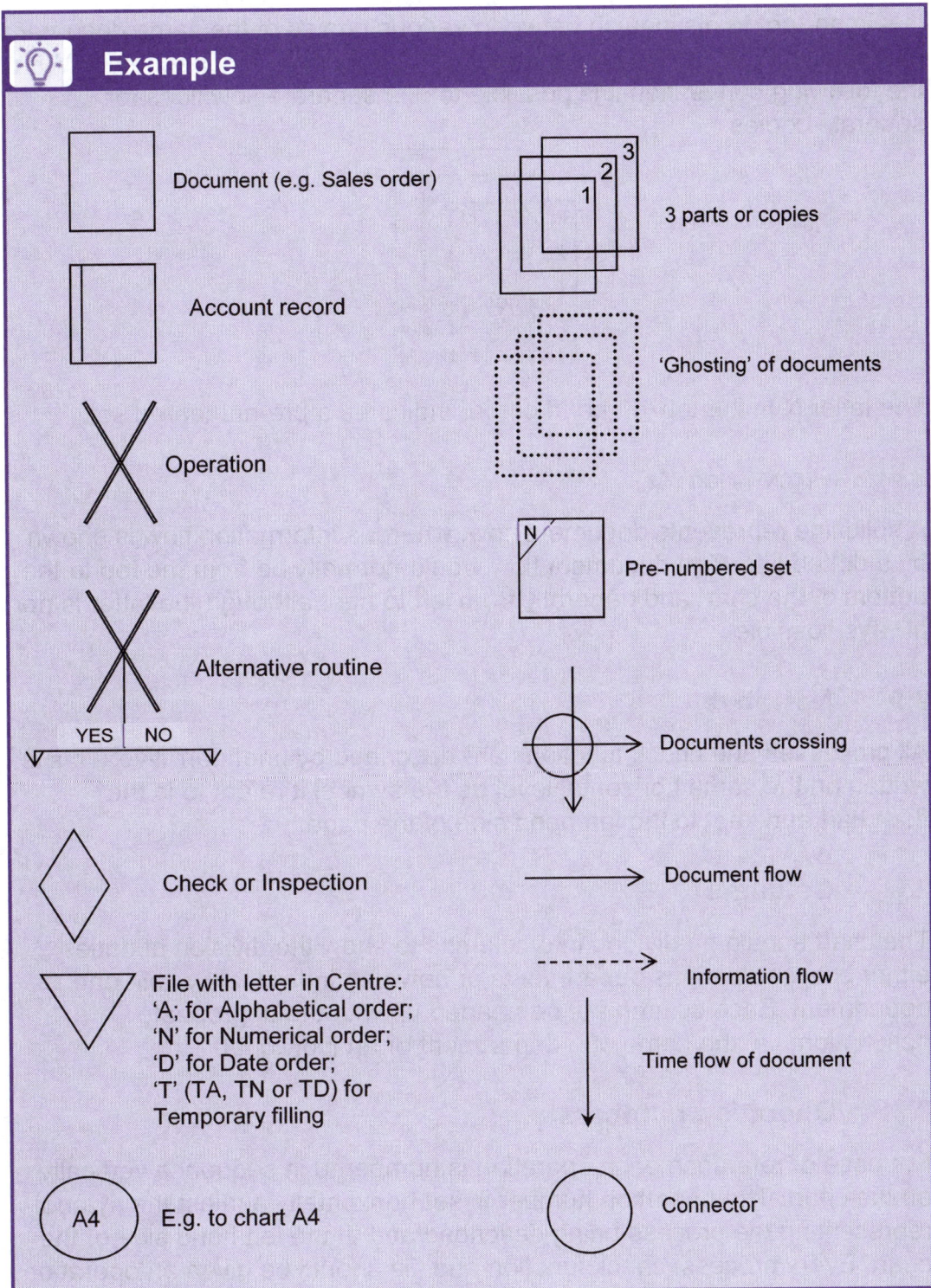

2.3 Multiple copies

It is important to distinguish between various copies of the same document particularly if they are to be separated and processed independently. With the following convention it is possible to use separate flow lines for separate copies.

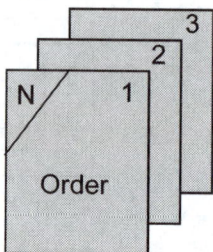

The letter N in the top left hand corner indicates a pre-numbered set.

2.4 Flow lines

A solid line represents document flow, whereas information flow is shown by a dotted line. The document flow would normally be from the top to the bottom of the chart and generally from left to right although the latter is not always possible.

2.5 Narrative

All processes and check functions are described by brief narrative. This is written on the same horizontal level as the symbol it refers to in the flowchart and kept to the left hand side of the page.

2.6 Columns

The chart should be divided into columns to show the division of duties either between various departments or between individuals within one department. Each column will be headed up with the appropriate description, i.e. the name of a department or an individual.

2.7 Operation numbers

For ease of reference each operation is numbered in sequence vertically on the chart. The operation number is set horizontally against the symbol representing the process being described and at the left hand side of the chart. Every process, check function and file should be given an operation number.

2.8 Annotation

To distinguish between permanent and temporary files it is possible to mark a temporary file with the letter 'T' as follows:

Even more information concerning the structure of the file can be added by coding.

A – alphabetical order
N – numerical order
D – date order

Thus ▽T represents a temporary file in alphabetical order

Thus ▽D represents a permanent file in date order

2.9 'Ghosting'

When a document appears in the system for the first time it will be shown as a solid square symbol with the name of the document printed inside. Normally there is no need to show the document again, its progress can be seen by following the document flow line, but where the document is carried forward to another chart or when copies that have previously been processed together are split up, it is useful to repeat the document symbol with dotted lines as

[Invoice]

2.10 Internal control procedures

Checks are denoted by ◇ These usually indicate internal control procedures which may be tested by the auditor later.

2.11 Rules for clarity

- No diagonal lines. Avoid intersecting lines. If this is impossible show a 'bridge' as follows:

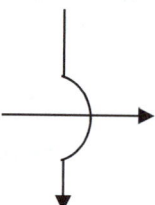

- Remember vertical lines represent the passage of time horizontal solid lines the transfer of documents between departments or individuals and horizontal broken lines the transfer of information. Documents can therefore only be processed on a vertical line.

- There should only be one operation number at a given horizontal level.

- Avoid excessive detail and narrative on the face of the chart. Keep in a column on the left hand side and be as brief as possible.

- Avoid unusual abbreviations (but can use a 'key' or symbols.)

- Avoid too many columns. Split a large system into smaller logical sections and draw a separate chart for each section.

- If a document may be processed in alternative ways according to some predetermined criteria the line of flow may be split as follows:

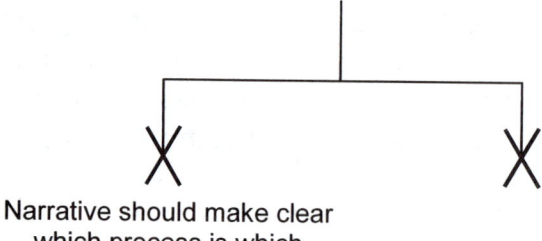

Narrative should make clear which process is which

2.12 Illustration of a flowchart

The following process will vary according to the extent of computerisation within the business as some of these documents may be stored electronically and passed to team members in soft copy, rather than in paper form.

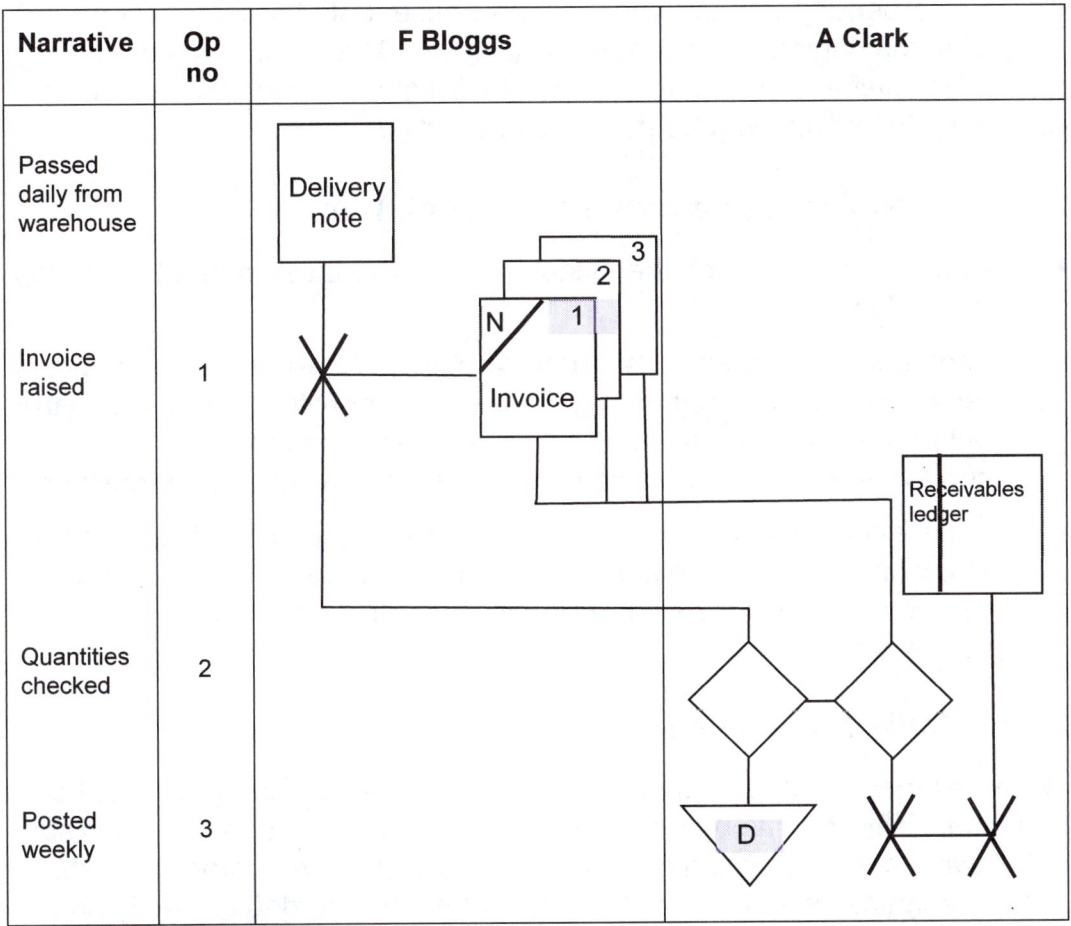

We will now interpret this simple flowchart.

When goods are delivered a delivery note is completed and is passed daily to F Bloggs. F Bloggs, on receipt of the delivery note, raises a three part pre-numbered invoice.

The delivery note and all three copies of the invoice are sent to A Clark for the quantities to be checked. One copy of the invoice will be sent to the customer, the delivery note and second copy of the invoice will be filed in date order and the remaining copy will be posted on a weekly basis by A Clark to the receivables ledger.

2.13 Collecting information

Information must be collected so that the flowchart can be constructed or indeed a narrative description of the system made. In practice this requires the exercise of powers of enquiry. Information is collected by asking staff how the system operates in practice. This entails going into, for example, the sales order department, into the warehouse, onto the factory floor and observing the company procedures in practice. The auditor cannot merely talk to the chief accountant about how the auditor believes the system is operating as this may not be the case in practice.

2.14 Constructing an information/audit trail

- Enquire who operates the system (principally those named at the top of the flowchart).

- Interview each person. Ask them what they do, what documents they receive, what documents they prepare and how frequently they carry out procedures. Discussions with operational staff must be conducted in a manner which maintains good working relationships.

- Take a copy of each document raised (e.g. despatch note), note how many copies are made and to whom they are distributed. Ascertain what entries are made in permanent records as a result of transactions.

2.15 Walk-through checks

Whatever method of recording the system is used, its accuracy must be confirmed. This is done by means of a 'walk-through test', which consists of following one transaction right through the system from start to finish. Any error indicates that the system has not been recorded correctly and this must be put right before any audit tests are designed. It is also usually a good idea to agree flowcharts with the client. The walk-through test and the client's confirmation of the system should be documented on the current working paper file.

Example

Walk-through test

Client: Noel Co	**Prepared by:** ABC
Year end: 31 December 20X6	**Date:** 17.5.X6
Subject: Sales walk through test	

Customer order
- Date: 3.4.X6
- No: 12345
- Goods description: Product x
- Quantity: 3 boxes
- Agreed price: £15

Despatch note
- Date: 4.4.X6
- No: 23456
- Goods agreed to order: ✓
- Quantity agreed to order: ✓
- Evidence of check by gate staff: ✓

Invoice
- Date: 4.4.X6
- No: 34567
- Goods agreed to order and despatch note: ✓
- Quantity agreed to order and despatch note: ✓
- Price agreed to price on order: ✓

Checked
- Invoice correctly entered in Receivables ledger ✓

Conclusion
The system is correctly recorded on the flowchart

3 Internal controls

3.1 Definition of a system of internal control

> **Definition**
>
> A **system of internal control** comprises the control environment (the general attitude to controls taken by the organisation) and control procedures. It includes all the policies and procedures (internal controls) adopted by the directors and management of an entity to assist in achieving their objective of ensuring, as far as practicable, the orderly and efficient conduct of its business, including adherence to internal policies, the safeguarding of assets, the prevention and detection of fraud and error, the accuracy and completeness of the accounting records, and the timely preparation of reliable financial information. Internal controls may be incorporated within computerised accounting systems. However, the system of internal control extends beyond those matters which relate directly to the accounting system.

Controls may be **direct** or **indirect**. Direct controls are controls that are precise enough to address risks of material misstatement at the assertion level. Indirect controls are controls that support direct controls (i.e. controls that are not sufficiently precise to prevent, detect or correct misstatements but which support other controls and may therefore have an indirect effect on the likelihood that a misstatement will be detected or prevented on a timely basis).

According to ISA 315 (Revised) *Identifying and assessing the risks of material misstatement*, there are 5 components of a system of internal control:

1. Control environment
    - This is the attitude and awareness of the directors.
2. The entity's risk assessment process (see below)
3. The information system and communication
    - This refers to the controls over the software and hardware.
4. Control activities (see below)
5. The entity's process to monitor the system of internal control
    - Are the controls still appropriate and effective?

3.2 The entity's risk assessment process

The main aim of risk assessment is to protect the business from unforeseen circumstances that could negatively impact the profitability of the company and stop it achieving its strategic goals.

Companies need mechanisms in place to identify and then assess those risks. In doing so, companies can rank risks in terms of their relative importance by scoring them with regard to their likelihood and potential impact. This could take the form of a 'risk map' or 'risk matrix'.

This enables the company to assess the likelihood or probability of a risk occurring and the likely impact to the business.

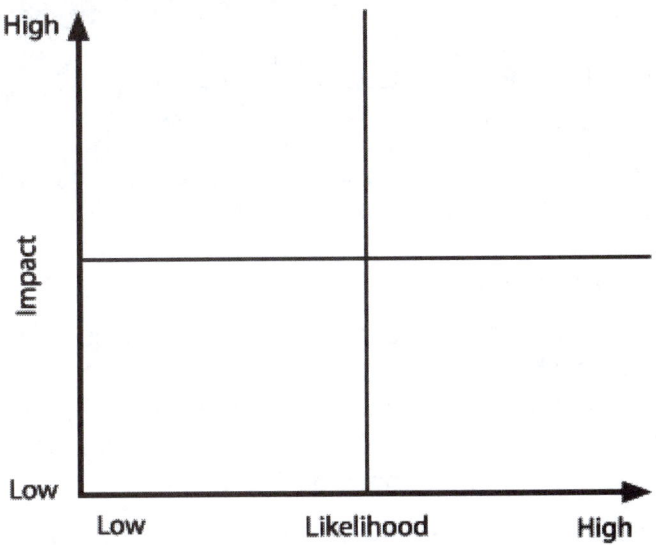

A risk that ranks highly likely to occur and high potential impact to the business would be prioritised as requiring immediate action. A company may be able to manage the risks they have identified by implementing effective systems and controls. A risk that is considered both low likelihood and low impact might be ignored.

The following risk matrix has reportedly been used in areas of the UK National Health Service (NHS). Likelihood and consequence are ranked from 1 to 5 (many other combinations can be used). The ratings for likelihood and consequence are multiplied to give a risk score, or numerical grade, for each scenario enabling easy prioritisation of the risks. Bands of a given level of risk run diagonally across the matrix.

		Likelihood				
		1 Rare	2 Unlikely	3 Possible	4 Likely	5 Almost Certain
Consequence	5 Catastrophe	5 Moderate	10 High	15 Extreme	20 Extreme	25 Extreme
	4 Major	4 Moderate	8 High	12 High	16 Extreme	20 Extreme
	3 Moderate	3 Low	6 Moderate	9 High	12 High	15 Moderate
	2 Minor	2 Low	4 Moderate	6 Moderate	8 High	10 High
	1 Negligible	1 Low	2 Low	3 Low	4 Moderate	5 Moderate

3.3 Control activities

'Control procedures' are those policies and procedures in addition to the control environment which are established to achieve the entity's specific objectives. They include, in particular, procedures designed to prevent or to detect and correct errors. The latter may be a particular focus of high level controls in small or owner-managed entities.

ISA 315 (Revised 2019) *Identifying and assessing the risks of material misstatement* refers to the following categories of control activities:

Authorisation and approvals – An authorisation affirms that a transaction is valid and typically takes the form of an approval by a higher level of management or of verification and a determination if the transaction is valid.

An example of an authorisation and approval control is a supervisor approving an expense report after reviewing whether the expenses seem reasonable and within policy.

An example of an automated approval is when an invoice unit cost is automatically compared with the related purchase order unit cost within a pre-established tolerance level. Invoices within the tolerance level are automatically approved for payment. Those invoices outside the tolerance level are flagged for additional investigation.

Reconciliations	– Controls that compare two or more data elements. If differences are identified, action is taken to bring the data into agreement. Reconciliations generally address the completeness or accuracy of processing transactions.
Verifications	– Controls that compare two or more items with each other or compare an item with a policy, and will likely involve a follow-up action when the two items do not match or the item is not consistent with policy. Verifications generally address the completeness, accuracy or validity of processing transactions.
Physical or logical controls	– Controls that encompass the physical security of assets such as secured facilities over access to assets and records, banking cash immediately, authorisation for access to computer programs and data files, electronic tagging of inventory and portable non-current assets.
Segregation of duties	– Assigning different people the responsibilities of authorising transactions, recording transactions and maintaining custody of assets. Segregation of duties is intended to reduce the opportunities to allow any person to be in a position to both perpetrate and conceal errors or fraud in the normal course of the person's duties.

The above list is not exhaustive but does cover the main areas an auditor looks at when completing an internal controls review.

3.4 Auditing in a computer environment

It is likely that the auditor will have to consider accounting systems which are based on a computer.

In order to be able to conclude whether accounting records produced by a computer form a reliable basis for the preparation of the financial statements, the auditor must understand and be able to audit the system.

Planning implications – additional factors to consider

- Controls in the computerised system.
- Potential loss of 'audit trail'.
- Likely weaknesses and breakdowns in computer systems.
- The timing of audit work to ensure data is available in readily useable format.

Controls

In addition to manual controls (user controls), computer systems include

- Programmed controls (in the software) over the data being processed.
- Information technology controls (in the IT department) over the implementation, security and use of programs and data.

Some user controls and programmed controls are known as 'information processing controls'.

Information processing controls are aimed at ensuring the completeness and accuracy of the accounting records and the validity of the entries processed.

Some examples of 'information processing controls' could include:

- processing invoices by batch rather than individually, and a manual check being performed to ensure the batch of invoices has been processed completely

- manual calculations and recording of the total of the batch of invoices before inputting to the system, and subsequent check to the total value of items recorded per the system.

Example of a batch control sheet

ABC

Batch N°	421
Date	1 March 20X6
Total value of batch	£28,541.40
N° of invoices in batch	24
Invoice numbers included	10072–10095

This batch control sheet would be attached to the invoices it relates to (i.e. those numbered 10072–10095) and checks should be performed to ensure:

1. the sequence of invoices in the batch is complete
2. the total value of invoices is correct
3. ensure processed accurately to the computer system, both that the sequence of invoices is complete and the total per batch agrees to system.

Other examples of information processing controls

- Random checks being performed on a one to one basis of input with output.
- Periodic printouts of data for manual review for reasonableness (e.g. a bank reconciliation, aged receivables report).
- Monthly agreement of the computer's closing balances with the balances on the control accounts in the nominal ledger.

Information Technology controls

These include controls over:

- the design and implementation of new systems and systems maintenance
- program and data file security
- computer operations and systems software.

Examples of such controls could include:

- password protection – a programmed recognition of a valid identification to activate a terminal. The same technique could be used to restrict user's access to certain files.
- physical access controls:
    - over the computer room (e.g. security coded locks)
    - over terminals (e.g. keys)
- adequate training of all users
- up-to-date user manuals
- adequate supervision of staff using the systems
- regular maintenance of the computer, perhaps under a service agreement from the software supplier
- regular backing-up of copies of data files, and their secure storage
- virus checkers being installed and regularly updated.

Loss of 'audit trail'

The results of computer processing may not be printed out in detail. Difficulties arising include:

- totals and analyses being printed without supporting details
- it not being apparent whether reports of 'exceptions' (e.g. customer accounts in excess of credit limits) or rejected data are complete

Accounting systems and internal controls: Chapter 2

- control procedures being carried out without visible evidence of it having taken place (e.g. if input data is corrected on a visual display by an operator).

The phrase **'loss of audit trail'** does not necessarily constitute a weakness in the system (e.g. 'reporting by exception' should assist management in controlling the business). The term 'loss of visible evidence' is therefore preferred.

Overcoming loss of visible evidence

Techniques which the auditor can plan to use to overcome the problems include the following:

- Requesting printouts of complete information to check makeup of totals and analyses.

- Manually checking data before it is processed to test a programmed procedure.

- Simulating a report condition (e.g. withholding an input document to create a 'no data' report), with the client's permission.

- Clerical recreation of totals from source documents (this may be time consuming and expensive).

- Testing totals rather than tracing individual items (e.g. comparing analyses with previous periods and budgets).

- Using alternative tests (e.g. testing inventory count procedures when movements making up inventory balances cannot be tested).

Automated tools and techniques (computer-assisted audit techniques)

Automated tools and techniques are sometimes referred to as computer-assisted audit techniques (CAATs).

AUDIT AND ASSURANCE

In addition to reviewing the controls surrounding computer systems, auditors might use automated tools and techniques throughout the audit. These tend to fall in to two categories.

	Test data	Audit software
Description	Auditor data is put into the client's system Data: real or dummy System: live or a copy (Note: An integrated test facility creates a fictitious entity in a database to process test transactions simultaneously with live input.)	Client data is put into the auditor's system
Use	Test the controls in the system	Basic data analysis Substantive testing
Examples	The auditor enters data e.g. (a) A timesheet with hours outside the normal range to check that the system rejects it. (b) A valid purchase invoice to check that it is allocated to the correct account.	Re-performance of addition or ageing of transactions Preparation of reports Calculations of ratios Sample selection

Test your understanding 1

Two types of automated tools and techniques are test data and audit software. For each of the procedures listed below, select the type of automated tools and techniques would be used to perform that procedure.

1   Comparison of the cost and net realisable value of inventory items to determine the lower value.

2   Input of data with false inventory code numbers to check that the system rejects such data.

3   Extraction of inventory balances over £5,000 in order to carry out further testing.

Within the next chapter, you will find further discussion on automated tools and techniques and the impact of technology on auditing.

3.5 Preliminary assessment

One of the external auditor's objectives in ascertaining and recording the accounting system is to make a preliminary evaluation of the system of internal control.

The degree of reliance which the external auditor feels can be placed on the internal controls will determine the sorts of test to be carried out on the system (to determine its adequacy as a basis for preparing financial statements).

3.6 Extent of internal controls

The extent of the system of internal control will depend on what is appropriate to the entity. Factors which may have an influence include:

- the nature, size and volume of transactions
- the degree of personal control by management
- the geographical distribution of the entity, and
- the cost effectiveness of operating certain controls, with respect to the benefits expected to be derived from them.

Thus the external auditor's approach to evaluating the system of internal control will depend on the type of business.

3.7 Small businesses

Auditors obtain an appropriate level of audit evidence to support their audit opinion regardless of the size of the entity. However, many internal controls relevant to large entities are not practical in a small business; for example, in small businesses accounting procedures may be performed by few persons who may have both operating and custodial responsibilities and, consequently, segregation of duties may be severely limited.

Inadequate segregation of duties may, in some cases, be offset by other control procedures and close involvement of an owner or manager in strong supervisory controls where they have direct personal knowledge of the entity and involvement in transactions – though this in itself may introduce other risks.

In circumstances where segregation of duties is limited and evidence of supervisory controls is lacking, the audit evidence necessary to support the auditors' opinion on the financial statements may have to be obtained entirely through the performance of substantive procedures and any audit work carried out in the course of preparing the financial statements.

3.8 Larger businesses

Procedures are likely to be more formalised than for a smaller business, and the internal controls in operation much more extensive and sophisticated. However, even where this is the case, the auditor may choose not to rely on such controls if, for example, their preliminary evaluation shows that they are ineffective.

4 Preliminary evaluation of internal controls

4.1 Introduction

In order to make the decision about whether or not to place reliance on the internal controls of the business, the auditor makes a preliminary evaluation of their operation. This may be carried out using internal control questionnaires (ICQs or checklists) and/or evaluations (ICEs or questionnaires).

4.2 Internal control questionnaires (ICQs)

Definition

Internal control questionnaires (ICQs) are checklists of questions designed to:

- discover the existence of internal controls, and
- identify possible areas of weakness.

The questions are framed in order to highlight situations where:

- there is no subdivision of duties between essential functions
- controls do not exist, or
- essential aspects of management supervision of controls do not exist.

The questionnaire is phrased consistently so that, for example, a 'yes' answer indicates a strength, and a 'no' answer a weakness. This makes it easier to evaluate the completed questionnaire. Weaknesses can then be cross referenced to the relevant part of the audit programme.

Example

Steps required for drafting appropriate questions for an ICQ.

Step 1 – Identify the cycle e.g. sales

What do we start with?	Opening receivables
What do we do to change it?	Transactions
What do we end up with?	Closing receivables

Step 2 – Consider overall audit approach

Opening balances – Agree to prior year working papers.

Transactions – Controls help ensure completeness and accuracy.

Therefore:

Closing balances – Auditor can obtain comfort as to completeness and accuracy.

Step 3 – Break down the transaction types into components

Customer order → sales order → despatch note → invoice → receivables ledger → statement

Step 4 – Ask 'what could go wrong?'

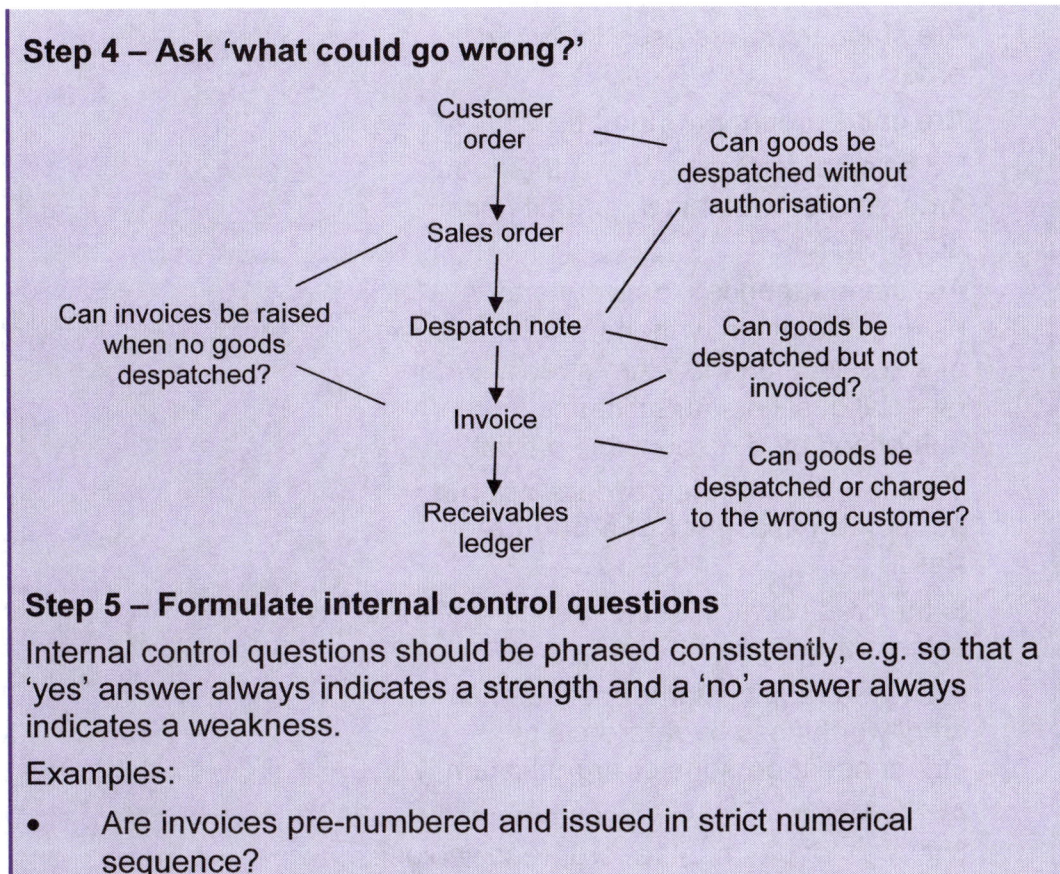

Step 5 – Formulate internal control questions

Internal control questions should be phrased consistently, e.g. so that a 'yes' answer always indicates a strength and a 'no' answer always indicates a weakness.

Examples:

- Are invoices pre-numbered and issued in strict numerical sequence?

4.3 Example of an internal control questionnaire

The following is an example of an internal control questionnaire.

Example

Sales and trade receivables

Client:	Normanton Co		
Year end:	30 September 20X6	Prepared by:	B.E. Mignano
Cycle:	Sales	Date:	7.9.X6

		Yes/No or N/A	Flowchart reference
1	**To ensure that all orders received are processed in such a way that keeps errors to a minimum.**		
	Are persons responsible for preparation of sales orders independent of credit control, custody of inventory and recording sales transactions?		

Are standard forms used to record orders?

Are sales orders pre-numbered?

Do sales order clerks check the goods ordered are available in quantity and quality required?

Are standard prices, delivery and payment terms in written form for the use of sales order clerks? Are special orders (special qualities, quantities, prices) authorised by a responsible official?

2 **To ensure that sales orders are not accepted in respect of a bad credit risk.**

Is the credit controller independent of the sales order clerks?

Are new credit customers vetted for creditworthiness by reference to independent persons or organisations?

Are orders from existing customers checked for payment record, receivables ledger balance and credit limit?

Are credit limits set by responsible officials for all credit customers?

Is the credit approval evidenced on the sales order by the signature of a responsible official?

Is the work of a credit control clerk independently checked?

3 **To ensure that goods are only despatched to customers after proper authorisation.**

Is warehouse/despatch department independent of sales order preparation, credit control and invoicing?

Do warehouse personnel release goods from the warehouse on the basis of sales orders signed by authorised sales order and credit control personnel?

Is the despatch of goods evidenced by the preparation of a goods despatch note?

Are goods despatch notes pre-numbered?

Are two copies of the goods despatch notes sent to the customer for one to be returned as evidence of receipt? Is a copy of the despatch note sent to the inventory control department to update inventory records?

Is inventory counted periodically and compared with inventory records?

4 **To ensure that all goods despatched are invoiced at authorised prices and terms.**

Is sales invoicing independent of sales order preparation, credit control, warehouse and despatch departments? Are copies of sales orders received by sales invoicing?

Is a sequence check carried out on sales orders?

Is a sequence check carried out on goods despatch notes?

Are goods despatch notes matched with sales orders and unmatched orders followed up?

Do invoicing clerks have details of current prices, terms and conditions, including special agreements with particular customers? Are sales invoices independently checked before despatch?

5 **To ensure that all sales invoices are properly recorded in individual customers' accounts in the receivables ledger.**

Is the receivables ledger clerk independent of sales order preparation, credit control, warehouse, despatch and sales invoicing?

Is a receivables ledger control account maintained independent of the receivables ledger clerk?

> Are differences between extracted list of receivables ledger balances and control account balances investigated by a responsible official?
>
> Are monthly statements of amounts outstanding prepared and despatched to customers?
>
> Is an aged receivable listing prepared and reviewed by a responsible official?
>
> Are receivables ledger balances made up of identifiable sales invoices and other items?
>
> Are irrecoverable receivable write-offs and discounts authorised by a responsible official other than the receivables ledger clerk?

4.4 Internal control evaluations (ICEs/Questionnaires)

An ICE may be used as well as or instead of an ICQ. See the specimen on the next page.

In practice, many audit firms make no distinction between an ICQ and an ICE (even to the extent of calling one an ICEQ!). However, an ICE is usually more detailed than an ICQ as it links the control to the effect this will have on the audit and the resulting substantive work.

4.5 Principal features of an ICE

- Contains only those direct control questions on which reliance is to be sought.

- Records the direct control which satisfies the direct control question (an ICQ may well be required to distinguish the direct control from the indirect controls).

- Describes the nature and extent of the tests of controls.

- Records the test conclusion and how substantive procedures are affected.

AUDIT AND ASSURANCE

Definition

An **Internal Control Evaluation** contains the direct control questions, the direct control which satisfies this question and details of the audit to test the direct control.

Example of internal control evaluation

Client:	Albany Co
Year end:	30.5.X6

	Initials	Date
Prepared by	WANV	27/7/X6
Reviewed by		

Direct control question	Direct control	System ref	Tests of controls	WP ref	Substantive procedures	WP ref	Conclusions
Can goods be ordered without authorisation?	All orders are authorised before being placed.		Select a sample of GRNs and confirm that the PO is: – attached/cross-referenced – signed by the buyer; and – supported by a signed purchase requisition.		For the same sample: – agree quantities received to quantities ordered; and – confirm part of short deliveries (e.g. to credit note).		
Can goods be received without authorisation?	All GRNs are matched with purchase orders before goods are accepted.						

Accounting systems and internal controls: **Chapter 2**

5 Reliance on internal controls

5.1 Introduction

Where the preliminary assessment has indicated that there are internal controls upon which the auditor wishes to rely, the auditor will design and carry out tests of controls.

Definition

Tests of controls are audit procedures designed to evaluate the operating effectiveness of controls in preventing, or detecting and correcting material misstatements.

The auditor seeks assurance from these tests that the controls have been operating effectively throughout the period and consequently that:

- the accounting records are complete and accurate, and
- all entries are valid.

5.2 If favourable

The auditor may restrict substantive procedures to be carried out.

(**Note:** Substantive procedures may never be eliminated completely – see below).

5.3 If unfavourable

The auditor may extend tests of controls to determine whether the breakdowns in controls which have been recorded are only isolated incidents. If the original results are particularly unfavourable, or the additional tests of control in this area reveal further breakdowns, a wholly substantive approach must then be adopted.

5.4 Limitations on the effectiveness of internal controls

As mentioned above, even where the system of internal control is extensive, and tests of control have revealed that such controls have operated effectively throughout the period, some substantive procedures must still be carried out. This requirement stems from the fact that no system of internal control can guarantee the completeness and accuracy of the records by itself, due to inherent limitations on their effectiveness such as the following:

- The usual requirement that the cost of an internal control is not disproportionate to the potential loss which may result from its absence.

- Most systematic internal controls tend to be directed at routine transactions rather than non-routine transactions.

- The potential for human error due to carelessness, distraction, mistakes of judgement and the misunderstanding of instructions.

- The possibility of circumvention of internal controls through collusion with parties outside or inside the entity.

- The possibility that a person responsible for exercising an internal control could abuse that responsibility, for example by overriding an internal control.

- The possibility that procedures may become inadequate due to changes in conditions or that compliance with procedures may deteriorate over time.

Test your understanding 2

The external auditor may seek to place reliance on internal controls in order to restrict substantive testing. In each of the following circumstances select whether the external auditor is likely to place reliance or place no reliance on internal controls.

1. A company where the processing of accounting transactions is undertaken by one person.

2. A company which has an internal audit function which monitors operational and financial controls.

3. A company which has internal controls with a history of management override.

6 Management and supervision

6.1 Professional scepticism and professional judgement

During the course of an audit, the auditor will hold a number of discussions with the client. It is very important that throughout these discussions, the auditor maintains their professional scepticism.

Definition

Professional scepticism is an attitude that includes a questioning mind, being alert to conditions which may indicate possible misstatement due to error or fraud, and a critical assessment of audit evidence.

Professional scepticism does not mean that auditors should disbelieve everything they are told; however they must have a questioning attitude.

Definition

Professional judgement is the application of relevant training, knowledge and experience in making informed decisions about the courses of actions that are appropriate in the circumstances of the audit.

All discussions held with the client must be documented by the auditor to ensure there is evidence that these discussions took place and the information and explanations received.

Test your understanding 3

External auditors use a variety of methods for documenting systems of control, including flowcharts, internal control questionnaires and internal control checklists. For each of the following descriptions, select whether it represents a flowchart, internal control questionnaire or internal control checklist.

1 A listing of controls necessary to provide reasonable assurance of effective internal control within a given transaction cycle.

2 A pictorial presentation of the processing steps within a given transaction cycle.

Test your understanding 4

For each of the following statements, select whether they are true or false.

1. If the controls of a company are considered to be very strong, the auditor can avoid doing any substantive testing.
2. A walk through test is a type of substantive test.

7 Summary

The following are the key points arising in this chapter which you should have noted.

Accounting systems

- Factors affecting adequacy of accounting systems.

Internal control

- Considerations affecting the extent of internal controls.
- Factors affecting the auditor's reliance on internal controls.
- Limitations of internal controls.

Flowcharting

- How to draft and interpret a flowchart.

Walk-through tests

- How to confirm the accuracy of the system recorded.

Checklists and questionnaires

- Purpose and principal features.

Professional scepticism

Test your understanding answers

Test your understanding 1

1. Audit software.
2. Test data.
3. Audit software.

Test your understanding 2

1. No reliance.
2. Reliance.
3. No reliance.

Test your understanding 3

1. Checklist.
2. Flowchart.

Test your understanding 4

1. False.
2. False.

Planning, controlling and recording

Introduction

Planning an audit is essential to the effective running of the assignment. There are a number of factors to consider when planning an audit which we will see in this chapter.

ASSESSMENT CRITERIA

The concept of risk (3.1)

The concept of materiality (3.2)

Audit procedures (3.3)

The role of audit working papers (3.4)

Audit approach (4.4)

CONTENTS

1. Planning
2. The client/auditor relationship
3. The engagement letter
4. Planning the assignment
5. Audit planning memorandum
6. Quality management
7. Audit risk
8. Materiality
9. Analytical procedures
10. The audit approach
11. Recording audit work
12. Impact of technology on auditing

Planning, controlling and recording: **Chapter 3**

1 Planning

1.1 Introduction

ISA 300 *Planning an audit of financial statements* states:

The auditor should plan the audit so that the engagement will be performed in an effective manner.

Planning entails developing a general strategy and a detailed approach for the expected nature, timing and extent of the audit.

In addition to dealing with the significant aspects of planning an audit, this chapter also discusses the impact of technology on auditing. Technological advances can be very beneficial for auditors, often helping to increase efficiency during the audit process.

1.2 Audit plan and audit programme

Auditors formulate the general audit strategy in an overall audit plan, which sets the direction for the audit and provides guidance for the development of the audit programme. The audit programme sets out the detailed procedures required to implement the strategy.

1.3 Objectives

Planning is necessary for audits of entities of all types and sizes. The objectives of planning the audit work, which takes place before the detailed audit work begins, include:

- ensuring that appropriate attention is devoted to the different areas of the audit
- ensuring that potential problems are identified, and
- facilitating review.

Planning also assists in the proper assignment of work to members of the audit team and their briefing, and in the co-ordination of work done by other auditors and experts, so that the audit may be performed in an efficient and timely manner.

1.4 Procedures

An understanding of the entity's business and, as far as practicable, of the nature and scope of the work they are to carry out is necessary for all members of the audit team before the audit field work starts.

The auditors' experience with the entity and knowledge of its business assist in the identification of events, transactions and practices which may have a material effect on the financial statements.

Auditors may need to discuss elements of the overall audit plan and certain audit procedures with the entity's management and staff to improve the effectiveness of the audit and to co-ordinate audit procedures with the work of the entity's personnel, including internal auditors. The overall audit plan and the detailed audit procedures to be performed, however, remain the auditors' responsibility.

2 The client/auditor relationship

2.1 Knowing the client

An auditor has a duty of care to carry out their work with a reasonable standard of skill and care and therefore should not take on engagements which the auditor cannot properly fulfil. (See Chapter 15)

Consequently the auditor must:

- understand how the business operates, its strengths and its weaknesses, the markets served, the products it supplies
- have a good working relationship with the key members of the management team
- have a clear understanding of the nature of the services provided by the auditor to their client
- be aware of what can be regarded as 'best practice' and be able to implement the latest professional developments.

In the case of companies audited in prior years, most of the information required for planning will be available in the permanent file, working papers and other files.

2.2 New audits

On being asked to accept appointment as auditor to a new client, there are various matters that the auditor should consider before accepting such an appointment (see Chapter 13 for details of appointment).

- Does the auditor have the capability and resources to carry out the audit? The auditor will need to determine the following:
    - size, location and nature of business of the prospective client
    - timing of the audit
    - number and degree of experience of the staff required

- current commitments of the firm
- firm's experience in the audit of such a business.

- Is the auditor independent of the client? The auditor must establish the independence of the firm.
- Are there any other reasons for not accepting appointment?

Communication with the existing auditor may reveal professional reasons why the audit should not be accepted. (See Chapter 13 for changes in professional appointment).

3 The engagement letter

Definition

An **engagement letter** is a letter from the auditor to the client setting out the terms of the assignment.

3.1 Introduction

The purpose of the engagement letter is:

- to set out the terms under which the assignment is to be carried out; and hence
- to minimise the chances of misunderstanding between client and external auditor.

3.2 Procedures

Auditors should:

- agree the terms of their engagement with new clients in writing
- thereafter, regularly review the terms of engagement and if appropriate agree any changes in writing.

3.3 New audits

The agreement of an engagement letter is in the interests of both auditors and client. It is therefore desirable that the contents be agreed prior to the audit appointment (and the letter sent soon after) and, in any event, before the commencement of the first audit assignment. Subsequently, the regular review of the engagement letter helps the auditors and the client avoid misunderstandings with respect to the engagement.

3.4 Recurring audits

As part of the annual planning process, auditors consider whether a new engagement letter is required. The following factors may make the agreement of a new letter appropriate:

- any indication that the client misunderstands the objective and scope of the audit
- a recent change of management, board of directors or audit committee
- a significant change in ownership, such as a new holding company
- a significant change in the nature or size of the client's business
- any relevant change in legal or professional requirements.

It may be appropriate to remind the client of the original letter when the auditors decide a new engagement letter is unnecessary for any period.

3.5 Principal contents of the engagement letter

The engagement letter should:

- document and confirm acceptance of the appointment; and
- include a summary of the responsibilities of the directors and of the auditors, the scope of the engagement and the form of any reports.

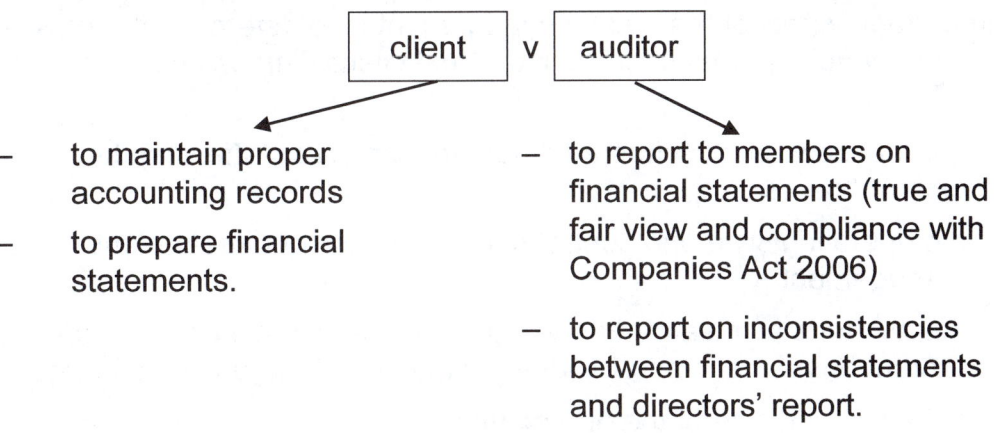

- to maintain proper accounting records
- to prepare financial statements.

- to report to members on financial statements (true and fair view and compliance with Companies Act 2006)
- to report on inconsistencies between financial statements and directors' report.

The letter should outline the main stages in the audit. The remaining content hinges around areas where particular misunderstandings may occur, including the following:

- fees and billing arrangements
- procedures where the client has a complaint about the service
- where appropriate, arrangements concerning the involvement of:
    - other auditors and experts in some aspect of the audit
    - internal auditors and other staff of the entity

- arrangements, if any, to be made with the predecessor auditors, where the audit is being performed by a new auditor
- where appropriate, the country by whose laws the engagement is to be governed
- a reference to any further agreements between the auditors and the client
- a proposed timetable for the engagement.

Representations by management may be requested in writing. If the auditor does not clarify this up front, the directors may be reluctant to provide written representations. (See Chapter 11 for more detail).

Accounting and taxation services should be distinguished from audit.

Fees are usually based on time spent and level of staff involved i.e. variable not fixed.

4 Planning the assignment

4.1 Audit approach

An important aspect of the auditor's judgement is to determine the most appropriate audit approach for the individual client. This will be based on the following:

- general economic factors and industry conditions affecting the entity's business
- the operating style and control consciousness of directors and management
- the auditor's cumulative knowledge of the accounting system and system of internal control and any expected changes in the period
- the scale and size of the organisation
- the volumes and value of transactions
- the geographical spread of business operations.

The auditor must have a thorough understanding of the affairs of the business and its recent financial history. This is done by reviewing files of working papers and regular contact with the client.

4.2 Obtaining the knowledge

In the first audit the necessary information must be collected before planning can commence. A starting point is to consider the industry in which the business operates in broad terms. The following matters should be noted:

- typical kinds of business within the industry (e.g. large international)
- the broad functions involved (e.g. manufacturing, distribution, wholesaling)
- any particular features of the business important to management (e.g. long-term contracts)
- typical sources of income (e.g. room lettings in a hotel)
- typical kinds of expenditure (e.g. food in a restaurant)
- the kinds of records kept (e.g. ledgers, registers, manual or computerised)
- management information needs.

Such information is vital if the auditor is to discuss the industry, its problems and solutions with management in a credible manner.

4.3 Client liaison

The auditor should obviously pay attention to the client's requirements in carrying out the audit. The client will wish to avoid audit visits at critical times of the year (e.g. when quarterly accounts are being prepared). The auditor should consult with their client in order to ascertain the following dates:

- to which accounts are to be made up for the period under review
- by which final accounts will be prepared together with supporting schedules
- on which the directors intend to meet in order to approve the financial statements
- of the AGM when audited accounts must be laid before the members
- by which accounts must be filed at the Companies Registry (Companies House in the UK).

4.4 Time and fee budgets

The auditor should aim to provide their client with an efficient and cost effective service. Budgetary planning is an important part of the overall audit plan in order to ensure that:

- the work is completed efficiently
- the costs of carrying out the audit are monitored
- the client's fee can be negotiated on a reasonable basis (this is now often a sensitive issue in good client/auditor relationships)
- forward planning for staff requirements is facilitated.

4.5 Staffing

The audit budget will also assist the auditor to determine the manpower requirements. It is important to select the right mix of skills so that the audit work is competently performed. Other factors to consider:

- staff members' prior experience of the client, and
- personal qualities of staff (e.g. potential personality clashes with client or other audit staff).

4.6 The planning meeting

Once staff have been selected they should be briefed at a planning meeting. The matters discussed at the meeting must be documented in the form of minutes and should cover the following:

- a description of key features of the client
- the names of contacts
- any special features that may be encountered on the audit
- the general instructions to staff on their responsibilities
- any issues of confidentiality and security.

Many firms use a planning memorandum, see later.

4.7 Timing of audit visits

The timing of the audit visits varies according to the type of enterprise and specific deadlines.

When dealing with a large public company audit there is a need to ensure that the work is reasonably spread so that undue pressure is not placed upon the auditor in the critical period between the date of the statement of financial position and the date of the directors' meeting to finalise the accounts. Instead, work will be spread over the period prior to the year-end date.

4.8 First interim visit

- To review accounting systems.
- To document any new systems or changes that have occurred.
- To ascertain and evaluate internal controls using standard checklists, questionnaires etc.
- To confirm the system by means of walk-through tests on one or two transactions.

4.9 Second interim visit

- To test processing systems of the major transaction cycles of purchases, sales and payroll to ensure that the controls are sound.
- To test the records (on the basis of the above) in order to form an opinion as to whether the processing is accurate and the records are reliable.

4.10 Year-end inventory count

To witness the physical inventory count (see Chapter 6).

4.11 Final audit visit

After the year-end date, the auditor can devote time to verifying assets and liabilities and carrying out a review of the financial statements so as to be in a position to sign the auditor's report.

It is common, however, to find that the audits of small companies (whose control systems are limited) are performed in a single phase commencing after the year-end date.

5 Audit planning memorandum

5.1 Introduction

Most audit firms prepare an audit planning memorandum which sets out factors to be taken into account, the methods by which the audit objectives will be achieved and the organisational matters which need to be considered.

5.2 Typical contents

Terms of the engagement

The work to be done (i.e. audit work, accounting work to be done for the client, tax work, letters to be sent). Including reports required and client expectations.

The client and its background

History, products, locations, especially noting factors like a new managing director, a new computer, a new product.

Important figures and ratios

From previous years audit working papers and, if available, from management and draft accounts.

Audit risk areas

These might include inventory and work in progress or dealings with a fellow group company (see later in this chapter). This may include the requirement for involvement of specialists.

Preliminary estimate of materiality

(See section 8 in this chapter).

Client assistance

Assistance from the client may be required in providing documents and analyses, providing computer time, arranging visits to branches. Also the extent to which internal audit may be involved.

The audit approach

Extent of reliance on internal control, the use of tests of control and substantive procedures (see later in this chapter).

Timetable

Key audit dates e.g. of interim, year-end and final audits and of deadlines to meet (e.g. AGM).

Staffing requirement

Time budget and audit fee estimate. This may be included in a separate memorandum.

5.3 Confidentiality matters

The following matters illustrate the nature of confidential information which may be encountered in the planning process.

- **Risk assessment** – some factors which increase the auditor's perception of risk may appear to cast aspersions on the integrity of the client's staff and/or management (see later in this chapter for more detail).

- **Sensitive issues** – for example, new product development, plans for business acquisitions etc. These must be kept confidential within the client-auditor relationship.

- **Audit approach** – where locations are to be visited on a surprise basis (e.g. to attend the inventory count or count cash) it is inappropriate to warn the client in advance by incorporating details in an audit planning memorandum which is shown to the client.

- **Nature and scope of audit tests to be performed** – if there is suspicion of irregularities being perpetrated by the client's staff, their detection by the auditor may be thwarted.

- **Budgets and fees** – although the audit fee is negotiated with the client, it is usually inappropriate to disclose budgeted hours and charge-out rates of the audit team. Pressure from an audit client to curtail audit work and reduce fees would impair objectivity (see Chapter 14).

Example – AUDIT PLANNING MEMORANDUM

HASTINGS & WARWICK

Client: Peppers Co   Prepared by: K.E.D.   Date: 5.6.X6

Period: Y/e 31 July 20X6   Reviewed by: Date:

Audit plan

1. Terms of engagement including reports required and client expectations

   Normal Companies Act audit (voluntary audit); we write up nominal ledger and prepare draft statutory accounts from client records.

2	The company and its business	New company set up in 20X4 to retail PCs and related software packages – provides some consultancy services. Financed mainly by proprietors and overdraft until £100,000 new capital injected by Capital Venture Co in January 20X6. Turnover about £1,200,000 (£650,000 last year).
3	Special audit problems	Possible obsolete inventory due to changes in technology; NX50 software may be unsaleable. Billing of sales is likely to give rise to errors – new systems are invoiced in advance of delivery; consultancy work is billed retrospectively and there is little by way of 'work in progress' records.
4	Results of analytical procedures	Client produces management accounts comprising sales analysis and cash flows (not reproduced); these are in line with the forecasts done in the report to Capital Venture Co.
5	Evaluation of audit risk	In view of the rapid growth of the business, the importance placed on the accounts by Capital Venture Co and the problems in recording sales, this audit should be treated as higher than normal risk. No reliance can be placed on the accounting systems nor on any analytical procedures.
6	Preliminary estimate of materiality	£7,000 based on estimate of turnover of £1.2m and likely profit of around £120,000–£250,000.

AUDIT AND ASSURANCE

7	Audit approach	No attempt to rely on internal controls or analytical procedures. The following specific procedures should be carried out: • Reconcile purchases and sales of computer systems and check that cut off is correct, bearing in mind that it is the company's practice to invoice before delivery. • Review consultants' diaries for the last 3 months to check that all assignments are included in WIP or billings. For other procedures and objectives, see the audit programme which has already been prepared (not reproduced).
8	Other matters	The company moved to new leasehold premises in April; we need to take particular care that leasehold improvements are treated as tax efficiently as possible (see attached letter – not reproduced).
9	Budget and fee	Budget £15,500, excluding VAT
10	Timetable and staffing	G. Smith and J. Taylor to complete by 2.10.X6.

Audit plan approved   Date

Manager _____ _____

Partner _____ _____

5.4 Matters of security

All audit staff should be briefed in the observance of the client's security procedures. For example:

- presenting temporary passes for door security
- completing registers (e.g. for computer utilisation).

Audit staff should take precautions to protect themselves when handling cash or other valuables. For example, when counting cash:

- a responsible member of the client's staff must be in attendance throughout so the auditor is never left unattended with client monies
- if possible, the room should be locked to prevent interruption
- it is advisable that the auditor does not have any cash in their possession
- the responsible official should sign a declaration that the cash has been returned intact into their custody.

6 Quality management

6.1 Methods of control

Direction, supervision and review are the principal methods for controlling the audit.

6.2 Procedures for controlling the audit

- Audit assistants are informed of their responsibilities and the objectives of the procedures they are to perform.
- Audit directions are communicated via briefing meetings, internal oral communications, audit manuals and checklists and the audit planning memorandum.
- Work should be done by staff with suitable skill and experience.
- The audit partner should be in constant contact with team members, ensuring that supervision is carried out by themselves or their manager.
- The audit plan should be monitored by regular reports on work done so that the partner or manager is alerted to any changes from the agreed sequence of tasks.

- The procedures for carrying out audit field work should be documented in a manual of instruction and followed by audit staff.
- The work carried out by audit staff should be properly documented and reviewed by a more senior person.
- Troublesome points should be brought to the attention of partners, and staff should be sufficiently skilled to be alerted to unusual matters so that they are followed up.
- There should be written evidence that audit work has been reviewed.

7 Audit risk

7.1 Introduction

Most audit firms adopt a 'risk-based' approach to auditing.

Auditors should:

(a) obtain an understanding of the accounting and system of internal control sufficient to plan the audit and develop an effective audit approach; and

(b) use professional judgement to assess the components of audit risk and to design audit procedures to ensure it is reduced to an acceptably low level.

7.2 Risk-based audit approach

A risk-based approach to auditing:

- encourages a rational and systematic approach (which is essential to performing a high quality audit in the current climate of litigation)
- gives a plausible reason for keeping the level of audit testing to a minimum in certain cases (as commercial pressure on audit fees has forced firms to perform more cost-effective audits).

7.3 Audit risk

Definition

Audit risk is the risk that the auditor will form an inappropriate opinion, either on the financial statements as a whole, or in relation to a particular account balance or area.

This means that the auditor would issue a modified opinion where, in fact, an unmodified opinion was appropriate, or the converse (which is highlighted more frequently in litigation) an unmodified opinion when modification was required.

Some firms quantify their overall acceptable level of audit risk as a matter of practice policy and as the basis for mathematical derivation of detection risk and sample sizes (see Chapter 4).

Audit risk is made up of inherent risk, control risk and detection risk.

7.4 Inherent risk

Definition

Inherent risk is the risk that derives from the characteristics of the company or entity which is to be audited, or the circumstances of the audit or assignment.

- A company which operates in a high technology industry could be regarded as risky due to the impact of specialist technical advances on inventory values and trading base.

- A new client could be perceived as high risk owing to the auditor's lack of experience of the company and its management.

- An audit which is performed to a tight reporting deadline is performed without the same reliance on hindsight in the form of post year-end events which confirm the statement of financial position picture.

7.5 Control risk

Definition

Control risk is the risk that the client's internal controls will fail to prevent or detect and correct material misstatements on a timely basis.

Any initial assessment of control risk will be confirmed (or otherwise) by the results of adequate tests of control.

7.6 Detection risk

Definition

Detection risk can be formally defined as the risk that the auditor's substantive procedures will fail to detect any remaining errors or omissions. This could be due to the inappropriate nature, extent or timing of audit procedures.

Having assessed inherent risk and control risk, detection risk is then the balancing figure set to achieve an acceptable total audit risk. Detection risk is the only element of audit risk that the auditor can control.

7.7 The audit risk model

Inherent risk and control risk exist independently of the audit and must be assessed by the auditor in order that detection risk (which is under the auditor's control) can be 'managed' to achieve an acceptable level of overall audit risk.

Where inherent risk and control risk together are high, detection risk must be minimised (rendered low) by the audit procedures performed. The auditor can respond by varying the nature, extent and/or timing of audit work.

7.8 Minimising detection risk

Methods of varying detection risk	Examples of audit work where inherent/control risk are high
1 Change the nature of audit work.	Obtain third party confirmation in preference to relying on internal documentation.
2 Change the extent of audit work.	Submit more items to scrutiny in audit test.
3 Change the timing of audit work.	Perform a circularisation closer to the year-end rather than at the interim.

7.9 Recognising risk

Audit risk can be assessed at two levels: the overall financial statement (or 'entity') level and the individual account balance and class of transactions level.

7.10 Entity level

An assignment would be judged risky if the circumstances of the client or of the assignment as a whole meant that the financial statements as a whole were more prone to material error. Examples have been suggested in the previous section in relation to inherent risk e.g. a company in a high technology industry.

Control risk could be judged to be high at the overall financial statement level, for example in a company with poor or no general controls over its computer environment.

The consequence is that more (or more reliable) audit work will be required in respect of account balances generally, in order that audit evidence is sufficient.

7.11 Account balance and class of transactions level

This means that on a generally low risk assignment (e.g. the recurring audit of an established company in a stable industry), areas with high inherent risk can be identified. These could include the audit of inventory, especially if these are manufactured by the client. These are high risk due to judgements involved in attributing overheads.

Inventory is also high risk where they do not form part of the day to day accounting records and where physical count and subsequent valuation form the basis of the inventory figure in the accounts. The direct profit impact of the valuation increases the possibility of deliberate management bias. The area of provisions would also be judged risky due to the degree of subjectivity involved.

Poorly programmed procedures relating to a specific computer application (e.g. receivables ledger processing) would increase control risk at the individual account balance level. Here, audit procedures can be extended, or more reliable sources of evidence sought, in respect of the particular account balance identified.

7.12 High inherent risk factors

Factors contributing to high inherent risk	
At overall financial statement level	**At individual account balance level**
1 Tight reporting deadline.	1 Items which are not part of the accounting records on a day to day basis (e.g. inventory).
2 Non-audit assignment.	2 Items which are essentially judgmental (e.g. provisions).
3 Newly formed company.	3 Items which are complex in calculation.
4 New client.	4 Cash-based transactions.
5 Client in financial services sector.	5 Transactions with related parties.
6 Client in high-tech industry.	
7 Existence of a large number of business locations.	
8 Poor quality management.	
9 Strained financial circumstances.	
10 Dominant influence by proprietor or a director.	
11 Impending change of ownership.	
12 Need for additional capital.	

Test your understanding 1

Outline the 3 components of audit risk and give an example of each.

8 Materiality

Definition

Materiality is an expression of the relative significance or importance of a particular matter in the context of financial statements as a whole. A matter is material if its omission, misstatement or obscurement would reasonably influence the decisions of an addressee of the auditor's report. Materiality may also be considered in the context of any individual primary statement within the financial statements or of individual items included in them. Materiality is not capable of general mathematical definition as it has both qualitative and quantitative aspects.

Performance Materiality is the amount or amounts set by the auditor at **less** than materiality for the financial statements as a whole to reduce to an acceptably low level the probability that the aggregate of uncorrected and undetected misstatements exceeds materiality for the financial statements as a whole.

8.1 Why is materiality important?

Materiality is important both to the auditor who expresses an opinion on the financial statements and to the preparer of the accounts.

- The auditor must direct their attention to material items as any errors or omissions will have an impact on the truth and fairness of the financial statements and therefore on the audit opinion.

- For the accountant, the Companies Act 2006 does not define materiality. However, it states that: 'amounts which are not material in the context of any requirements of the Act may be disregarded for that purpose'.

Clearly it is important that the auditor and accountant are able to calculate materiality given its importance to both the profession and the law.

8.2 When is something material?

There are essentially three considerations:

- the size of the item
- the nature of the item
- the likely influence on a user of financial statements.

8.3 Size of the item

ISA 320 *Materiality in planning and performing an audit* recognises and permits the use of benchmark calculations of materiality. However, it must be stressed, that these should be used in the initial assessment of materiality. The auditor must then use judgement to modify materiality so that it is relevant to the unique circumstances of the client.

A traditional calculation basis is as follows:

	Value	Comments
Profit before tax	5 – 10%	Users usually interested in profitability of the company.
Revenue	0.5 – 1%	Materiality relates to the size of the business, which can be measured in terms of revenue.
Total assets	1 – 2%	Size can also be measured in terms of the asset base.

When deciding on an appropriate benchmark the auditor must consider:

- the elements of the financial statements
- whether particular items tend to be the focus of users
- the nature of the entity, its life cycle and its environment
- the ownership of the financing structure, and
- the relative volatility of the benchmark.

8.4 Nature of the items

Again, it is necessary to consider the impact on the user. Certain items in the accounts are capable of precise determination, for example directors' emoluments, share capital and related party transactions. Any error, however small, in respect of these items would be considered material and must be adjusted.

Other items are not capable of precise determination, for example, the inventory provision. With regard to such items, some degree of latitude is acceptable. Auditors are also alert to the nature of misstatements relating to qualitative aspects of a matter. Examples of qualitative misstatements are the inadequate or inaccurate description of an accounting policy when it is likely that a user of the financial statements could be misled by the description.

> **Test your understanding 2**
>
> Select whether the following statements, in respect of materiality, are true or false.
>
> 1. An amount may be material by nature because it is a big amount of money.
> 2. An amount may be material by nature because it indicates future developments or other significant events.
> 3. An amount may be material by nature because its disclosure is compulsory.

8.5 Likely influence on a user

The definition of materiality is user-orientated. Different users will base their assessment of materiality on different criteria; for example, a bank considering a loan application will consider matters to be material if they affect the company's:

- profit before interest (affects interest cover), and
- net assets (affects solvency).

The auditor is reporting to the shareholders and therefore this group of users are of primary importance when setting materiality levels.

8.6 Materiality at the overall financial statement level

Calculations of materiality are not usually appropriate at this stage. Consideration about materiality will usually come down to the auditor's judgement. In exercising this judgement, the partner may dismiss, as immaterial at the entity level, audit adjustments proposed by the audit staff as exceeding materiality thresholds at the account balance level. This does not mean that the audit staff were wrong to propose the adjustments; it reflects that a different level of materiality is relevant to forming an opinion on the financial statements as a whole.

8.7 Evaluating the effect of misstatements

The auditor will:

- aggregate the effect of misstatements noted during audit work
- consider their impact on critical points (e.g. profit/loss)
- use their experience to assess whether or not the financial statements can still give a true and fair view if the misstatements remain uncorrected.

The aggregate of uncorrected misstatements comprises:

- specific misstatements identified by the auditors, including uncorrected misstatements identified during the audit of the previous period if they affect the current period's financial statements, and
- their best estimate of other misstatements which cannot be quantified specifically.

If the audit partner concludes that the misstatements may be material, consideration will be given to:

- reducing audit risk by extending audit procedures, or
- requesting the directors to adjust the financial statements.

In any event, the directors may want to adjust the financial statements for the misstatements identified. If the directors refuse to adjust the financial statements and the results of extended audit procedures do not enable the partner to conclude that the aggregate of uncorrected misstatements is not material, the auditor must consider the implications for the auditor's report.

9 Analytical procedures

9.1 Introduction

Definition

Analytical procedures means the analysis of relationships:

- between items of financial data, or between items of financial and non-financial data, deriving from the same period, or
- between comparable financial information deriving from different periods or different entities

to identify consistencies and predicted patterns or significant fluctuations and unexpected relationships, and the results of investigations thereof.

Analytical procedures involve the use of ratios, percentages and trend information which may allow the auditor to assess whether the figures subject to audit make sense.

Auditors must apply analytical procedures at the planning stage to assist in understanding the entity's business, in identifying areas of potential audit risk and in planning the nature, timing and extent of other audit procedures.

9.2 Information for analytical procedures

Analytical procedures at this stage are usually based on interim financial information, budgets and management accounts. However, for those entities with less formal means of controlling and monitoring performance, it may be possible to extract relevant financial information from the accounting system (perhaps when preparing the draft financial statements), VAT returns and bank statements. Discussions with management, focused on identifying significant changes in the business since the prior financial period, may also be useful.

Application of analytical procedures may indicate aspects of the entity's business of which the auditors were previously unaware and assist in determining the nature, timing and extent of other audit procedures.

Analytical procedures as substantive procedures are considered in detail in Chapter 4.

10 The audit approach

10.1 Introduction

The audit approach is a plan of action (general strategy) to tackle the critical aspects and meet the audit objective in a cost effective manner.

Where the auditor believes that the client's internal controls are strong, or relevant to the audit (e.g. because they address certain inherent risks identified by the auditor), tests of controls (also called compliance tests) may be performed. If these indicate that controls are operating satisfactorily, the amount of detailed checking (substantive procedures) may be reduced.

10.2 Alternative audit approaches

The general audit approaches, outlined below, reflect the alternatives:

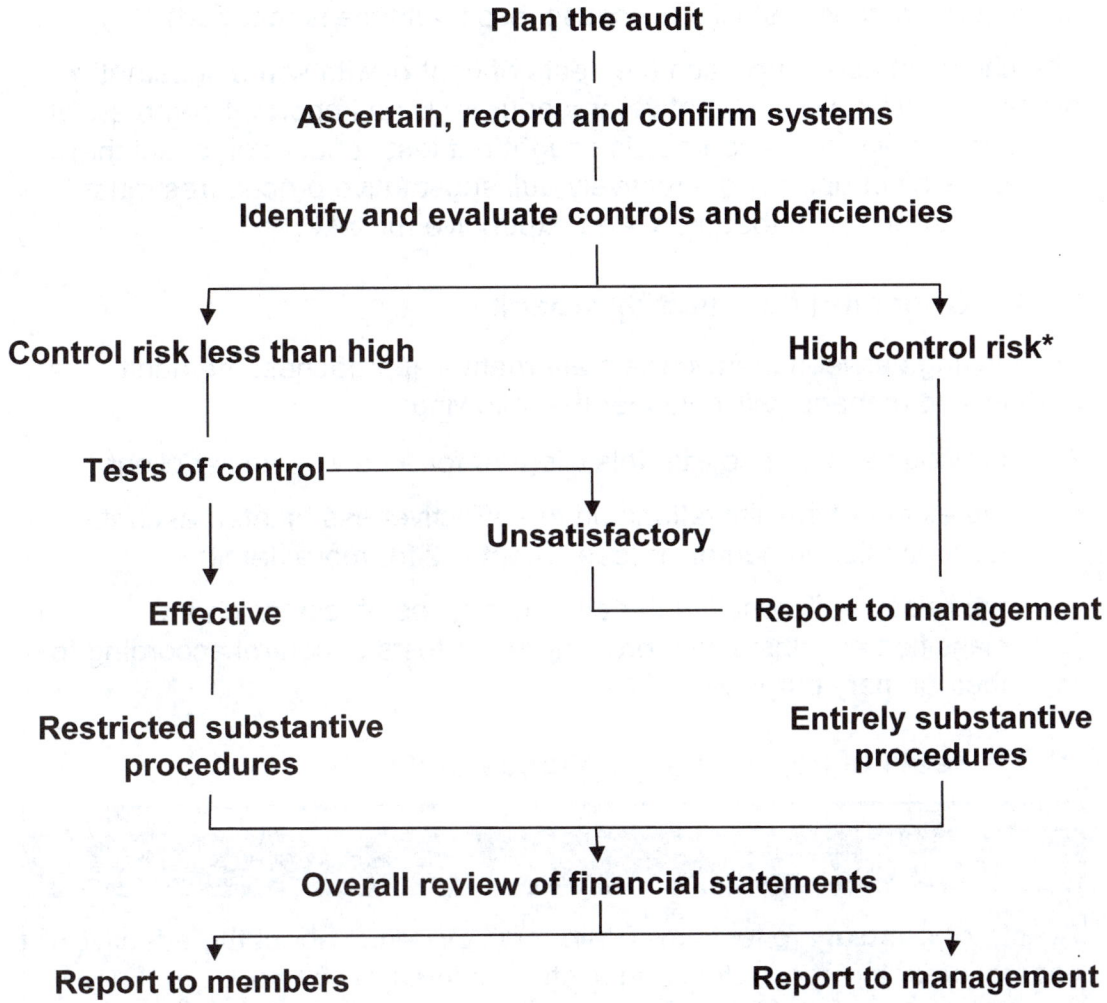

* Remember, high control risk does not mean that controls are necessarily weak. If an entirely substantive approach is considered more cost-effective (i.e. no reliance is sought to be placed on internal controls), then control risk is assessed as high in the audit risk model.

10.3 Substantive or compliance tests?

Compliance tests are tests of controls. Substantive tests are tests of the accuracy of the recording of transactions and balances.

In some cases (e.g. the audit of a small business where controls are known to be weak or poorly evidenced) the evaluation of controls may be very superficial and the auditor may proceed very quickly with entirely substantive procedures.

In other cases, the identification and preliminary evaluation of internal controls may be more thorough, as the decision whether to test controls becomes more critical (e.g. due to cost savings where substantive procedures can be restricted because less staff time is required).

The choice of audit approach (i.e. tests of control with some substantive procedures v wholly substantive procedures) is an important commercial decision. If reliance on controls is sought but tests of control reveal that controls are not operating effectively, full substantive procedures must then be performed in that area – an expensive mistake.

10.4 Choosing the audit approach

In choosing between the two main alternative approaches, the audit partner and manager will consider the following:

- previous experience with this client or for a new or similar client
- the extent of any limitations on the effectiveness of internal controls for example, human error (see Chapter 2 for more detail)
- the relative efficiency of the two main types of test which are classified as substantive procedures or tests of control according to their primary purpose.

10.5 Tests of controls (compliance tests)

Definition

Tests of control are tests to obtain audit evidence about the effective operation of the accounting and system of internal control.

Evidence is sought to indicate that properly designed controls identified in the preliminary assessment of control risk exist and have operated effectively throughout the relevant period.

This form of testing is usually regarded as more efficient where an account balance is made up of a high volume of individually low value transactions.

10.6 Substantive procedures

Definition

Substantive procedures are tests carried out to obtain audit evidence to detect material misstatements in the financial statements.

There are generally two types of substantive procedures:

(a) analytical procedures, and

(b) other substantive procedures, such as tests of details of transactions and balances, review of minutes of directors' meetings and enquiry.

This type of testing is usually regarded as more efficient where an account balance is made up of a low volume of individually high value transactions. The nature and extent of these tests are indicated in Chapter 4. Numerous examples are to be found in Chapters 5 and 6 which follow.

Where the auditor examines internal controls the quality of the report to management is often improved (see Chapter 12).

11 Recording audit work

11.1 Working papers

Working papers are the material that auditors prepare or obtain, and retain in connection with the performance of the audit. Working papers may be in the form of data stored on paper, electronic media or other media. Working papers support, amongst other things, the statement in the auditors' report as to the auditors' compliance or otherwise with Auditing Standards, and thus record compliance with Auditing Standards to the extent that this is important in supporting their report.

Working papers record:

- the planning and performance of the audit
- the supervision and review of the audit work, and
- the audit evidence resulting from the audit work performed which the auditors consider necessary and on which they have relied to support their report.

As such, working papers are important evidence of the quality of work performed if disputes later emerge.

ISA 230 *Audit documentation* says the auditor should document matters which are important in providing audit evidence to support the auditor's opinion and evidence that the audit was carried out in accordance with ISAs.

11.2 Features of working papers

- They should be clearly labelled with the name of the client.
- The objective and purpose of all work should be clearly stated.
- The accounting period under review should be shown.
- The date the working paper was prepared and the name of the person who prepared it should be stated.
- The date the working paper was reviewed and the name of the person who reviewed it should be stated.
- All working papers should be prepared in a permanent form.
- Where the firm's audit manual prescribes any standard form of documentation the working papers should be prepared on a basis which is consistent with the standards laid down.

Working papers should be of a standard which allows any person who is unconnected with the audit to follow the objectives of and results obtained from the tests.

11.3 Permanent audit file

Matters of continuing importance affecting the company or the audit should be kept in a separate permanent file, suitably indexed.

Typically this will include:

- Copies of the Memorandum and Articles of Association.
- Copies of other documents of continuing importance:
    - the engagement letter
    - minutes of important board or general meetings
    - debenture deeds
    - mortgages and charges
    - title deeds of freehold and leasehold properties
    - trade agreements
    - agreements for licences and royalties.
- Descriptions of the nature and history of the client's business, its locations and products.
- Organisation charts, with extra details for the finance department.
- A list of the main accounting records, showing where they are kept and of what type (e.g. handwritten or computerised).
- Copies of previous financial statements.

- Copies of previous reports to management (reports from auditors to the client detailing the deficiencies found in the accounting system).
- A list of the client's investments (if any).
- A list of the client's other professional advisers.
- Details of the client's insurance cover.
- Tables of significant ratios.
- Descriptions of accounting systems in flow chart and narrative form.
- Internal control evaluation data: questionnaires and checklists.
- Details of principal accounting policies.
- Accounts completion checklist.

11.4 Current audit file

The current year's file will relate primarily to the set of accounts or statements being audited.

Typically, this will include:

- A copy of the **accounts or statements** on which the auditors are reporting, authenticated by directors' signatures or otherwise.
- An **index** covering all the working papers.
- A **schedule for each item** in the statement of financial position, preferably including comparative figures, showing its make-up and how existence, ownership and value or liability have been verified. These schedules should be cross referenced to documents arising from external verification such as bank letters and the results of circularisation of receivables and attendance at physical inventory count.
- A **schedule supporting each item** in the statement of profit or loss account, preferably including comparative figures, and such other items in the trading or subsidiary accounts as may be necessary.
- A **checklist** concerning compliance with statutory disclosure provisions.
- A **record showing queries raised** during the audit and their clearance, with notes where appropriate for attention the following year. Queries not cleared at the time should be entered on to a further schedule for the attention of the person reviewing the audit and for reference to the client if necessary. Material queries which cannot be settled satisfactorily by immediate reference to the client may require a modification of the auditor's report, and should be fully documented and supported by a note of all discussions with the client and any explanations given.

- A **record of extracts** of minutes of meetings of the directors and shareholders. These should be cross-referenced where relevant to the auditors' working schedules.

- Copies of **communications to the client** setting out any material deficiencies or matters with which the auditors are dissatisfied in respect of the accounts or control procedures. Such communications should be sent even where the particular matter has been discussed informally with one or more of the company's officials. (See extracts in Chapter 12)

Letters of representation – written confirmation by the client of the information and opinions expressed in respect of certain matters such as, inventory values and amounts of current and contingent liabilities. (See Chapter 11 for a sample letter).

- **Job administration** data which includes:
    - details of partner and staff employed
    - dates when phases of audit were completed
    - time summaries of work carried out by the audit staff
    - details of performance monitored against budget.

- The **audit planning memorandum**.

- **Working papers** created to show the results of tests and evaluation of systems, records of control weakness and the action taken. (See earlier in this chapter for extracts)

- **Schedules showing the result of audit tests** carried out on transactions and balances. An important aspect of the current file is careful indexing and cross-referencing between items in the accounts and items in the schedules so that the collected working papers demonstrate that there is sufficient audit evidence. (See Chapters 5 and 6 for examples)

- The completed **audit programme**.

AUDIT AND ASSURANCE

Test your understanding 3

Select whether the following statements, in respect of an external auditor's working papers, are true or false.

1. Working papers are prepared by the external auditor because there is a legal requirement to do so.

2. The objective of working papers is to provide evidence that the audit was planned and performed in accordance with International Standards on Auditing.

3. Working papers should contain the name of who performed the audit work and the date it was performed.

Test your understanding 4

When planning an audit of financial statements, the auditor is required to consider how factors such as the entity's operating environment and its system of internal control affect the risk of misstatement in the financial statements.

Select whether the following factors are likely to increase or reduce the risk of misstatement or have no effect.

1. The entity is committed to employing personnel with appropriate accounting and financial reporting skills.

2. The entity is to be sold and the purchase consideration will be determined as a multiple of reported profit.

3. The entity's management does not intend to remedy deficiencies in internal controls identified by the external auditor.

12 Impact of technology on auditing

12.1 Data analytics

In the previous chapter, we saw how automated tools and techniques (sometimes known as computer-assisted audit techniques, CAATs) can help auditors. We looked specifically at techniques using test data and audit software. As automated tools and techniques are likely to be tailored to the specific client, they often require significant investment and, as a result, are not widely used across all audits.

Technological development means it is now possible to capture and analyse entire datasets allowing for the interrogation of 100% of the transactions in a population – data analytics (DA). Whilst DA can be developed for bespoke issues, a key characteristic is that the development of standard tools and techniques allows for more widespread use. Some of the more widely used DA tools started out as bespoke automated tools and techniques which have been developed for wider application.

Definition

Audit data analytics is the science and art of discovering and analysing patterns, deviations and inconsistencies, and extracting other useful information in the data of underlying or related subject matter of an audit through analysis, modelling and visualisation for the purpose of planning the audit.

Definition

Big data refers to data sets that are large or complex.

Big data technology allows the auditor to perform procedures on very large or complete sets of data, rather than samples.

12.2 Benefits of data analytics

Benefits of data analytics include:

- Audit procedures can be performed more quickly and to a higher standard. This provides more time to analyse and interpret the results rather than gathering the information for analysis.

- Audit procedures can be carried out on a continuous basis rather than focussed on the year end.
- The use of DA may result in more frequent interaction between the auditor and client over the course of the year.

The use of big data will:

- provide opportunities to test entire populations of audit-relevant data as opposed to using sample-based testing.
- enable a higher quality of relevant audit evidence to be collected.
- enable faster and more comprehensive identification of business risks and fraud occurrence.

The quality of the audit can be enhanced by the use of DA. DA enables the auditor to obtain a greater understanding of the entity and its environment. Professional scepticism and professional judgement are improved when the auditor has a better understanding.

12.3 Impact of the use of technology in auditing

The increasing use of technology will impact:

- **Risk assessment** – DA may improve the risk assessment process.
- **Quality management** – audit firms will need to consider how specialist teams are supervised and how they interact with the audit teams they support e.g. firms will need to consider the integrity of the DA software to ensure it does what it is supposed to do.
- **Group audits** – technology may help by enabling better analytical procedures to be performed in respect of components. Also, the audit procedures may be more centralised enabling the group auditor to perform more procedures rather than relying on the work of the component auditor.
- **Smaller audit firms** – smaller firms may not be able to make the required investment to develop DA tools, for example. Audits of public sector entities may prove challenging as home-grown systems are more prevalent and data capture may be more difficult.
- **Ethics** – due to auditors having access to large volumes of client data, there may be a need to update the Code of Ethics to enhance the requirements for confidentiality.
- **Auditing standards** – there is likely to be a need to revise a number of auditing standards such as ISA 240 (Fraud), ISA 320 (Materiality), ISA 300 (Planning), ISA 500 (Audit Evidence), ISA 520 (Analytical Procedures) and ISA 530 (Audit Sampling).

12.4 Challenges that impact the use of technology in auditing

Auditors must be alert to the possibility that the data used in their data analytics may be incomplete or from an unreliable source. The use of DA will not replace the need for auditors to use professional scepticism and professional judgement.

Challenges include:

- **Data acquisition and retention** – the entity's data will need to be transferred to the auditor raising concerns over data security and privacy as well as perhaps creating storage problems for such large data sets.

- **Legal and regulatory challenges** – regulations may prohibit data leaving the jurisdiction the entity is located. This may pose an issue if the IT facilities of the client are located in a different country.

- **How regulators and oversight authorities maintain oversight** – these bodies tend to have limited experience themselves of inspecting audits using DA.

- **Investment in retaining and reskilling auditors** – changing the auditor's mindset from traditional audit methods requires time and investment.

12.5 Audit quality

Audit quality is a driver for the increased use of technology in auditing. The use of large volumes of data can:

- deepen the auditor's understanding of the entity
- facilitate testing the highest risk areas through stratification
- enhance the use of professional scepticism
- improve consistency on group audits
- enable the auditor to test entire datasets
- improve audit efficiency
- increase the possibility of identifying fraud.

12.6 Artificial intelligence

Definition

Artificial intelligence (AI) is an area of computer science that emphasises the creation of intelligent machines that work and react like human beings.

Some of the activities that computers with artificial intelligence are designed for include:

- voice recognition
- planning
- learning
- problem solving.

Most recent advances in AI have been achieved by applying machine learning to very large data sets. Machine learning algorithms detect patterns and learn how to make predictions and recommendations by processing data and experiences, rather than by explicit programming instruction. The algorithms themselves then adapt to new data and experiences to improve their function over time.

Artificial intelligence and accountancy

It is evident that, in many cases, systems can carry out tasks that result in far more accurate and consistent outputs than could be achieved by humans.

AI brings many opportunities for accountants to improve their efficiency and deliver more value to businesses. In the longer term, AI brings opportunities for more extensive developments, as systems increasingly carry out decision-making tasks that would otherwise be carried out by humans.

There is no doubt that AI will contribute to significant beneficial changes across all areas of accounting. It will equip accountants with powerful new capabilities, as well as enabling machines to deal with an increasing amount of tasks and judgements.

Examples of how auditors may use machine learning include:

- to code accounting entries
- to recognise what constitutes 'normal' activities in order to improve fraud detection
- to forecast revenues with the use of predictive models

- to improve access to, and analysis of, unstructured data, such as contracts, emails and multimedia content.

Having identified many of the opportunities that AI can bring to the profession, we must appreciate that machines will never act as a direct replacement for human intelligence. The ways in which humans and computers can work together in the most efficient way is therefore a key consideration.

 Test your understanding 5

For each of the following statements select whether they are true or false, in respect of artificial intelligence (AI).

1   AI is a set of computer programmes that produce output that would be considered to reflect intelligence if it were to be generated by humans.

2   AI is the embodiment of human intellectual capabilities within a computer.

12.7 Blockchain technology

 Definition

A **blockchain** has been described as a decentralised, distributed and public digital ledger that is used to record transactions across many computers so that the record cannot be altered retroactively without the alteration of all subsequent blocks and the consensus of the network.

Alternatively, it has been defined by the Bank of England as a technology that allows people who do not know each other to trust a shared record of events.

Benefit of a blockchain

The main benefit of a blockchain is security. In the digital era, cyber security is a key risk associated with the use of IT systems and the internet. This is because traditional systems have been 'closed', and so modifications to data have been carried out by just one party. If the system is hacked, there is little control over such modification to prevent it from happening.

A blockchain provides an effective control mechanism aimed at addressing such cyber security risks. It is a record-keeping mechanism that is 'open' or public, as it is a form of distributed ledger; it has been described as a form of collective bookkeeping.

Relevance of blockchain to auditors

Ultimately, blockchain provides an unalterable, transparent record of all audit-related data.

Examples of how blockchain can benefit the audit profession include:

- reducing the cost of maintaining and reconciling ledgers

- providing absolute certainty over the ownership and history of assets, the existence of obligations and the measurement of amounts owed to a business and owed by a business

- freeing up time to allow staff to concentrate on other responsibilities such as planning, valuation and reporting etc., rather than record-keeping.

12.8 Cloud computing

Cloud computing is computing based on the internet. It avoids the need for software, applications, servers and services stored on physical computers. Instead, it stores these with cloud service providers who store these things on the internet and grant access to authorised users.

Due to the information being stored in such a way that it is always accessible, users can log in and perform accounting practices on any computer on the planet with an internet connection.

Benefits of cloud computing to the auditor

Benefits include:

- **Storing and sharing data** – cloud services can often store more audit-relevant data than traditional, local physical drives and the data can be shared more easily amongst the audit team (regardless of physical location).

- **Flexibility** – work can be done more flexibly as audit team members no longer need to be 'plugged into' work networks or facilities to access the data they need.

- **Collaboration** – the cloud facilitates better workforce collaboration – documents, plans etc. can be worked on by many different users simultaneously.

- **Increased competitiveness** – smaller audit firms can get access to technology and services that, without significant financial investment, may otherwise only be available to the largest organisations. This can allow small firms to compete better with larger rivals.

- **Reduced maintenance** – there is no longer need on the part of the audit firm for regular maintenance and (security or software) updates of IT services; the cloud provider will take care of this.

- **Back-ups** – cloud computing can be used to back-up data. This adds an extra layer of security and removes the need for physical devices to store backed-up data.

- **Improved data security** – for example, if in the past a member of the audit team were to lose a laptop with sensitive data on it, this would be a high risk security event for the audit firm and potentially their clients. Keeping this data stored in the cloud should reduce such risks associated with hardware.

12.9 Cyber security

Definition

Cyber security is the protection of internet-connected systems, including hardware, software and data, from cyber attacks.

A cyber attack is a malicious and deliberate attempt by an individual or organisation to breach the information system of another individual or organisation. Usually, the attacker seeks some type of benefit from disrupting the victim's network.

In a computing context, security comprises cyber security and physical security – both are used by organisations to protect against unauthorised access to data and systems.

Key risks to data of cyber attacks

If the data on an organisation's computer system is accessed without authorisation or damaged, lost or stolen, it can lead to disaster.

A number of different technical methods are deployed by cybercriminals. There are always new methods proliferating, and some of these categories overlap, but these are the terms that you are most likely to hear discussed.

- **Malware** – short for malicious software. It is software designed to cause damage to a single computer, server or computer network. Worms, viruses and trojans are all varieties of malware, distinguished from one another by the means by which they reproduce and spread.

These attacks may render a computer or network inoperable, or grant the attacker access so that they can control the system remotely.

- **Phishing** – a technique by which cybercriminals craft emails to fool a target into taking some harmful action. The recipient might be tricked into downloading malware that is disguised as an important document, for example, or urged to click on a link that takes them to a fake website where they will be asked for sensitive information like usernames and passwords.

- **Denial of service attacks** – a brute force method to try stop an online service from working properly. For example, attackers might send so much traffic to a website or so many requests to a database that it overwhelms the system's ability to function, making it unavailable to anybody.

- **Man in the middle attacks** – a method by which attackers manage to interpose themselves secretly between the user and a web service that they are trying to access. For example, an attacker might set up a Wi-Fi network with a login screen designed to mimic another organisation's network; once a user logs in, the attacker can harvest any information that user sends, including passwords.

Test your understanding 6

For each of the following statements, choose whether they are a common example of 'phishing', by selecting true or false.

1. You receive an email from an acquaintance who you are rarely in contact with that contains only a web link.

2. You receive an email that appears to be from your bank asking you to enter your account number and password, but the web address looks unfamiliar.

3. You receive a text message claiming that you have won a contest asking you to click on the link.

Protection of IT systems and software within a business

There are various methods that can be used to keep data secure.

Potential threat	Solution
Natural disasters – e.g. fire, flood.	• Fire procedures – fire alarms, extinguishers, fire doors, staff training and insurance cover. • Location e.g. not in a basement prone to flooding. • Physical environment e.g. air conditioning, dust controls. • Back-up procedures – data should be backed up on a regular basis to allow recovery.
Malfunction – of computer hardware or software.	• Fire procedures – fire alarms, extinguishers, fire doors, staff training and insurance cover. • Location e.g. not in a basement prone to flooding.
Viruses – a small program that once introduced into the system spreads extensively.	• Virus software should be run and updated regularly to prevent corruption of the system by viruses. • Formal security policy and procedures. • Regular audits to check for authorised software.
Hackers – deliberate access to systems by unauthorised persons.	• Firewall software – should provide protection from unauthorised access to the system from the internet. • Passwords and usernames – limit unauthorised access to the system.
Electronic eavesdropping – e.g. users accessing private information not intended for them.	• Data encryption – data is scrambled prior to transmission and is recovered in a readable format once transmission is complete. • Passwords and usernames (as above).
Human errors – unintentional errors from using computers and networks.	• Training – adequate staff training and operating procedures.

13 Summary

In this chapter we have examined the client/auditor relationship and considered planning, controlling and recording in more detail. You should have noted the following points in particular:

- features of a good auditor/client relationship
- purposes of the interim and final visits to the client
- contents of a planning memorandum
- contents of working papers and the permanent and current files
- benefits to auditors of advancement in technology.

You should also understand the impact on the audit approach of:

- the level of risk (both inherent and control) present
- materiality of different areas of the financial statements
- the auditor's previous knowledge of the client
- the type and extent of internal controls within the client's system
- relative costs involved when choosing between the two main approaches of reliance on controls and substantive procedures.

Test your understanding answers

Test your understanding 1

Inherent risk – the risk that derives from the characteristics of the company or entity which is to be audited.

e.g. company operating in a hi-tech industry.

Control risk – the risk that the client's internal controls will fail to prevent or detect and correct material misstatements on a timely basis.

e.g. company employs temporary staff on a rolling basis who are not fully trained in how the systems work.

Detection risk – the risk that the auditor's substantive procedures will fail to detect any remaining errors or omissions.

e.g. sample sizes chosen to test were too small or not representative of the population.

Test your understanding 2

1. False. Some items may be material by nature, regardless of size.
2. True.
3. True.

Test your understanding 3

1. False.
2. True.
3. True.

AUDIT AND ASSURANCE

 Test your understanding 4

1 Reduce.
2 Increase.
3 Increase.

 Test your understanding 5

1 True.
2 True.

 Test your understanding 6

1 True.
2 True.
3 True.

AUDIT AND ASSURANCE

Audit evidence, techniques and procedures

Introduction

In this chapter, we will consider gathering sufficient and appropriate audit evidence. We will also evaluate various sampling techniques and look at factors affecting sample size. We will move on to discuss how we can evaluate the results from our chosen samples and examine the use of analytical procedures within an audit assignment.

ASSESSMENT CRITERIA

The concept of risk (3.1)

Methods used to obtain audit evidence (4.1)

Different sampling techniques (4.3)

Audit approach (4.4)

Matters to be referred to a senior colleague (5.1)

CONTENTS

1. Audit evidence
2. Audit sampling
3. Evaluation of sample results
4. Analytical procedures

Audit evidence, techniques and procedures: **Chapter 4**

1 Audit evidence

> **Definition**
>
> **Audit evidence** is the information used by the auditor in arriving at the conclusions on which the audit opinion is based.

1.1 Introduction

Auditors should obtain sufficient, appropriate audit evidence to draw reasonable conclusions on which to base the audit opinion.

Audit evidence is obtained in a number of ways, including from an appropriate mix of tests of control and substantive procedures (see below). In some circumstances, evidence may be obtained entirely from substantive procedures and enquiries made to ascertain the adequacy of the accounting system as a basis for the preparation of the financial statements.

1.2 Sufficient, appropriate audit evidence

Sufficiency and appropriateness are interrelated and apply to audit evidence obtained from both tests of control and substantive procedures.

- Sufficiency is the measure of the quantity of audit evidence.
- Appropriateness is the measure of the quality or reliability of audit evidence and its relevance to a particular assertion (e.g. 'inventory exists at the year-end date').

Usually, audit evidence is persuasive rather than conclusive, and therefore auditors often seek audit evidence from different sources or of a different nature to support the same assertion.

Auditors seek to provide reasonable, not absolute, assurance that the financial statements are free from material misstatement. In forming their audit opinion, auditors do not normally examine all of the information available. Appropriate conclusions can be reached about a financial statement assertion using a variety of means of obtaining evidence, including sampling (see below).

1.3 Auditors' judgement

The auditors' judgement as to what is sufficient appropriate audit evidence is influenced by factors such as the following:

- assessment of the nature and degree of risk of misstatement at both the financial statement level and the account balance or class of transaction level
- nature of the accounting system and system of internal control, including the control environment
- the materiality of the item being examined
- experience gained during previous audits and the auditors' knowledge of the business and industry
- the findings from audit procedures, and from any audit work carried out in the course of preparing the financial statements, including indications of fraud or error (fraud is considered in Chapter 15)
- the source and reliability of information available.

1.4 Tests of control ('compliance tests')

In obtaining audit evidence from tests of control, auditors should consider the sufficiency and appropriateness of audit evidence to support the assessed level of control risk. Aspects of the relevant parts of the accounting system and system of internal control about which auditors seek to obtain audit evidence are:

(a) **Design:** the accounting system and system of internal control are capable of preventing or detecting material misstatements, and

(b) **Operation:** the systems exist and have operated effectively throughout the relevant period.

1.5 Substantive procedures

In obtaining audit evidence from substantive procedures, auditors should consider the extent to which that evidence, together with any evidence from tests of controls, supports the relevant financial statement assertions. These are the representations of the directors that are embodied in the financial statements, for example:

- **Completeness:** all assets, liabilities, equity interests, transactions and events that should have been recorded have been recorded, and all related disclosures that should have been included in the financial statements have been included.

- **Occurrence:** transactions and events that have been recorded or disclosed have occurred, and such transactions and events pertain to the entity.

- **Accuracy, valuation and allocation:** assets, liabilities and equity interests have been included in the financial statements at appropriate amounts and any resulting valuation or allocation adjustments have been appropriately recorded, and related disclosures have been appropriately measured and described.

- **Existence:** assets, liabilities and equity interests exist.

- **Rights and obligations:** the entity holds or controls the rights to assets, and liabilities are the obligations of the entity.

- **Accuracy:** amounts and other data relating to recorded transactions and events have been recorded appropriately, and related disclosures have been appropriately measured and described.

- **Cut-off:** transactions and events have been recorded in the correct accounting period.

- **Classification:** assets, liabilities, equity interests, transactions and events have been recorded in the proper accounts.

- **Presentation:** assets, liabilities, equity interests, transactions and events are appropriately aggregated or disaggregated and clearly described, and related disclosures are relevant and understandable in the context of the requirements of the applicable financial reporting framework.

Audit evidence is usually obtained to support each financial statement assertion. Audit evidence regarding one assertion (e.g. existence of inventory) does not compensate for failure to obtain audit evidence regarding another (e.g. its valuation). Tests may, however, provide audit evidence about more than one assertion (e.g. testing subsequent receipts from receivables may provide some audit evidence regarding both their existence and valuation).

1.6 Directional testing

If an item in the financial statements is misstated, it may be overstated or understated. When testing for overstatement (existence) a different approach is used from testing for understatement (completeness).

When testing for overstatement, the auditor would begin by looking at the balance in the accounts and then work backwards towards the supporting evidence. This can be explained by way of an example.

> **Example**
>
> Invoice 1 is a fraudulent purchase invoice for £5,000 and should not have been posted. As a result, purchases are overstated by £5,000. To find this misstatement, the auditor can either:
>
> - examine every purchase invoice and try to identify the fraudulent one; or
> - look at the figure in the financial statements and find supporting evidence.
>
> If the fraudulent invoice had been hidden by the client in some way, it would not be possible to find it by examining every purchase invoice and so the auditor should start from the financial statements and work backwards.

When testing for understatement, the auditor will start by looking at the supporting evidence and agree this to the figure in the financial statements. Again, let's look through an example:

> **Example**
>
> Invoice 2, a sales invoice for £5,000, has been omitted and therefore revenue is understated by £5,000. If the auditor were to select a sample from the financial statements, this will be of no use as the item is not there to test. Therefore, the auditor will select items from the population and agree this to the financial statements.

1.7 Audit objectives

Programmes of detailed audit procedures are sometimes drawn up by auditors by reference to 'audit objectives'. Such objectives may provide a satisfactory way of enabling auditors to satisfy themselves that the planned work will result in appropriate evidence being obtained, provided that the objectives cover all the relevant financial statement assertions made by the directors.

1.8 Nature, timing and extent

The nature, timing and extent of substantive procedures depends on:

- the auditors' assessment of the control environment and accounting systems generally and of the inherent and control risks, and
- any evidence obtained from audit work performed during the preparation of the financial statements.

Where tests of control provide satisfactory evidence as to the effectiveness of the accounting system and system of internal control, the extent of relevant substantive procedures may be reduced, but not entirely eliminated (see Chapter 2).

Substantive procedures may be incorporated within other procedures. For example, tests of control may be designed as dual purpose tests to provide evidence of a substantive nature, and such evidence may also be obtained as part of the work carried out to make preliminary assessments of risks of error.

1.9 Reliability of evidence

The reliability of audit evidence is influenced by its source: internal or external, and by its nature: visual, documentary or oral.

The following generalisations may help in assessing reliability:

Type of evidence	
External	Audit evidence from external sources is more reliable than that obtained from the entity's records.
Auditor	Evidence obtained directly by auditors is more reliable than that obtained indirectly or by inference.
Entity	Evidence obtained from the entity's records is more reliable when related control systems operate effectively.
Written	Evidence in the form of documents (paper or electronic) or written representations are more reliable than oral representations.
Originals	Original documents are more reliable than photocopies.

Audit evidence is more persuasive when items of evidence from different sources or of a different nature are consistent. When audit evidence from one source is inconsistent with that from another, auditors determine what additional procedures are necessary to resolve the inconsistency.

Auditors consider the relationship between the cost of obtaining audit evidence and the usefulness of the information obtained. However, the existence of difficulty or expense is not in itself a valid basis for omitting a necessary procedure.

> **Test your understanding 1**
>
> Order the following sources of evidence in terms of their reliability for an auditor, listing the most reliable first.
>
> 1. Recalculation of the depreciation charge by the auditor
> 2. Bank confirmation letter
> 3. Written representation letter from the client

1.10 Procedures for obtaining audit evidence

Audit evidence is obtained by one or more of the following procedures: inspection, observation, enquiry and third party confirmation, computation/re-performance and analytical procedures.

The choice of which procedures is partly dependent upon the periods of time during which the audit evidence sought is available and the form in which the accounting records are maintained (e.g. manual, computer printout, etc.)

1.11 Inspection

Inspection consists of examining records, documents or tangible assets. Inspection of records and documents provides audit evidence of varying degrees of reliability depending on their nature and source (see above) and the effectiveness of internal controls over their processing. Three major categories of documentary audit evidence, listed in descending degree of reliability as audit evidence, are:

- evidence created and provided to auditors by third parties (e.g. a bank loan confirmation)
- evidence created by third parties and held by the entity (e.g. suppliers' statements)
- evidence created and held by the entity (e.g. monthly statements for customers).

Inspection of tangible assets provides reliable audit evidence about their existence but not necessarily as to their ownership or value. Further procedures will be needed to gather evidence on these matters.

1.12 Observation

Observation consists of looking at a process or procedure being performed by others e.g. the observation by auditors of the counting of inventory by the entity's staff or the performance of internal control procedures, in particular those that leave no audit trail (i.e. visible evidence).

1.13 Enquiry and external confirmation

Enquiry consists of seeking information of knowledgeable persons inside or outside the entity. Enquiries may range from formal written enquiries addressed to third parties (e.g. to the entity's solicitor) to informal oral enquiries addressed to persons inside the entity. Responses to enquiries may provide auditors with information not previously possessed or with corroborative audit evidence.

External confirmation consists of the response to an enquiry to corroborate information contained in the accounting records (e.g. obtaining direct confirmation of debts by communication with receivables).

1.14 Computation

Computation consists of checking the arithmetical accuracy of source documents and accounting records or performing independent calculations.

1.15 Analytical procedures

Analytical procedures consist of the analysis of relationships between items of financial data, or between items of financial and non-financial data, deriving from the same period, or between comparable financial information deriving from different periods or different entities, to identify consistencies and predicted patterns or significant fluctuations and unexpected relationships, and the results of investigations thereof. For details see later in this chapter.

 Test your understanding 2

State whether the following statements are true or false:

1   A controls test is a type of substantive test.
2   Substantive testing must always be performed during an audit.
3   Testing for completeness is an example of a substantive test.

2 Audit sampling

2.1 Introduction

The auditor is not required to carry out a complete check of all the transactions and balances of a business because:

- the cost would be uneconomical
- the complete check would take so long that accounts would be outdated before users saw them
- users of accounts do not require 100% accuracy
- a complete check would be so tedious that the audit staff would become ineffective and errors could be missed
- a complete check would not add much to the worth of figures if, as would be normal, few errors were discovered (the emphasis in auditing should be on the completeness of records and the true and fair view).

In most areas a 100% check is not necessary and a test check is made by the examination of a sample of items taken from the whole population of transactions or balances.

In the following areas a 100% check is still necessary:

- unusual, one-off, or exceptional items
- high risk areas
- categories which are few in number but of great importance (e.g. land and buildings)
- categories with special importance where normal materiality levels do not apply (e.g. directors' emoluments and loans).

Definition

'Audit sampling' means the application of audit procedures to less than 100% of the items within an account balance or class of transaction to enable auditors to obtain and evaluate audit evidence about some characteristic of the items selected in order to form or assist in forming a conclusion concerning the population which makes up the account balance or class of transactions.

2.2 Benefits of audit sampling

These include:

- developing a consistent approach to audit areas
- providing a framework within which sufficient appropriate audit evidence is obtained
- forcing clarification of audit thinking to determine how the audit objectives will be met
- minimising the risk of 'over-auditing'
- facilitating quicker review of working papers.

2.3 The decision to sample

When planning the audit procedures to be adopted, the decision to sample account balances and transactions is influenced by:

- materiality and number of items in the population
- inherent risk of errors arising
- relevance and reliability of evidence available through non-sampling procedures
- costs and time involved.

To obtain the overall level of assurance required, a cost-effective combination of sampling and non-sampling procedures should be determined.

2.4 Stages in sampling

If the auditor chooses to use sampling then the following stages will be required:

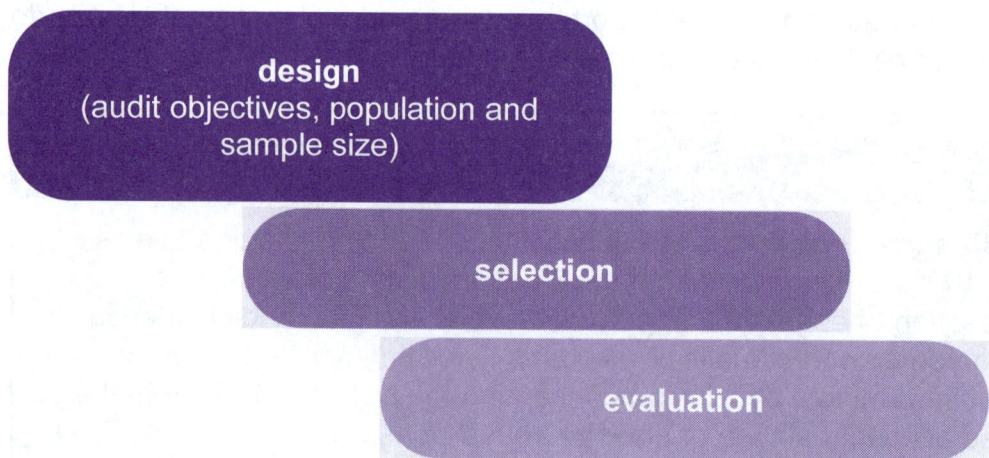

2.5 Design of the sample

When designing the size and structure of an audit sample, auditors should consider the specific audit objectives, the nature of the population from which they wish to sample, and the sampling and selection methods.

2.6 Audit objectives

Auditors first consider the specific audit objectives to be achieved and the audit procedures which are most likely to achieve those objectives. In addition, when audit sampling is appropriate, consideration of the nature of the audit evidence sought and possible error conditions or other characteristics relating to that evidence assists auditors in defining what constitutes an error and what population to use for sampling.

For example, when performing tests of control over purchasing procedures, auditors may be concerned with matters such as whether an invoice was clerically checked and properly approved.

Alternatively, when performing substantive procedures on invoices processed during the period, auditors are concerned with matters such as the proper reflection of the payable and of the monetary amounts of such invoices in the financial statements.

2.7 Population

The population is the entire set of data from which auditors wish to sample in order to reach a conclusion. Therefore the population from which the sample is drawn has to be appropriate and complete for the specific audit objective.

If the audit objective is to test for overstatement of receivables, the population may be defined as the receivables listing.

When testing for understatement of payables, the population is not the payables listing but rather subsequent disbursements, unpaid invoices, suppliers' statements, unmatched goods received notes or other populations that can provide evidence of understatement of payables.

2.8 Sampling units

The individual items that make up the population may be described as sampling units. The population can be divided into sampling units in a variety of ways. For example, if the audit objective is to test the validity of receivables, the sampling unit may be defined as customer balances or individual customer invoices. In monetary unit sampling each £1 of, for example, a receivables balance listing is the sampling unit. Auditors define the sampling unit in order to obtain an efficient and effective sample to achieve the particular audit objectives.

Audit evidence, techniques and procedures: Chapter 4

2.9 Sample size

When determining sample sizes, auditors consider sampling risk, the amount of error that would be acceptable (tolerable misstatement) and the extent to which they expect to find errors (expected error).

2.10 Factors influencing sample size for tests of controls

Factor	Impact on sample size
Sampling risk	• The greater the reliance on the results of a test of control using audit sampling, the lower the sampling risk auditors are willing to accept and, consequently, the larger the sample size. • The lower the assessment of control risk, the more likely auditors are to place reliance on audit evidence from tests of control. • A high control risk assessment may result in a decision not to perform tests of control.
Tolerable misstatement	• The higher the tolerable misstatement rate the lower the sample size and vice versa.
Expected error	• If errors are expected, a larger sample usually needs to be examined to confirm that the actual error rate is less than the tolerable misstatement rate. • High expected error rates may result in a decision not to perform tests of control.
Number of items in population	• Virtually no effect on sample size unless population is small.

2.11 Factors influencing sample size for substantive tests

Factor	Impact on sample size
Inherent risk	• The higher the assessment of inherent risk, the more audit evidence is required to support the auditors' conclusion.
Control risk	• The higher the assessment of control risk, the greater the reliance on audit evidence obtained from substantive procedures. • A high control risk assessment may result in the decision not to perform tests of control and reliance entirely on substantive procedures.

Detection risk	• Sampling risk for substantive tests is one form of detection risk. The lower the sampling risk auditors are willing to accept, the larger the sample size.
Tolerable misstatement	• The higher the monetary value of the tolerable misstatement the smaller the sample size and vice versa.
Expected error	• If errors are expected, a larger sample usually needs to be examined to confirm that the actual error rate is less than the tolerable misstatement rate.
Population value	• The less material the monetary value of the population to the financial statements, the smaller the sample size that may be required.
Number of items in population	• Virtually no effect on sample size unless population is small.
Stratification	• If it is appropriate to stratify the population this may redirect the sample and lead to a smaller sample size (see later).

Test your understanding 3

State whether the following statements are true or false:

1 100% testing may be appropriate in certain circumstances – particularly where there is a small population of high-value items.

2 At least 50% of each account balance has to be tested while selecting a sample.

3 There is no requirement to use sampling specified in any International Standards on Auditing (ISAs).

2.12 Sampling risk

Fundamental to audit sampling is sampling risk. This may be regarded as a component of detection risk, the other component being non-sampling risk.

Sampling risk arises from the possibility that the auditors' conclusion, based on a sample, may be different from the conclusion that would be reached if the entire population were subjected to the same audit procedure.

Auditors are faced with sampling risk in tests of controls and in substantive procedures.

Sampling risk is essentially the risk that the auditor's sample from a population will not be representative. In other words it will, by chance, include too many or too few errors to give a realistic impression of the population as a whole. Sampling risk reduces as samples become larger.

2.13 Tests of control

Sampling risk can arise in tests of control. If the sample contains a disproportionately high number of errors then the auditor might get the false impression that a control has not operated and control risk will be evaluated as too high. Conversely, the auditor might attach too low a control risk if there are too few compliance errors in the sample.

2.14 Substantive procedures

There are two possible aspects to sampling risk when carrying out substantive procedures:

- The risk of concluding that a recorded account balance or class of transactions is materially misstated when it is not, because the error in the sample is greater than the error in the population as a whole.

- The risk of concluding that a recorded account balance or class of transaction is acceptable when it is materially misstated, because the error in the sample is less than the error in the population as a whole.

Sample size is affected by the degree of sampling risk that auditors are willing to accept from the results of the sample, which depends upon the importance of the results of the audit procedure involving sampling to the auditors' conclusions.

The greater their reliance on the results, the lower the sampling risk auditors are willing to accept and the larger the sample size needs to be.

2.15 Measuring sampling risk

When an audit sample is designed using a statistical sampling method (see later), it is possible to measure sampling risk. In practice, only the risk of accepting a population which does contain material errors is measured. The risk is expressed as a percentage; for example a risk of 5% means that there is a 1 in 20 chance of a material error going undetected. It is the policy of many auditors to accept a 5% risk of failure to detect a material error in any given test. This figure is a judgement based on experience.

2.16 Non-sampling risk

Non-sampling risk is the risk that auditors might use inappropriate procedures or might misinterpret evidence and thus fail to recognise an error.

Non-sampling risk arises because, for example, most audit evidence is persuasive rather than conclusive. Furthermore, inexperienced or over-stretched audit staff might make mistakes in the evaluation of evidence and reach invalid conclusions. Audit firms attempt to reduce non-sampling risk to a negligible level by appropriate planning, direction, supervision and review.

2.17 Tolerable misstatement

Tolerable misstatement is the maximum error in the population that auditors are willing to accept and still conclude that the audit objective has been achieved. Tolerable misstatement is considered during the planning stage and, for substantive procedures, is related to the auditors' judgement about materiality. The smaller the tolerable misstatement, the larger the sample size as a proportion of the population.

- In **tests of control**, the tolerable misstatement is the maximum rate of deviation from a prescribed control procedure that auditors are willing to accept in the population and still conclude that the preliminary assessment of control risk is valid.

- In **substantive procedures**, the tolerable misstatement is the maximum monetary error in an account balance or class of transactions that auditors are willing to accept so that, when the results of all audit procedures are considered, they are able to conclude, with reasonable assurance, that the financial statements are not materially misstated.

2.18 Expected error

If auditors expect error to be present in the population, a larger sample than when no error is expected generally has to be examined to conclude that the actual error in the population is not greater than the planned tolerable misstatement. The size and frequency of errors is important in assessing the sample size. Larger sample sizes arise, for the same overall error, if there are a few large errors compared to where there are many small ones. Smaller sample sizes result when the population is expected to be error free. If the expected error rate is high then sampling may not be appropriate. In determining the expected error in a population, auditors consider such matters as the size and frequency of errors identified in previous audits, changes in the entity's procedures and evidence available from other procedures.

2.19 Selection of the sample

Auditors should select sample items in such a way that the sample can be expected to be representative of the population in respect of the characteristics being tested.

For a sample to be representative of the population, all items in the population are required to have an equal or known probability of being selected.

While there are a number of selection methods, the methods commonly used are random or systematic selection.

2.20 Random selection

This method ensures that all items in the population have an equal chance (i.e. same statistical probability) of selection (e.g. by use of random number tables or a computer program).

2.21 Systematic selection

This method (which is also called interval selection) involves selecting items using a constant interval between selections, the first interval having a random start.

This method is suitable for both tests of control and substantive procedures and is particularly useful for sampling from non-monetary populations.

Example

A systematic sample of 125 of the despatch notes issued during the year is to be made. The first despatch note raised in the year was 11,129 and the last was 18,671.

Solution

Sampling interval: $\dfrac{\text{Population}}{\text{Sample size}} = \dfrac{18{,}671 - 11{,}129}{125} = 60$

Random start: 36 (between 0 and 60)

Selection procedure   DN number

11,165	(11,129 + 36)
11,225	(11,165 + 60)
11,285	(11,225 + 60)
: etc.	:

When using systematic selection, auditors must ensure that the population is not structured in such a manner that the sampling interval corresponds with a particular pattern in the population.

2.22 Stratified sampling

Stratified sampling can be used if the population naturally falls into strata or layers. So, for example, if a sample were to be taken for receivables balances, the population of receivable balances might be split into the following strata:

Up to £5,000

£5,000 to £30,000

Over £30,000

An appropriate size of sample would then be taken from each of these groups using random or systematic sampling.

> **Test your understanding 4**
>
> A sample of sales invoices are to be tested to ensure that they agree to customer orders and despatch notes. A sample of 200 is required and is to be selected using the systematic sampling method with a random start number of 44. The first sales invoice in the year was number 110652 and the last sales invoice number in the year was 126435.
>
> **Task**
>
> Determine the invoice number of the first four invoices to be tested in the sample.

2.23 Haphazard selection

In haphazard selection, the auditors select the sample without following a structured technique. This may be an acceptable alternative to random selection provided auditors are satisfied that the sample is representative of the entire population. This method requires care to guard against making a selection which is biased (e.g. towards items which are easily located) as they may not be representative.

2.24 Block sampling

With block sampling, a number of adjacent transactions or items will be selected, e.g. all sales invoices in a particular week, or all receivables with a name beginning with a particular letter. The main disadvantage of this method is that it may not show characteristics that are representative of the whole population. However, block sampling can result in significant cost savings in audit time.

3 Evaluation of sample results

3.1 Introduction

Having carried out, on each sample item, those audit procedures which are appropriate to the particular audit objective, auditors should:

- analyse any errors detected in the sample, and
- draw inferences for the population as a whole.

3.2 Analysis of errors

In analysing the errors detected in the sample, auditors first confirm that an item in question is in fact an error. In designing the sample, auditors define those conditions which constitute an error by reference to the audit objectives.

For example, in a substantive procedure relating to the recording of receivables, a mis-posting between customer accounts does not affect the total receivables. Therefore, it may be inappropriate to consider this an error in evaluating the sample results of this particular procedure, even though it may have an effect on other areas of the audit such as the assessment of irrecoverable receivables.

When the expected audit evidence regarding a specific sample item cannot be obtained, auditors may be able to obtain sufficient, appropriate audit evidence through performing alternative procedures. For example, if a positive receivables confirmation has been requested but no reply received, auditors may be able to obtain sufficient appropriate audit evidence of the receivable by reviewing subsequent payments from the customer. If they are able to perform satisfactory alternative procedures, the item is not treated as an error.

Auditors also consider the qualitative aspects of the errors. These include the nature and cause of the error and the possible effect of the error on other phases of the audit. In analysing the errors discovered, auditors may observe that many have a common feature, for example type of transaction, location, product line or period of time. In such circumstances, they may decide to identify all items in the population which possess the common feature, thereby producing a sub-population, and extend audit procedures in this area. The auditors may then perform a separate analysis based on the items examined for each sub-population, so that they have sufficient appropriate audit evidence for each sub-population.

3.3 Inferences to be drawn for population as a whole

Auditors project the error results of the sample to the population from which the sample was selected, ensuring that the method of projection is consistent with the method used to select the sampling unit.

The projection of the sample involves estimating the probable error in the population (by extrapolating the errors found in the sample) and estimating any further error that might not have been detected because of the imprecision of the technique. This is in addition to the consideration of the qualitative aspects of any errors found.

Auditors consider whether errors in the population might exceed the tolerable misstatement. To accomplish this, they compare the projected population error to the tolerable misstatement taking into account the results of other audit procedures relevant to the specific control or financial statement assertion. The projected population error used for this comparison in the case of substantive procedures is net of adjustments made by the entity. When the projected population error exceeds the tolerable misstatement, they re-assess the sampling risk and, if that risk is unacceptable, consider extending the audit procedure or performing alternative audit procedures, either of which may result in them proposing an adjustment to the financial statements.

3.4 Statistical sampling

Statistical sampling involves:

- the use of random sample selection, and
- probability theory to:
    - determine the sample size
    - evaluate quantitatively the sample results, and
    - measure the sampling risk.

In practice, a high level of mathematical competence is required if valid conclusions are to be drawn from sample evidence. However, most firms that use statistical sampling have drawn up complex plans which can be operated by staff without statistical training. These involve the use of tables, graphs or computer methods.

The main advantages of using statistical sampling are as follows:

- It imposes a more formal discipline to planning the audit of a population.
- It objectively determines sample sizes.
- It evaluates test results more precisely.
- It quantifies the sampling risk.
- The use of judgement is not precluded, since it is required to set objectives and evaluate results.

3.5 Non-statistical sampling

Non-statistical sampling is any approach which does not fulfil all the conditions set out above in the definition of statistical sampling. This includes not only non-random selection but choosing a sample size on a judgement basis. This approach has the following advantages:

- The approach has been used for many years; it is well understood and refined by experience.

- The auditor can bring greater judgement and expertise into play.

- Non-random selection may be quicker and more cost effective as special knowledge of statistics is required.

- In tests of controls the qualitative aspects of error evaluation cannot be statistically analysed.

There are some potential disadvantages to non-statistical sampling:

- Sampling risk cannot be quantified.

- Sample sizes may be too small to satisfy stated objectives.

- Sample sizes may be larger than necessary.

- Personal bias in the selection of samples is unavoidable.

4 Analytical procedures

4.1 Nature of analytical procedures

Analytical procedures include the consideration of comparisons of the entity's financial information with, for example:

- comparable information for prior periods

- anticipated results of the entity, from budgets or forecasts

- predictive estimates prepared by the auditors, such as an estimation of the depreciation charge for the year; and

- similar industry information, such as a comparison of the entity's ratio of sales to trade receivables with industry averages, or with the ratios relating to other entities of comparable size in the same industry.

Analytical procedures also include consideration of relationships:

- between elements of financial information that are expected to conform to a predicted pattern based on the entity's experience, such as the relationship of gross profit to sales, and
- between financial information and relevant non-financial information, such as the relationship of payroll costs to number of employees.

Various methods may be used in performing the above procedures. These range from simple comparisons to complex analyses using advanced statistical techniques. Analytical procedures may be applied to consolidated financial statements, financial statements of components (such as subsidiary undertakings, divisions or branches) and individual elements of financial information.

4.2 Purpose of analytical procedures

Analytical procedures are used by auditors:

- to assist in planning the nature, timing and extent of other audit procedures
- as substantive procedures when their use can be more effective or efficient than other procedures in reducing detection risk for specific financial statement assertions, and
- as part of the overall review of the financial statements when completing the audit.

4.3 Analytical procedures at the planning stage

Auditors must apply analytical procedures at the planning stage to assist in:

- understanding the entity's business
- identifying areas of potential audit risk, and
- planning the nature, timing and extent of other audit procedures.

Analytical procedures at this stage are usually based on interim or draft financial information, budgets and management accounts. However, for those entities with less formal means of controlling and monitoring performance, it may be possible to extract relevant financial information from the accounting system (perhaps when preparing the draft financial statements), sales tax returns and bank statements. Discussions with management, focused on identifying significant changes in the business since the prior financial period, may also be useful.

Application of analytical procedures may indicate aspects of the entity's business of which the auditors were previously unaware and assist in determining the nature, timing and extent of other audit procedures.

> **Example**
>
> Albatross Co had 100 employees last year with total wages of £840,000 and 100 employees this year with a wage bill of £950,000, an increase of 13%. We know that the annual pay rise was 6% and the level of business has remained approximately constant.
>
> **Solution**
>
> At first sight, the figures do not appear to make sense because the increase is substantially greater than expected. There may, however, be satisfactory explanations. For example, there may have been a change in sales mix with previously bought-in goods being replaced by goods manufactured in house, resulting in substantial authorised overtime. This could be verified by looking at the sales figures for different products as well as the payroll. Alternatively there could have been a switch to more skilled, and hence more expensive, labour; this could be verified from payroll and production records.
>
> If no such explanation is available, it is possible that the payroll has been inflated by an error or irregularity, for example:
>
> - mis-posting in the nominal ledger
> - dummy employees on the payroll
> - unauthorised overtime being paid
> - employees being paid at higher rates of pay than authorised.
>
> Substantive tests will therefore be directed towards finding any errors of this nature.

4.4 Types of analytical procedures

For a manufacturing company analytical procedures may include:

- **comparing sales** for each major product with budget and previous years actual sales, and assessing the reasonableness of explanations for variances shown in the monthly sales report.

- **comparing monthly figures** for each major product to establish trends and seasonal fluctuations. This may help to verify explanations about the performance of individual products.

- **comparing sales quantities** for each major product, in relation to budgets and previous years.

- **reconciling sales quantities to production schedules** and opening and closing inventory for each major product.

- **comparing ratios** such as gross profit, inventory turnover, receivables collection period, with budget and previous years (gross profit and inventory turnover may be calculated on an individual product basis).
- **examining price lists** to establish the effect of changes in prices.

If the results of these procedures are satisfactory, sample sizes for sales and receivables may be reduced.

4.5 Analytical procedures at the detailed testing stage

The decision about whether to use analytical procedures as substantive procedures and the nature, timing and extent of their use is based on the auditors' judgement about the expected effectiveness and efficiency of the available procedures in reducing detection risk for specific financial statement assertions. Auditors usually enquire of management as to the availability and reliability of information needed to apply analytical procedures and the results of any such procedures performed by the entity. It may be efficient to use analytical data prepared by the entity, provided the auditors are satisfied that such data is properly prepared.

4.6 Factors affecting use

When intending to apply analytical procedures as substantive procedures, auditors consider a number of factors such as the following:

- The **plausibility** and **predictability** of the relationships identified for comparison and evaluation. For example, there is a strong relationship between certain selling expenses and turnover in businesses where the sales force is paid by commission.
- The **objectives** of the analytical procedures and the extent to which their results are reliable.
- The **degree to which information can be disaggregated**, for example analytical procedures may be more effective when applied to financial information on individual sections of an operation or to financial statements of components of a diversified entity, than when applied to financial information relating to the entity as a whole.
- The **availability of information,** both financial (such as budgets or forecasts) and non-financial (such as the number of units produced or sold). The relevance of the information available, for example whether budgets are established as results to be expected rather than as goals to be achieved.
- The **comparability** of the information available, for example broad industry data may need to be supplemented to be comparable with that of an entity that produces and sells specialised products.

- The **knowledge gained** during previous audits, together with the auditors' understanding of the effectiveness of the accounting system and system of internal control and the types of problems that in prior periods have given rise to accounting adjustments.

4.7 Reliability of information

The reliability of the information used in analytical procedures is likely to be enhanced if it comes from sources independent of, rather than internal to, the entity. If the information is produced internally, its reliability is enhanced if it is produced independently of the accounting system or there are adequate controls over its preparation. The necessity for evidence on the reliability of such information depends on the results of other audit procedures and on the importance of the results of analytical procedures as a basis for the auditors' opinion.

4.8 Extent of reliance

The extent of reliance that auditors place on the results of analytical procedures when used as substantive procedures may also depend on the following factors.

- **Other audit procedures** directed towards the same financial statement assertions. For example, other procedures auditors undertake in reviewing the collectability of receivables, such as the review of subsequent cash receipts or a receivables circularisation, may confirm or dispel questions arising from the application of analytical procedures to an aged profile of customers' accounts.

- The **accuracy** with which the expected results of analytical procedures can be predicted. For example, auditors normally expect greater consistency in comparing the relationship of gross profit to sales from one period to another than in comparing discretionary expenses, such as research or advertising.

- The **frequency** with which a relationship is observed (e.g. a pattern repeated monthly as opposed to annually).

The application of analytical procedures is based on the expectation that relationships between data exist and continue in the absence of known conditions to the contrary. The presence of these relationships provides audit evidence as to the financial statement assertions relating to the data produced by the accounting system. However, reliance on the results of analytical procedures depends on the auditors' assessment of the risk that the analytical procedures may identify relationships as expected whereas, in fact, a material misstatement exists.

4.9 Proof in total

Proof in total is where the value of one item can be verified directly by reference to another item of data, the validity of which has already been established. In some circumstances, this may by itself provide the required level of assurance.

- Commission expense = (audited) sales × known commission %

- Sales = (audited) opening inventory + purchases − closing inventory × known mark-up

- Interest expense = (confirmed) balance of loan outstanding × interest rate, per loan agreement

4.10 Reasonableness tests

Reasonableness tests may contribute to the sufficiency of evidence when used in conjunction with other substantive tests.

- Closing receivables = Opening receivables + credit sales − cash receipts

- Depreciation = Average cost (or NBV, if reducing balance) of non-current assets − fully depreciated assets + purchases × Average depreciation rate

- Payroll costs = Average no. of employees × average wage × (1 + employers' NI rate)

4.11 Analytical procedures at the overall review stage

When completing the audit, auditors must apply analytical procedures in forming an overall conclusion as to whether the financial statements as a whole are consistent with their knowledge of the entity's business.

The conclusions drawn from the results of such procedures are intended to corroborate conclusions formed during the audit regarding individual components or elements of the financial statements and to assist in arriving at the overall conclusion as to whether the financial statements as a whole are consistent with the auditors' knowledge of the entity's business. However, they may also identify areas requiring further procedures. For instance, if the auditor cannot explain a material fluctuation in a balance, this may indicate that they do not have sufficient, appropriate audit evidence.

4.12 Investigating significant fluctuations or unexpected relationships

The investigation of significant fluctuations and unexpected relationships normally begins with enquiries of management, followed by corroboration of management's responses:

- by comparing them with the auditors' knowledge of the entity's business and with other evidence obtained during the course of the audit; or

- if the analytical procedures are being carried out as substantive procedures, by undertaking additional audit procedures where appropriate to confirm the explanations received.

If management is unable to provide an explanation or if the explanation is not considered adequate, auditors determine the audit procedures to be undertaken to obtain an explanation for the fluctuation or relationship noted.

Test your understanding 5

Task 1

A manufacturing business operates at a gross profit margin of 33%. The audited figure for cost of sales (i.e. opening inventory + purchases – closing inventory) is £583,406. What would you expect the sales figure to be?

Task 2

A class of non-current asset had a cost of £380,700 at the start of the year and a total cost of £420,600 at the end of the year. Within those totals there were assets costing £68,400 which were fully depreciated at the start of the year. This class of non-current assets is depreciated at 25% straight line on cost.

Carry out a reasonableness test for the depreciation charge for the year.

AUDIT AND ASSURANCE

 Test your understanding 6

The objective of a substantive test will determine the population from which the sample for testing is selected.

For each of the objectives set out below, select the population from which the sample should be selected.

1. Obtain evidence of the existence of a non-current asset.
2. Obtain evidence of the completeness of the trade payables balance.

 Test your understanding 7

For each of the following, select whether they are a test of control or a substantive procedure:

1. Vouching of an addition to the non-current assets to the purchase invoice.
2. Observation of the order process in respect of a new customer placing an order.
3. Comparison of this year's receivables figure with the previous year's figure.

5 Summary

Audit evidence

You should now be able to specify the nature and reliability of sources of audit evidence and apply the procedures by which audit evidence is obtained.

Audit sampling

You should appreciate what constitutes audit sampling and the factors which affect its use. In particular, you should be able to design, select and evaluate a sample for a specified audit objective.

Analytical procedures

You should understand how analytical procedures contribute to the planning, testing and review stages of the audit. You should be able to design proofs in total and reasonableness tests for specified audit areas.

Test your understanding answers

Test your understanding 1

2, 1, 3

Test your understanding 2

1. False.
2. True.
3. True.

Test your understanding 3

1. True.
2. False.
3. True.

Test your understanding 4

Sampling interval = $\dfrac{\text{Population}}{\text{Sample size}} = \dfrac{126{,}435 - 110{,}652}{200}$

= 79

Invoice 1 (110,652 + 44) Invoice no: 110696
Invoice 2 (110,696 + 79) Invoice no: 110775
Invoice 3 (110,775 + 79) Invoice no: 110854
Invoice 4 (110,854 + 79) Invoice no: 110933

Test your understanding 5

Task 1

Anticipated sales = £583,406 × $\frac{100}{67}$

= £870,755

Task 2

Average cost = $\frac{380,770 + 420,600}{2}$ = £400,650

Consider: (Average cost – fully depreciated assets) × depreciation rate

= (£400,650 – £68,400) × 25%

= £83,062

Test your understanding 6

1. Non-current asset register.
2. Goods received records.

Test your understanding 7

1. Substantive procedure.
2. Test of control.
3. Substantive procedure.

AUDIT AND ASSURANCE

Audit verification work 1 – General principles

Introduction

This chapter looks at how the auditor can verify evidence and how this evidence corresponds to the financial statement assertions.

ASSESSMENT CRITERIA
Methods used to obtain audit evidence (4.1)
Audit approach (4.4)
Audit assertions (4.5)

CONTENTS
1 Audit verification techniques
2 Review of financial statements

1 Audit verification techniques

1.1 Introduction

At this, the verification stage of the audit, the auditor is typically presented with a set of draft financial statements prepared by the client. The role of the auditor is to generate evidence to allow a conclusion to be reached as to whether the information contained in those financial statements, and the way the information is presented and disclosed, give a true and fair view.

We know already that audit evidence is generated by the auditor performing audit tests. Here, in verification work, the auditor will use substantive testing procedures, designed to give evidence relating to the figures in the financial statements, rather than control tests, dealing with the systems that produced those figures. However, the testing procedures available to the auditor here are the same as those we saw earlier. As a reminder, audit-testing procedures available to the auditor are:

Inspection

This covers the physical review or examination of records, documents and tangible assets. An example in substantive testing is examining purchase invoices to ensure that they have been properly recorded and analysed in the financial statements.

Observation

This procedure is mainly applicable to tests of control, but may also be used in substantive testing, such as the auditor observing the client's inventory count to gain evidence that the inventory figure in the financial statements had been arrived at accurately.

Enquiry

Seeking relevant information from knowledgeable persons inside or outside the entity.

An example in substantive testing is asking management for an explanation as to why a receivable has, or has not, been treated as an irrecoverable receivable.

Computation

Checking the arithmetical accuracy of records or performing independent calculations, for example computing or re-computing the depreciation charge for the year.

Analytical procedures

You should note that these procedures are mainly used in substantive testing rather than as a test of controls. They may help the auditor to understand relationships between figures in the financial statements. This is sometimes referred to as the business approach to auditing.

Re-performance

This involves re-performing client procedures e.g. test checking inventory counts.

External confirmation

- This refers to the auditor obtaining a direct response (usually written) from an external, third party.
- Examples include:
  - circularisation of receivables
  - confirmation of bank or loan balances in a bank letter
  - confirmation of actual/potential penalties from legal advisers; and
  - confirmation of inventories held by third parties.
- May give good evidence of existence of balances, e.g. receivables confirmation.
- May not necessarily give reliable evidence of valuation, e.g. customers may confirm receivable amounts but, ultimately, be unable to pay in the future.

1.2 Choice of verification techniques

There are no specific rules that exist as to the type(s) of techniques that the auditor should use in a given set of circumstances.

This is principally a matter of audit judgement and the nature of the audit objective(s). The auditor has to look at each individual item in its own right, identify the audit objective(s) for that particular item and then decide the most reliable audit evidence available. The circumstances and evidence available will affect the type of technique(s) the auditor uses.

1.3 Audit objectives and financial statement assertions

As just stated, the type(s) of technique(s) used depend on the audit objectives that the auditor is seeking to achieve.

The general objective to be achieved by audit verification work is to establish whether the financial statements present a true and fair view.

We can identify a number of more detailed objectives which underlie this overall objective. These more detailed objectives allow the auditor to design a series of substantive tests on each audit area (inventory, receivables, etc.) which will build up the overall bank of evidence necessary to support the overall audit opinion.

In carrying out substantive audit tests (verification work) the auditor will be looking for evidence on:

- **Completeness:** all assets, liabilities, equity interests, transactions and events that should have been recorded have been recorded, and all related disclosures that should have been included in the financial statements have been included (i.e. they are not understated).

- **Occurrence:** transactions and events that have been recorded or disclosed have occurred, and such transactions and events pertain to the entity.

- **Accuracy, valuation and allocation:** assets, liabilities and equity interests have been included in the financial statements at appropriate amounts and any resulting valuation or allocation adjustments have been appropriately recorded, and related disclosures have been appropriately measured and described.

- **Existence:** assets, liabilities and equity interests exist. (i.e. they are not overstated). Auditors spend a great deal of time confirming the existence of assets such as tangible non-current assets, inventory, receivables and cash. Clearly this is fundamental to the true and fair view principle.

- **Rights and obligations:** the entity holds or controls the rights to assets, and liabilities are the obligations of the entity.

- **Accuracy:** amounts and other data relating to recorded transactions and events have been recorded appropriately, and related disclosures have been appropriately measured and described.

- **Cut-off:** transactions and events have been recorded in the correct accounting period.

- **Classification:** assets, liabilities, equity interests, transactions and events have been recorded in the proper accounts in accordance with relevant legislation and accounting standards (e.g. the CA 2006 and relevant IFRS® Standards and IAS® Standards).

- **Presentation:** assets, liabilities, equity interests, transactions and events are appropriately aggregated or disaggregated and clearly described, and related disclosures are relevant and understandable in the context of the requirements of the applicable financial reporting framework.

The above objectives link into a concept known as the financial statement assertions. This concept takes the view that draft accounts presented by the client to the auditor are making a number of statements, or assertions. The role of substantive testing is to verify these assertions.

Test your understanding 1

State whether the following statements are true or false:

1 Rights and obligations would be relevant when testing sales transactions.

2 The auditors will test completeness if they want to see if there are any further liabilities that need to be included in the financial statements.

2 Review of financial statements

2.1 Content of financial statements

It is important that you are clear as to exactly what the financial statements consist of under modern accounting practice.

They comprise the following:

(a) The primary statements

    (i) Statement of financial position

    (ii) Statement of profit or loss

    (iii) Statement of changes in equity

    (iv) Statement of cash flows

(b) The notes to the accounts

The main principles underlying the preparation and presentation of company financial statements are now set out by the International Accounting Standards Board's Framework for the Preparation and Presentation of Financial Statements.

The major points from this document are summarised below:

The elements of financial statements

The starting point here is definitions of assets and liabilities. The other elements are then defined in terms of these.

Assets are resources controlled by the entity as a result of past events and from which future economic benefits are expected to flow to the entity.

Liabilities are present obligations of the entity arising from past events, the settlement of which is expected to result in an outflow from the entity of resources embodying economic benefits.

Owners' equity is arrived at by deducting liabilities from assets (capital = assets – liabilities).

Revenue is determined in terms of increases in owners' equity.

Expenditure is determined in terms of decreases in owners' equity.

Recognition in financial statements

Recognition essentially means the recording process. The principles here address such questions as when is it acceptable to recognise (record) an asset or liability and when should assets and liabilities be de-recognised (i.e. no longer recorded in financial statements). The main points to note are:

Assets and liabilities should be recognised when there is evidence of their existence AND they can be reliably measured.

They should be derecognised when the right (assets) or obligations (liabilities) no longer exist.

2.2 The timing of audit procedures

Whereas tests of control can be (and usually are) performed by the auditor before the client's year end (interim audit), substantive audit procedures and verification work will be performed primarily at or very soon after the client's year end, as these procedures normally rely on the availability of draft financial statements.

Verification of the individual assets and liabilities by the auditor extends into the post year-end period (i.e. the period between the year-end date and the date of approval of the financial statements). The auditors will use this to their advantage when seeking to verify amounts stated for contingent liabilities, and for post year-end events (these are explained in a later chapter).

3 Summary

This chapter has introduced you to the application of standard audit testing procedures to substantive testing as used at the final stage of the audit. These procedures are used by the auditor to generate evidence that will enable the auditor to reach a conclusion on the financial statement assertions.

In carrying out these procedures the auditor should be aware of the theoretical framework within which financial statements are prepared (the IASB's Conceptual Framework) and the particular audit problems resulting from accounting estimates.

We are now ready to move on to look at the application of these testing procedures to major areas of the financial statements.

Test your understanding answers

 Test your understanding 1

1. False.
2. True.

AUDIT AND ASSURANCE

Audit verification work 2 – Inventory

Introduction

The following five chapters focus on audit field work across a number of areas. In this chapter we will look at the area of inventory. We will consider auditors work on inventory and the risks associated and we will end with reviewing an audit programme for inventory.

ASSESSMENT CRITERIA
Methods used to obtain audit evidence (4.1)
Audit approach (4.4)
Audit assertions (4.5)

CONTENTS
1 Inventory: Financial statement and audit implications
2 The auditor's work on the inventory count
3 The auditor's work on inventory valuation
4 Problem areas in the audit of inventory
5 An audit programme for inventory

1 Inventory: Financial statement and audit implications

Inventory is perhaps the area on a typical statement of financial position, which has, historically given auditors more problems than any other. Many of the leading negligence cases involving auditors revolved around the approach taken to the audit of inventory. The implication is that inventory is often a high-risk area, requiring careful audit planning and often a high degree of judgement in carrying out audit procedures.

1.1 The importance of inventory and work-in-progress

The term inventory and work-in-progress includes raw materials, bought in parts, work-in-progress (manufactured goods in an incomplete state) and finished goods.

This asset is very important from the audit viewpoint for the following reasons:

(a) Misstatement of inventory balances has a direct effect on the reported profit of two accounting periods – closing inventory of one year is, of course, opening inventory of the next year. As a result of the subjective nature of many aspects of the inventory figure in the financial statements it is the easiest asset for management to manipulate.

(b) Inventory can be very difficult for an auditor to access.

- There may be thousands of different lines of inventory – the average UK supermarket carries approximately 40,000 different product lines and, of course, large quantities of each and in varying locations.

- There may be some inventory items of a very specialist nature e.g. pharmaceutical or engineering companies may present this type of problem to the auditor.

(c) The quantities of inventory held at a given moment may be difficult to establish. It may not be possible to cease inventory movements during the inventory count with the effect that accurate inventory quantities may be hard to establish.

(d) Valuation may be difficult especially with specialist inventory and obsolete inventory. As a consequence net realisable values may be hard to establish. The amount of overheads that can be attributed to inventory may be subjective in nature.

(e) Inventory losses from pilferage, wastage, etc. may be difficult to control.

1.2 Inventory valuation

IAS 2 *Inventories* requires that inventory should be measured at the lower of cost and net realisable value on an item by item basis.

You should be familiar with this from your financial accounting studies. See Chapter 17 Financial Reporting Topics for help with the key requirements of IAS 2, should you need it.

Definition

The **cost of inventory** 'shall comprise all costs of purchase, costs of conversion and other costs incurred in bringing the inventory to their present location and condition' (IAS 2, para 10).

Definition

Net realisable value is 'the estimated selling price in the ordinary course of business less the estimated costs of completion and the estimated costs necessary to make the sale' (IAS 2, para 6).

1.3 Inventory quantities

In addition to valuing the inventory correctly, it is clearly important that the company can determine accurately the physical quantity of inventory on hand at any point in time.

Many companies will maintain accounting records of inventory, but from the audit point of view, the inventory records substantiated by physical inventory counts are important as inventory records by themselves are notoriously unreliable.

We are now going to examine in detail the audit work involved in reaching a conclusion on these two aspects of the final inventory figure in the financial statements – the quantity of inventory in hand at the year-end date and the valuation to be placed on that inventory.

Audit verification work 2 – Inventory: **Chapter 6**

2 The auditor's work on the inventory count

2.1 Available inventory count methods

The two principal methods of systems of inventory count available to clients are continuous and periodic.

- Under a continuous system, some items of inventory are counted say every week or every month through the accounting period.

- Under a system of periodic inventory count, all inventory is counted at the same time, typically at the year-end date.

It is clearly important that the auditor should be aware of which system is in operation by the client in order that suitable audit arrangements can be made.

2.2 Continuous inventory counting

Where suitable accounting records of inventory are maintained, it is often backed up by a programme of continuous inventory counting as part of general inventory control procedures. In a continuous inventory counting system, inventory is counted on a regular on-going basis throughout the accounting period.

If such a programme of continuous inventory counting is in operation by a client, the auditor should ensure that:

(a) Each item of inventory is physically inspected and counted at least once a year, and more frequently in the case of items liable to loss.

(b) Inventory records are kept up to date.

(c) The records are amended as a result of physical counting, and that there are appropriate reports and investigation procedures for discrepancies.

(d) Two people carry out each count, and there is a rotation of pairing of the checkers.

Providing the continuous inventory count procedures in place by a client are acceptable, auditors may use the information provided for audit purposes, even though this system means that all the inventory on hand at the year-end date was not counted at that date.

There are several advantages to be gained from a well organised system of continuous inventory checking:

(a) Disruption caused by the inventory count is minimised as each inventory count takes a shorter period of time to complete.

(b) More regular inventory counts will allow for earlier identification of errors and obsolete inventory.

(c) Increased discipline is imposed over storekeepers caused by the surprise elements of random checks. This should result in a higher level of control being exercised over inventory.

2.3 Periodic inventory counts

Under this system, inventory is counted only once in each accounting period.

The count will usually be undertaken on or near the financial year end. If undertaken shortly before or after the financial year end, the time gap between the physical count and financial year end should be kept to a minimum, so as to minimise the risk of inaccuracies arising in the final inventory figure.

Test your understanding 1

A potential client, Sofia, has approached your firm as she is setting up a new company selling computer stationery. She has asked for advice on inventory count methods and informs you that she has heard of periodic and continuous inventory counting, but doesn't understand what these terms mean.

Explain the difference between these two methods.

2.4 Organisation of inventory counts

Regardless of the inventory count system in operation – continuous or periodic – it is vitally important both for financial reporting purposes and for audit purposes that the count is carried out accurately.

It is the responsibility of management, not the auditor, to establish appropriate procedures to be followed by staff in organising and conducting the inventory count.

However, the auditor should carefully review the inventory count arrangements that a client has in place.

Clear procedures should be drawn up by the client well in advance of the inventory count taking place. These instructions should be made available to client staff who are going to be involved in the count so that they have a chance to review them, become familiar with their contents and clarify any areas of doubt or uncertainty.

In addition, the auditor should review a copy of the procedures before the inventory count is held by the client. In reviewing the procedures, the auditor is assessing their adequacy – will the client's procedures, if carried out effectively, ensure that a full and accurate count is taken, which can then be used as the basis for the quantity of inventory on hand at the year-end to be reflected in the financial statements?

Set out below are the main features that should appear in inventory count instructions.

1 The organisation of the inventory

   (a) The inventory area is in a well organised, tidy condition in order to make the counting process as efficient as possible.

   (b) Goods are clearly described and suitably labelled.

   (c) Goods are protected against deterioration and misappropriation, for example restriction of access to stores.

   (d) Goods held for third parties i.e. goods not belonging to the company, and slow-moving, obsolete inventory, etc. are identified and separated.

   (e) There is an adequate plan of the area to be covered, which should be tidy.

2 Carrying out the inventory count

   (a) The procedures to be followed by each relevant department, branch, division, etc., reflecting the circumstances of each part of the business.

   (b) Competent supervisors should be appointed for each inventory area, with teams or pairs of technically competent counters allocated to the supervisors. One person from each team should be responsible for counting, the other for recording and checking the count. The storekeepers should not be responsible for counting unless their work is independently checked (segregation of duties!)

   (c) Inventory should be suitably marked to indicate that it has been counted e.g. chalk mark, docket/ticket, etc.

(d) A standardised pre-numbered form should be used for recording the inventory count, the issue and return of which should be controlled so that all inventory counted and areas are accounted for, and that proper accounting records are kept.

(e) Movement of inventory during the inventory count should be halted or closely controlled.

(f) Comparisons should be made as soon as practicable after the inventory count with the continuous inventory records so that any discrepancies may be investigated and adjusted.

2.5 The auditor's attendance at the inventory count

Standard audit practice requires the auditor to attend the client's inventory count if inventory is material to the financial statements and if the auditor is to rely on the inventory count as a source of evidence as to the physical quantities of inventory on hand. It follows from this that if:

- inventory is not material, or
- the accounting record rather than the inventory count is used as the source of inventory quantities,

then the auditor is not expected to attend the count. These exceptions are not encountered on a regular basis in practice.

The auditor's role

The auditor will usually attend the client's inventory count, the overall purpose of attendance being to assess the effectiveness of the client's inventory count procedures. Attendance at an inventory count is primarily a test of controls, not a substantive procedure. It is not the auditor's responsibility to count inventory, but the client's. The auditor will perform test counts but these tiny samples are not intended to be representative of the populations they are drawn from.

We can analyse the role of the auditor in connection with inventory counts under three headings:

- Before the inventory count
- During the inventory count
- After the inventory count.

Audit verification work 2 – Inventory: Chapter 6

Before the inventory count	During the inventory count	After the inventory count
The auditor should perform the following procedures: (a) Review prior year's working papers, familiarise with the nature, volume and location of inventory. The controlling and recording procedures over inventory should also be considered. (b) Identify problem areas in relation to the system of internal control and decide whether reliance can be placed on internal auditors. (c) If inventory held by third parties is material, or the third party is insufficiently independent or reliable, then arrange an inventory count attendance at the third party's premises, otherwise, arrange third party confirmation by way of letter to the auditor.	The main task here is to ensure that the client's staff are carrying out their duties effectively. Here, the auditor is using the audit testing procedure of observation. In addition to observing the inventory count process being carried out, the auditor should also: (a) Make two-way test counts from factory floor to inventory sheets (completeness), and from inventory sheets to factory floor (existence). These are checked with the figures counted by the client and discrepancies investigated. The test counts are used for follow up audit work later. (b) Make notes of items counted, damaged inventory and instances where the procedures are not being followed.	The auditor should perform the following procedures after the inventory count: (a) Check the cut off details obtained at the inventory count are accounted for in the correct period. (b) Review the final inventory sheets and follow up test counts to the final statements of inventory. This test is designed to ensure that inventory quantities that actually existed at the date of the count are reflected in the final financial statements. (c) Ensure that continuous inventory records (if applicable) are adjusted or reconciled to the physical count.

Before the inventory count	During the inventory count	After the inventory count
(d) If the nature of the inventory is specialised then the auditor will need to arrange expert help or to review the client's own arrangements for identifying and valuing the inventory. (e) Examine the client's inventory –taking instructions, as explained above: If found to be inadequate, the matter should be discussed with the client with a view to improving them prior to the inventory count.	(c) Examine and test control over the inventory sheets. The client should keep an inventory sheet register. (d) Examine cut-off procedures. (e) Pay particular attention to goods held on behalf of third parties (for example, goods on consignment) and how these are segregated and recorded. (f) Reach and record a conclusion as to whether or not the inventory count was satisfactory, and hence provides reliable evidence supporting the final inventory figure. If the auditor in attendance at the inventory count does not feel that the procedures are being carried out adequately, the auditor must bring this to management's attention immediately and seek to rectify the position as it may not be possible to obtain the relevant evidence at a later date.	

The cut-off concept

As financial statements are drawn up at a specific point in time, it is important that the right transactions are fully recorded in the right period. This is a simple but useful way of looking at cut off.

For example, if sales are recorded as a transaction of the current period by recognising a year end receivable, the corresponding cost of sales entry must also be made in the current period and the item must not be included in year-end inventory. This is an example of sales cut off.

Similarly, if goods are received during the current period and recorded in closing inventory, the year-end payable for the item must also be recorded. This is an example of purchases cut off.

Tests the auditor would carry out to ensure correct cut-off include the following.

(a) During the inventory count attendance, note the serial numbers of the last sales invoice, despatch note and goods received note generated before the inventory count.

(b) After the inventory count, check the year-end despatch notes to sales invoices and the sales daybook and vice versa to ensure that despatches and the related invoice both fall before the year end.

(c) Similarly for purchases, ensure year-end goods receipts notes and related purchase invoices are correctly treated in the current period.

(d) Take a sample of goods received and goods despatched just after the year end and ensure that the related inventory was not included in the count in the case of goods received, and that it was included, in the case of goods despatched.

Test your understanding 2

Explain the main reasons why the auditors attend the inventory count and state what action they would take if they identified that the client's laid down inventory count procedures were not being followed.

AUDIT AND ASSURANCE

3 The auditor's work on inventory valuation

The main objective of the auditor attending the inventory count is to obtain evidence relating to the existence of inventory. Attendance will provide some evidence relating to the valuation of inventory, for example, the auditor should record details of any inventory showing signs of obsolescence, but much more work will be required before the auditor can reach an overall conclusion on inventory valuation. This section deals with that audit work.

The auditors need to perform additional valuation tests. The audit work which the auditor will need to perform in respect of the valuation of inventory will depend on the type of inventory items under review.

3.1 Raw materials and consumable supplies

As these items of inventory are in their raw state (no work has yet been done on them by the client), the principal element of cost to consider is their purchase price from the material supplier. In addition there may be incidental costs such as delivery charges to consider.

Typical audit procedures applied to the verification of these inventory items will be as follows:

(a) Ascertain what elements of cost are included e.g. carriage in, duties, etc.

(b) Ascertain the method of valuing inventory.

(c) If standard costs are used, enquire into standards: how and when the standards were set, how these compare with actual costs and how variances are treated.

(d) Compare costs used with purchase invoices received, before the inventory count.

(e) Compare quantities with inventory records with a particular aim of finding items which have been in inventory for an unduly long period. Discuss these items with a responsible official in order to find out when they might be used, if at all, in order to ascertain a reasonable net realisable value. Consider the need for any write down of the value of these items of inventory.

(f) Follow up valuation of all damaged or obsolete inventory noted during observance of physical inventory count with a view to establishing a net realisable value, and again consider any write down which may be necessary.

3.2 Work-in-progress (i.e. part completed goods)

The range of costs to consider here will include labour costs and production overheads, in addition to materials, as some work has been done by the client on this type of inventory.

Typical audit procedures applied to the verification of these inventory items will be as follows:

(a) Ascertain what elements of cost are included. If overheads are included, ascertain the basis on which they are calculated and review this basis with the available costing and financial information. If labour is included, compare the calculations to costing and payroll records.

(b) Ascertain how the state of completion of the work in progress is measured and if estimates are made, on what basis they are made.

(c) Ensure that any materials costs exclude any abnormal wastage factors as abnormal costs should not be included under IAS 2.

(d) Ensure that any addition for overheads includes only normal expenses based on normal production capacity and that any costs arising from under-utilisation of production facilities, excessive waste or exceptional circumstances (i.e. abnormal costs again) are not carried forward in the inventory valuation.

(e) Enquire into any old, obsolete or damaged items and ensure that these are valued at a reasonable estimated net realisable value. Compare this with previous or subsequent sales of similar items.

3.3 Finished goods and goods for resale

Note that if these items have been manufactured or processed by the client, the cost will consist of the same elements as were identified in work in progress above. If the items were brought in by the client in their completed state, cost of the inventory will comprise the purchase price from the supplier.

Typical audit procedures applied to the verification of these inventory items will be as follows:

(a) Enquire into what costs are included, how these have been established and ensure that any overhead addition is based on normal costs and is reasonable in relation to the information disclosed by the draft accounts. If labour is included, compare the calculations to costing and payroll records.

(b) Compare the final cost with the client's official sales prices, bearing in mind any trade discounts which are normally granted off the list prices. This enables the auditor to ensure that inventory is valued at net realisable value if this is less than cost. For any such items, also check back and see if the relevant partly processed inventory and raw materials have also been written down.

(c) Follow up any items which inventory records show are more than, say, six months in inventory. Enquire into reasons for this and ascertain possible realisable value of such items.

(d) Follow up any inventory which at the time of observance of physical inventory taking were noted as being damaged or obsolete.

(e) Discuss with sales manager any possible policy of selling off certain lines at less than usual selling prices e.g. 'loss leaders' due to competition, substitute products on the market etc.

(f) Follow up valuation of all 'seconds' items and ensure that they are valued at a reasonable estimated net realisable value if less than cost.

4 Problem areas in the audit of inventory

4.1 Introduction

Certain practical matters which may cause difficulty in some audits are explained briefly below. Where relevant, the auditor should take them into consideration when verifying inventory.

4.2 Overheads

Definition

Overheads are expenses incurred in the manufacture of goods and include items like factory rates and lighting and heating.

Overheads should normally be included in the cost of goods being produced, based on the normal activity level of the company. An estimate of overheads to be incurred at this level of activity will need to be calculated, and allocated to the goods produced based on this activity level. If the company produces less goods than expected, then the unabsorbed overheads should be written off to the profit and loss account and not included in the inventory valuation.

In addition, most costing systems base overhead allocations on budgeted figures. These are obviously pre-determined figures, calculated before the actual overhead costs for the period are known and before the actual level of production is known. Activity levels in excess of that expected may require a reapportionment of overheads. If this is not done, it may result in an excessive amount of overhead being included in inventory valuation.

The overheads to be included in inventory should be only those relating to production – these are known as production overheads e.g. the factory rates, etc.

4.3   Choice of overhead allocation method

There are many different ways of including overheads into the cost of inventory. Each company must make its own decision about which method to use. The method must give a close approximation to the actual cost of overheads incurred in making the inventory.

The auditor will need to apply judgement in order to evaluate the appropriateness of the method used by the client.

4.4   Net realisable value

 Definition

Net realisable value is the estimated selling price in the ordinary course of business less the estimated costs of completion and the estimated costs necessary to make the sale.

As you are already aware, inventory should be valued at the lower of cost and net realisable value and it is not always easy to arrive at a figure for net realisable value. This is often another area where estimates will be used and where the auditor will need to assess the reasonableness of those estimates. A wide variety of sources of information may be available in order to assess net realisable value. These include:

- selling prices realised after the year end
- price lists.

Where net realisable value is found to be less than cost, the individual inventory lines affected should be revalued at the (lower) net realisable value. The only exception to this rule is for raw materials and components to be used in manufacture. These items may have their own net realisable value being less than cost. However, these items are not normally sold in their raw state. Because of this, no reduction in value is needed if it can be shown that the product made from these items can still be sold at above its cost.

There are several situations where net realisable value is more likely to be less than cost, including:

(a) increased costs of manufacture
(b) reduced selling prices of products
(c) deterioration of inventory (particularly foodstuff)
(d) obsolescence of products (perhaps due to technological changes)
(e) deliberate selling at loss (supermarket 'loss leaders')
(f) buying and production errors.

5 An audit programme for inventory

The following is an extract from a detailed audit programme for inventory.

Example

Audit programme
HASTINGS & WARWICK
AUDIT PROGRAMME

Sch Ref

CLIENT	PREPARED BY	DATE
	REVIEWED BY	DATE
	(Audit senior in charge)	
PERIOD	REVIEWED BY	DATE
	(Manager)	

AUDIT AREA – Inventory

| The purpose of the auditing procedures set out in this section of the programme is to obtain reasonable assurance that inventory is not materially misstated. | Work performed by | Ref to supporting working paper |

RELIANCE ON INTERNAL CONTROL PROCEDURES

1. Where we have placed reliance on the client's internal control procedures, test that the controls on which we are relying have been complied with, and record the details of such tests in the working papers.

TESTS OF DETAIL

EXISTENCE AND RIGHTS AND OBLIGATIONS

Planning our attendance at the inventory count

2   Where the date selected for the inventory count is an interim date we must be able to rely on the year-end book inventory records. Assess the past reliability of the book records by examining the materiality of differences disclosed by previous physical inventory-counts. If there are any doubts as to the reliability of the book records, discuss immediately with the manager whether we should request the client to conduct a year-end inventory count.

3   Review the adequacy of the client's inventory count instructions. Any serious shortcomings must be discussed immediately with responsible client officials so that they can be rectified before the inventory-count.

4   Select for test counting those inventory items expected to have the largest monetary value at the inventory count date.

5   Where the client maintains inventory of a technical nature which is not readily identifiable, or whose conditions we are not competent to ascertain, consider using independent experts.

6   Obtain a list of all inventory held by third party custodians. Ensure that the list is complete. In respect of these inventory:

   (a)   Establish the suitability of the custodian.

   (b)   Confirm the existence and title of such inventory directly with the custodians.

   (c)   Review the controls exercised by the client over this inventory (including cut-off) and consider whether there is any need for us to inspect them physically.

7   Arrange for the necessary audit staff to attend inventory counts at the various locations. Brief the audit staff and ensure that they have a copy of the client's instructions for the inventory count together with a list of the inventory items pre-selected in 4 above and the audit programme for procedures during inventory count which they will be required to complete.

   Make arrangements for the audit staff to be present at the end of the inventory count.

8   On completion of the inventory count obtain and review the audit working papers prepared during our attendance at the various locations, and summarise the adequacy and effectiveness of the inventory count.

Procedures subsequent to inventory count

9   Obtain the client's count records and test that they are complete and accurate, as follows:

   (a) Test for completeness, by comparing the numerical sequence of count records with the details recorded in our working papers at the time of the physical count.

   (b) Scrutinise the count records to ensure that they have not been altered subsequent to our attendance at the inventory-count by comparing the records with details recorded in our working papers at the time of the physical count (e.g. photocopies).

Testing continuous inventory count procedures

10 Review the instructions issued to inventory counters and the procedures adopted by the client, in order to determine whether such instructions and procedures are adequate. Pay particular attention to controls revealed on the ICQ for the inventory system where inventory is not physically counted at the year-end date.

11 Arrange to attend at least one of the continuous inventory counts during the year. Review the inventory count reports or the inventory records to ascertain the extent to which inventory have been counted during the year, and also to determine (by reviewing any differences disclosed) the accuracy of the inventory records. In the light of this review, determine the extent of the counting to be performed under 12 (a) and (b) below. Test that the differences disclosed by inventory count have been adjusted in the inventory records.

12 Carry out audit tests as follows:

   (a) Select from the inventory account at the year-end date a sample of inventory items, and check the quantities with the underlying inventory records and the valuation of the items with supporting documents.

   (b) Count a number of items that are in inventory, and check these by comparing them with the inventory account.

13 Summarise on a working paper our findings on the adequacy and effectiveness of the continuous inventory count procedures and on the reliability of the inventory records. Also indicate the approximate amount of the differences found during the year.

Checking quantities on inventory sheets

14 Test the casts of the inventory sheets by:

  (a) Casting the pages to which counted items have been traced and follow the totals through to the inventory summary.

  (b) Casting the final inventory summary, selecting individual page totals and casting these pages, at the same time selecting items for examination in procedure 15(a).

15 Test that the physical quantities shown on the final inventory sheets are neither overstated nor understated by performing the following procedures:

  (a) Overstatement: Agree the details of those items selected in procedure 14 (b) above with the client's count records, to ensure that the inventory sheets only incorporate count records from the inventory count.

  (b) Understatement: Agree items which were counted by us, or in our presence, with the final inventory sheets.

Testing the cut-off of inventory

16 Test that there was a proper cut-off at the inventory count date, as follows:

  (a) Select from the goods received reports for a few days either side of the inventory count date, and compare with the relevant inventory records (and vice versa) to ensure that goods received were recorded in the inventory records in the correct accounting period.

  (b) Select from the despatch records for a few days either side of the inventory count date, and compare with the relevant inventory records (and vice versa) to ensure that goods despatched were recorded in the inventory records in the correct accounting period.

  (c) Where necessary, test the cut-off on the internal movement of inventory.

VALUATION

Checking valuations and calculations on inventory sheets

17 Record in the working papers in detail the bases and methods of costing used, and obtain reasonable assurance that these bases and methods are being applied consistently, and are in accordance with generally accepted accounting practices and the stated accounting policies of the company.

18 Test the items selected in procedure 15 above as follows:

   (a) Prove the unit costs on the inventory sheets by reference to appropriate supporting records (such as suppliers' invoices, labour cost analyses, overhead allocations and other appropriate records).

   (b) Prove the extensions on the inventory sheets.

19 Where the costs have been obtained from standard cost records, review the variance reports or the entries in the variance accounts as appropriate in order to determine whether or not the standard costs are materially different from actual costs. If there are material differences, ascertain the reasons for these differences and consider the need to adjust the valuation of the inventory.

20 Examine the overheads included in the inventory valuation and ensure that:

   (a) Their inclusion is in accordance with generally accepted accounting principles.

   (b) They reflect the client's normal level of activity.

21 Ensure that inter-department or inter-branch profit included in inventory have been properly eliminated and that where inventory include goods purchased or transferred from group companies they have been identified as such and segregated on the inventory summary.

22 Check that the general ledger accounts have been adjusted to reflect the results of physical inventory count. Establish the reasons for any material differences disclosed.

TESTING THE NET REALISABLE VALUE OF INVENTORY

23 Apply the procedures set out in (a) to (e) below to ascertain whether or not inventory write-downs and provisions are adequate (but not excessive) so that inventory are stated at the lower of cost and net realisable value. In doing this, consider the following factors where applicable: the condition of the inventory, its saleability, the possibility of obsolescence, the levels of inventory in relation to current and expected sales or usage, the estimated costs of completing work in progress, and current and expected selling prices less reasonable costs of disposal.

(a) Test the amount at which inventory of finished products and of other items held for sale to customers is stated does not exceed the selling price less reasonable costs of disposal. Also test that the quantities held are not excessive. Compare inventory levels (where appropriate) with sales for the current year, with orders, and with sales forecasts.

(b) Test that work in progress is current and saleable. Also test that (where appropriate) it has been written down by the amount of any losses expected to arise on realisation – taking into account reasonable costs of completion and disposal.

(c) Test that the costs incurred to date on contract work in progress plus the estimated costs of completing the work do not exceed the net contract price. Inspect written contracts for significant projects undertaken during the year (whether complete or incomplete at the year-end date), noting prices, terms of delivery, possible penalties, and possible variations of the contract price. Where profit is taken on contracts in progress, review the bases and methods used in order to determine whether or not such bases are consistent with those used during the previous year and also reasonable and acceptable.

(d) Test that inventory of raw material and supplies which are defective, obsolete or surplus to production requirements have been adequately written down.

(e) Test that adequate provision has been made for any major purchase commitments which are surplus to requirements or which are at prices in excess of current replacement prices.

AUDIT AND ASSURANCE

TESTING INVENTORY IN TRANSIT

24 In respect of inventory in transit:

(a) Examine the basis for recording any inventory that is in transit.

(b) Check that the inventory has been subsequently received and was validly in transit.

OVERALL REVIEW

25 Compare the inventory at the year-end date with those of the previous year, and obtain explanations for any significant differences. Compare inventory turnover rates with those of previous years. Generally consider whether inventory are stated on appropriate bases consistent with those stated in the preceding year.

Test your understanding 3

Engco Co is a company which undertakes industrial maintenance services under short-term fixed-price contracts. All direct costs (labour and materials) relating to each contract are recorded in the company's job costing system which is integrated with the purchases and payroll applications. The job costing records are used by the Finance Director to estimate the value of work in progress for the monthly management accounts and the year-end financial statements. For the work in progress valuation, a percentage is added to the direct costs to cover overheads. The Finance Director determines the percentage by taking the production overheads figure in the management accounts as a percentage of direct costs in the management accounts.

Set out, in a manner suitable for inclusion in the audit plan, the audit procedures to be undertaken in order to ensure that work in progress is fairly stated in the financial statements.

Test your understanding 4

For the following statements, select whether they are true or false in respect of inventory:

1 Inventory must be valued at the higher of cost and net realisable value.

2 The auditor's attendance at the inventory count is a test of control.

3 Inventory is generally an immaterial balance on the financial statements.

6 Summary

Inventory is a material asset in the financial statements of many companies which is relatively easily manipulated. Auditors will often treat inventory as a relatively high risk area. This together with its materiality impact, means that auditors will devote a significant amount of audit time to inventory.

There are two main areas to consider:

- Audit evidence in relation to the existence of inventory is derived primarily from the auditor's attendance at inventory counts.

- Evidence is also required on the valuation of inventory, which should be in accordance with IAS 2 – the lower of cost (including relevant labour and overhead) and net realisable value.

Test your understanding answers

Test your understanding 1

Continuous inventory counting is where each line of inventory is counted throughout the year, and each inventory item is physically counted at least once a year. The frequency will be determined according to the risk level of the inventory item. This method requires that records are maintained up to date; these will be amended as a result of physical inspection where any errors are identified.

Periodic inventory counting is where all inventory is counted once a year, usually at the financial year end.

Test your understanding 2

The auditor's attendance at the inventory count is a key step in the audit process. Inventory is often a material statement of financial position item and the auditors will want to assess the effectiveness of the client's inventory count procedures. By doing this they will obtain confirmation as to whether controls are working effectively and they can then decide the extent of their reliance on such controls.

If the client's inventory count procedures are not being followed, the auditor should raise the matter with management immediately so that action can be taken on the occasion of the count to ensure that adequate audit evidence is obtained.

Audit verification work 2 – Inventory: **Chapter 6**

> **Test your understanding 3**
>
> Vouch a sample of entries for materials to invoices.
>
> Vouch a sample of entries for wages to payroll records.
>
> Trace a sample of invoices to costing records.
>
> Trace a sample of timesheet details to the costing records.
>
> Re-perform the overhead percentage calculation.
>
> For a sample of contracts in progress at the year-end compare actual costs to:
>
> - Contract price to identify losses.
> - Budget to identify cost overruns and potential losses.

> **Test your understanding 4**
>
> 1. False.
> 2. True.
> 3. False.

AUDIT AND ASSURANCE

Audit verification work 3 – Non-current assets

Introduction

This chapter focuses on tangible and intangible non-current assets. We will consider the various verification procedures used.

ASSESSMENT CRITERIA
Methods used to obtain audit evidence (4.1)
Audit approach (4.4)
Audit assertions (4.5)

CONTENTS
1 Non-current assets: an introduction
2 Verification procedures: tangible non-current assets
3 Verification procedures: intangible non-current assets

1 Non-current assets: an introduction

This chapter examines the audit verification procedures relating to all non-current assets. As you will probably be aware from your financial reporting studies, this includes two main categories of assets:

- tangible non-current assets
- intangible non-current assets.

These assets will often be a material item in a client's statement of financial position, particularly in the case of a manufacturing company and represent another area where auditor judgement will be required, notably in the area of depreciation.

Definition

Non-current assets are those assets which are held for continuing use in the business and are not intended for resale.

Non-current assets can be analysed as follows:

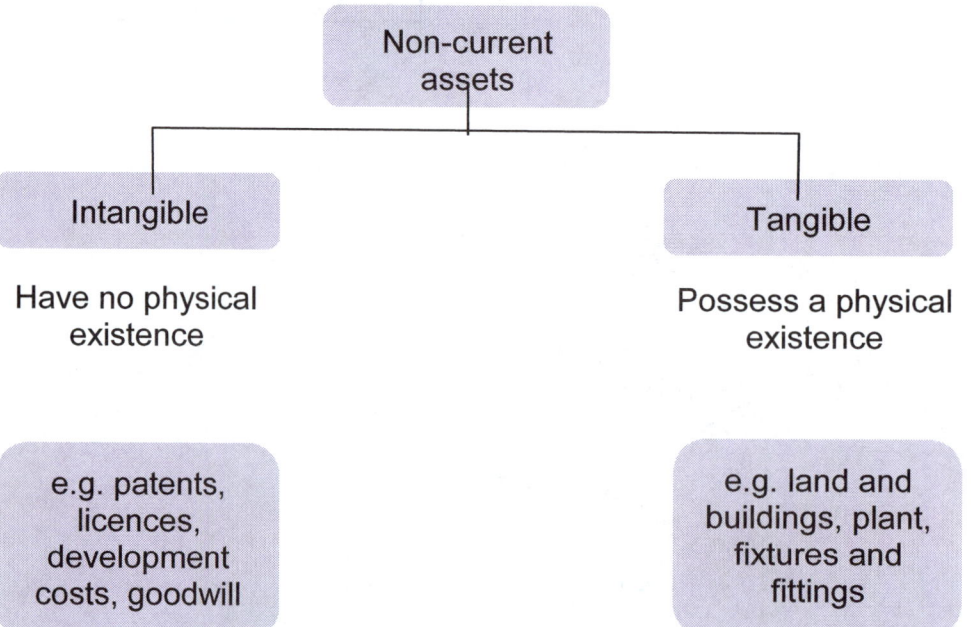

Any assets not intended for continuing use are treated as current assets regardless of when they will be realised.

1.1 Non-current assets – major disclosure requirements

In order to satisfy UK legislation, a schedule of non-current assets is required in published financial statements. This provision applies to all categories of non-current assets. An example is shown here relating to tangible non-current assets. A similar schedule would also be published in respect of intangible non-current assets.

	Land and buildings	Plant and machinery	Fixtures, fittings, tools and equipment	Payments on account and assets in course of construction	Total
Cost or valuation	£	£	£	£	£
At beginning of year	X	X	X	X	X
Additions	X	X	X	X	X
Disposals	(X)	(X)	(X)	(X)	(X)
At end of year					
Accumulated depreciation					
At beginning of year	X	X	X	X	X
Disposals	(X)	(X)	(X)	(X)	(X)
Provisions for the year	X	X	X	X	X
At end of year	X	X	X	X	X
Carrying amount: At end of year	X	X	X	X	X
At beginning of year	X	X	X	X	X

Statutory information requirements for tangible non-current assets.

The carrying amount of land and buildings comprises:

	20X5	20X4
	£	£
Freehold	X	X
Long leaseholds	X	X
Short leaseholds	X	X
	X	X

Where non-current assets are held under the revaluation model, the notes must disclose:

(a) the years in which the valuation took place, and for each year, the value of those assets

(b) for any valuation during the year the names of the valuers, or their qualifications, and the bases of valuation adopted.

It is also necessary to disclose the accounting policies as regards the depreciation and to account for any permanent fall in the value of assets.

The above movement schedule, as it is often called, is useful as an introduction to the audit work on non-current assets. It highlights some of the key areas where the auditor will focus attention, for example, additions and disposals.

1.2 Cost or valuation

Companies can choose to measure non-current assets in the statement of financial position using a cost model or a revaluation model. The most frequently encountered category of asset that is stated at valuation rather than cost is land and buildings.

The following points should be noted:

(a) The measurement basis used i.e. cost or valuation, must be disclosed in the accounts.

(b) If the assets are revalued the surplus on revaluation should be credited directly to other comprehensive income and accumulated in a revaluation reserve in equity.

(c) Revaluation of non-current assets in accounting practice is not compulsory unless there has been a permanent fall in value in which case the asset must be written down in the statement of financial position. Usually the debit is made in the statement of profit or loss account, but it can be taken to revaluation reserves in certain circumstances.

(d) Depreciation of revalued assets should be based on the revalued amount and current estimates of useful life.

(e) If the decision is made to revalue one asset or group of assets then all assets in that category must be revalued (e.g. all plant and machinery). These valuations must be kept reasonably up to date in subsequent periods.

The auditor should have special regard to ISA 620 *Using the work of an auditor's expert* when considering the accuracy of revaluations and the integrity/competence of the valuer.

1.3 Depreciation

Depreciation is a subjective area – it is important that the auditor considers the requirements of IAS 16 *Property, Plant and Equipment* and CA 2006 in respect of the appropriate accounting principles and the disclosure requirements for depreciation. See Chapter 17 Financial Reporting Topics for help with the key requirements for depreciation in IAS 16, should you need it.

1.4 Leases

Companies often choose to lease assets rather than purchase them. IFRS 16 *Leases* requires that a company recognises an asset and a liability for all leases, unless they are short-term or of low value.

1.5 Non-depreciation of non-current assets

You should note that some companies do not depreciate certain properties such as hotels and supermarkets on the grounds that the asset is constantly maintained to a high standard and that the residual value will always be higher than cost and that the property has an indefinite useful life (e.g. a well-kept 500-year-old pub).

This argument, although not frequently encountered, can be acceptable providing that refurbishment costs are charged to the statement of profit or loss in lieu of depreciation.

1.6 Internal control over non-current assets

It is the responsibility of the directors to establish a system of internal control over non-current assets with the following objectives:

(i) non-current assets are correctly recorded, adequately secured and properly maintained

(ii) acquisitions and disposals of non-current assets are properly authorised

(iii) acquisitions and disposals of non-current assets are for the most favourable price possible

(iv) non-current assets are properly recorded, appropriately depreciated, and written down where necessary.

You should note that a key feature of control systems over non-current assets is the existence of a non-current asset register, containing full details of each individual asset under the control of the company.

Audit verification work 3 – Non-current assets: **Chapter 7**

2 Verification procedures: tangible non-current assets

2.1 Verification procedures

IAS 16 *Property, Plant and Equipment* sets out the requirements for the recognition and subsequent treatment of property, plant and equipment. See Chapter 17 Financial Reporting Topics for help with the key requirements of IAS 16, should you need it.

Remember that audit verification procedures are designed to support the financial statement assertions of:

(a) completeness

(b) rights and obligations

(c) valuation

(d) existence

(e) classification

(f) presentation.

There follows a summary of the principal verification techniques which will be used to generate evidence on these assertions. The techniques shown below are related to each major category of tangible non-current assets, but you should note that there are common themes, that apply to all of the categories. The assertions to which each procedure relates is also identified.

2.2 Freehold and leasehold land and buildings

(a) Examine a sample of title deeds, land registry certificates, conveyancing documentation from solicitors and leases. Pay particular attention to any 'encumbrances' i.e. mortgages or other securities held over assets (rights and obligations, classification and presentation).

(b) Select a sample of entries in the non-current asset register and trace back to source documentation to ensure properly stated at cost (accuracy, valuation and allocation).

(c) Review company policies for depreciation and ensure appropriate in the light of the useful life of the building (commonly over 50 years) and ensure that land is not depreciated (accuracy, valuation and allocation).

(d) Select a sample of calculations of depreciation and ensure accurate and in line with company policy. Note that freehold land should not normally be subject to depreciation (accuracy, valuation and allocation).

(e) Review assets and establish the need for any write-down for permanent diminutions in value. Discuss with directors (accuracy, valuation and allocation).

(f) If freehold or leasehold assets are let to third parties, inspect tenancy agreements, and perform analytical procedures on rental income. Note that this procedure is an example of a useful general auditing technique allowing the auditor to relate together statement of financial position and statement of profit or loss account items – if there is an asset on the statement of financial position, is there any related statement of profit or loss account impact of the assets? (completeness of income).

(g) Ensure freehold land and buildings are stated in accordance with Sch4 CA 2006 at cost or valuation less accumulated depreciation. If valuation performed in year of audit, give name or qualification of valuer and basis of valuation (classification and presentation).

(h) Ensure assets held under leases are appropriately disclosed as long-term or short-term (classification and presentation).

(i) Physically inspect a sample of assets (existence).

(j) Ensure non-current asset register reconciles to nominal ledger (accuracy, valuation and allocation).

2.3 Plant, machinery, fixtures and fittings and motor vehicles

(a) Examine a sample of invoices, contracts, leases or other evidence of title to assets including vehicle registration documents (rights and obligations).

(b) Review company policies for depreciation and ensure appropriate in the light of the useful life of the assets (accuracy, valuation and allocation).

(c) Select a sample of calculations of depreciation and ensure accurate and in line with company policy (accuracy, valuation and allocation).

(d) Review assets and establish the need for any write-down for permanent diminutions in value. Discuss with directors (accuracy, valuation and allocation).

(e) Ensure that VAT is appropriately capitalised where it is not recoverable (accuracy, valuation and allocation).

(f) Ensure assets are stated in accordance with legislation and that the carrying amount of assets held under leases is disclosed separately (classification and presentation).

(g) Physically inspect a sample of assets (existence).

2.4 Assets in the course of construction

Such assets are built by the company for itself and can include plant and machinery as well as buildings. The tests are as above except that there are no title deeds or documents of title to examine. Instead the auditor may perform the following tests on the company's own records:

(a) Ensure the company's system for allocating costs to the asset is appropriate. Some tests of control may be necessary here. Such costs include raw materials, goods taken from trading inventory, costs of labour and sometimes interest costs.

(b) Ensure that the costs that are included relate to the project by taking a sample of costs included and tracing back to costings and source documentation.

The danger is always that costs that should be expensed through the statement of profit or loss account and reducing profits, are in actual fact being capitalised in the statement of financial position, thus turning losses into assets!

The following is an example of a detailed audit programme for tangible non-current assets.

Example

Audit programme

HASTINGS & WARWICK

AUDIT PROGRAMME

CLIENT _____ PREPARED BY _____ DATE _____

_____ REVIEWED BY _____ DATE _____

Sch Ref

AUDIT AREA – TANGIBLE NON-CURRENT ASSETS

The purpose of the auditing procedures set out in this section of the programme is to obtain reasonable assurance that tangible non-current assets are not materially misstated.	Work performed by	Ref to supporting working paper

RELIANCE ON INTERNAL CONTROL PROCEDURES

1 Where we have placed reliance on the client's internal control procedures, test that the controls on which we are relying have been complied with, and record the details of such tests in the working papers.

TESTS OF DETAIL

EXAMINING THE TRANSACTIONS DURING THE YEAR

2 Obtain or prepare working papers of non-current asset balances and a summary of the related general ledger transactions (including depreciation) and test that these have been properly prepared, as follows:

   (a) Agree the totals with the general ledger accounts.

   (b) Test the casts (additions) for overstatement.

   (c) Agree the totals with the subsidiary records of non-current assets (e.g. non-current asset registers).

3 (a) Select the non-current assets to be examined, as follows:

   (1) Select from the list of non-current assets at cost at the beginning of the financial year; and

   (2) Select additions to non-current assets in the financial year by selecting from the debit entries in the non-current asset control account in the general ledger. Test the casts of the debit entries in this account for overstatement.

(b) Test the additions selected in procedure (a) (2) above with the relevant supporting records and documents for:

  (1) Approval by the board of directors or by other designated officials or committees.

  (2) Other independent evidence of validity.

  (3) Correctness of the allocations to the general ledger accounts.

(c) For the items selected in procedure (a) (2) above, examine the paid cheque for the correctness of the relevant details.

(d) For each item selected under procedures (a) (1) and (2) above, perform the following procedures:

  (1) Where the non-current asset has not been disposed of, check that it is correctly included in the non-current asset control account at the year-end date.

  (2) Where the non-current asset has been sold or otherwise disposed of during the financial year, check with the supporting evidence (such as correspondence, scrapping note, etc.) and ensure that the profit or loss on disposal has been properly computed and has been correctly recorded in the general ledger accounts. Determine that the client has made a reasonable scrap recovery in the case of assets which have been scrapped.

CONFIRMING THE EXISTENCE AND OWNERSHIP OF NON CURRENT ASSETS

4 Confirm the existence and ownership of all non-current assets which have been examined 3 (D) (1) above, as follows:

(a) In respect of freehold property, inspect the title deeds or obtain confirmation from independent third-party custodians.

(b) In respect of leasehold property, inspect the leases or obtain confirmation from independent third-party custodians.

(c) In respect of plant and equipment and other non-current assets, review the evidence of physical counts, or inspect the assets, or use other appropriate procedures. If the asset is permanently idle or obsolete, review the value of this asset in the accounts.

CONFIRMING THE CARRYING AMOUNT OF NON CURRENT ASSETS

5   Test that depreciation has been correctly calculated by applying either procedure (a) or procedure (b) below:

   (a) Prove the amount of depreciation in total.

   (b) Test the amounts of depreciation on individual items selected in procedure 3 (a) above, by checking with the authorised depreciation rates and by checking the calculations in order to ensure that such items are not already fully depreciated. Also, test the casts of the depreciation records and the postings to the general ledger accounts.

6   Investigate and test the client's procedure which ensures that all amounts expended by the client on the acquisition of non-current assets are correctly recorded as non-current assets.

   Note: *The purpose of this procedure is to ensure that the test for understatement of the accumulated provision for depreciation (in paragraph 5 above) is based on a population of non-current assets that is not materially understated.*

7   Ensure that depreciation:

   (a) has been provided on a basis which is consistent with that of the previous year.

   (b) is adequate but not excessive, by reviewing gains and losses on disposals or by other appropriate methods.

PROPERTY VALUATION

8   (a) Review the details of any valuation of assets made in the year, whether or not such valuations have been reflected in the accounts.

   (b) Where there is reason to believe that the current market value of a property could be significantly different from the amount at which it is included in the accounts, and no valuation has been made in the current year, discuss with the manager the need to request the client to make such a valuation.

   (c) Assess whether or not a true and fair view is shown by the statement of financial position if the current market value is materially below the book value and, if appropriate, consult the manager or partner.

REVIEWING AND TESTING CAPITAL COMMITMENTS

9   Obtain or prepare a working paper of capital commitments.

10 Test that they are correctly stated.

11 Consider possible additional commitments. Discuss these with responsible client officials and include in the working papers the date and outcome of the discussions and the names and status of the officials concerned.

3 Verification procedures: intangible non-current assets

3.1 Intangible assets

An intangible asset is an asset without physical substance – such as a brand or a licence. If an entity purchases an intangible asset then it is initially recognised at cost. The intangible asset will be amortised over its useful life. The amortisation is charged to the statement of profit or loss.

IAS 38 *Intangible Assets* sets out the requirements for the recognition and subsequent treatment of intangible assets. See Chapter 17 Financial Reporting Topics for help with the key requirements of IAS 38, should you need it.

3.2 Trademarks, patents and brand names

IAS 38 allows intangibles to be measured using a revaluation model but only if an active market exists for that asset. An active market is where lots of identical assets are regularly bought and sold. This is rare for most intangibles.

Note that IAS 38 does not generally allow internally generated intangible assets to be capitalised (e.g. a brand that a company set up itself). This is because the cost of the brand cannot be distinguished from the general costs of running the business.

However, IAS 38 does allow internally generated intangible assets to be recognised if they arise from development activity.

3.3 Research and development expenditure

The accounting requirement on this area is the subject of IAS 38 *Intangible assets*.

Research and development expenditure are distinguished by the following definitions:

(a) Research is 'original and planned investigation undertaken with the prospect of gaining new scientific or technical knowledge and understanding' (IAS 38, para 8).

(b) Development is 'the application of research findings or other knowledge to a plan or design for the production of new or substantially improved materials, devices, products, processes, systems or services before the start of commercial production or use' (IAS 38, para 8).

The cost of all research must be written off in the statement of profit or loss account as incurred.

In contrast, development costs should be capitalised if **all** of the following conditions are met:

(a) The project is technically feasible so that it will be available for use or sale.

(b) The company intends to complete the project and use or sell the results.

(c) The company is able to use or sell the results of the project.

(d) The company expects to generate probable future economic benefits (e.g. by demonstrating the existence of a market for the output of the project).

(e) The company has adequate technical, financial and other resources to complete the development and to use or sell the intangible asset.

(f) The company is able to measure reliably the expenditure attributable to the intangible asset during its development.

In theory, the company must capitalise expenditure on projects which meet these criteria, although it would be a simple matter to prepare pessimistic forecasts about the expected outcome of the project so that all costs had to be written off as incurred.

Once commercial production has commenced, the development costs carried forward should be amortised over the period of production that will benefit from the development expenditure. This may be done on a time basis or using a 'unit of production' method.

Deferred development expenditure should be reviewed at the end of each accounting period and if the above six conditions can no longer be satisfied the expenditure should be written off immediately.

The main audit procedures that should be performed are to check that the conditions noted above have been complied with, but note that this is likely to be a high risk area of the audit because of the degree of technical knowledge required and the fact that the conditions from IAS 38 stated above require the use of forecasts and estimates.

Test your understanding 1

During the audit of Ahoy! Ltd, a fishing supplies company, the auditor discovered that although the company maintained a non-current asset register, no checking procedures other than a reconciliation with the nominal ledger are undertaken.

Prepare extracts suitable for inclusion in a report to management of Ahoy! Ltd, which set out:

(i)   the possible consequences; and

(ii) the recommendations that you would take in respect of this matter.

Test your understanding 2

The objective of a substantive test will determine the population from which the sample for testing is selected.

For each of the following objectives, select the population from which the sample should be selected.

Obtain evidence of the existence of a non-current asset

(non-current asset register/physical asset).

Obtain evidence of the valuation of a non-current asset

(non-current asset register/purchase invoice).

4 Summary

This chapter has dealt with the principal audit verification techniques applicable to the main categories of non-current assets – tangible, intangible.

As with all verification work, the audit work can be structured around the financial statement assertions. You will have noted that there is lot of regulation of the accounting treatment of non-current assets by IFRS® Standards and IAS® Standards – these requirements need to be fully reflected in the audit verification work.

Test your understanding answers

Test your understanding 1

(i) **Consequences**

Equipment recorded in the register may not exist

Equipment may be fully written down but still in use

Depreciation charges may be inappropriate

Equipment in existence may not be recorded.

(ii) **Recommendations**

Periodic reconciliation of:

- Physical equipment to register to ensure completeness.
- Entries in the register to physical equipment to ensure existence.

Differences to be investigated.

Monitoring of procedures to ensure checks are undertaken.

Regular (e.g. monthly) reconciliation of the non-current asset register to the nominal ledger.

Test your understanding 2

1 Non-current asset register

2 Purchase invoice

AUDIT AND ASSURANCE

Audit verification work 4 – Receivables, cash and bank

Introduction

In this chapter we will look at receivables and bank and cash. In particular, we will examine the use of receivables circularisation and bank letters as forms of evidence. We will end with looking at a relevant audit programme.

ASSESSMENT CRITERIA	CONTENTS
Methods used to obtain audit evidence (4.1) Audit approach (4.4) Audit assertions (4.5)	1 The audit of receivable balances – general principles 2 Direct circularisation procedures 3 The audit of bank and cash balances

Audit verification work 4 – Receivables, cash and bank: **Chapter 8**

1 The audit of receivables balances – general principles

1.1 Introduction

This chapter deals with verification procedures for the remaining principal current assets of a company – receivables and cash and bank balances.

The areas covered here represent useful examples of a number of standard audit verification principles, in particular the requirement for the auditor to collect reliable audit evidence. Written evidence is considered to carry a high degree of reliability – this type of evidence is central to verification work in these areas.

You should of course cover all aspects of the audit work on these important areas, but you might find it helpful in focusing your attention to bear in mind where the major audit problems might arise. In the case of receivables this is the subjective area of provisions for potential irrecoverable balances. In the case of cash and bank, the audit problem results from the fact that this is the asset most likely to be subject to misappropriation – strong control procedures should be in place backed up by rigorous audit testing. In the case of receivables, we are largely concerned that clients may want to overstate the figures and therefore the audit emphasis is usually on existence.

1.2 Internal control over receivables

The objectives of internal controls in this area are to ensure that:

(a) all goods despatched are invoiced

(b) invoicing is at correct price and discount

(c) goods are only despatched on credit to approved customers

(d) invoices are recorded and related to subsequent cash receipts

(e) receivables are controlled and outstanding receivables pursued

(f) credit notes are approved.

Note that there are very close links to the sales accounting system here.

In addition, internal controls over receivables should ensure that the possibility of any falsification of the receivables accounts is eliminated. Segregation of duties is an important part of the controls. So, for example, the cashier should not have access to the receivables ledger, and the receivables ledger clerk should not have access to cash received. Thus, the possibility of teeming and lading (i.e. stealing a receivables payment and then concealing the fact by juggling subsequent receipts so that a sum received a few days later from another receivable is credited to the first account, then a later receipt goes to the second account and so on indefinitely) could only be brought about by collusion. Collusion is an inherent limitation of any system of internal control.

1.3 The audit of receivables – general approach

In order to verify the figure in the financial statements for receivables the auditor would perform a number of substantive procedures as outlined below.

Control account

The auditor should obtain a list of the receivables balances in the receivables ledger from the client and agree the total with the control account. This acts as a check on the completeness and accuracy of the listing of receivables balances which will be extensively used in the following detailed audit verification work.

Year-end receivables account balances

(i) Obtain an aged receivables listing and discuss any significantly overdue balances with management to identify action to be taken, and whether or not the receivables are likely to be paid. This will assist the auditor in verifying the reasonableness of the provision for irrecoverable receivables.

(ii) Inspect the authorisation for receivables written off as irrecoverable and review external correspondence relating to these receivables.

(iii) Carry out direct confirmation of receivables balances. This is known as circularisation and will be considered further in the next section.

(iv) Ensure that the balances are made up of specific invoices relating to recent transactions and enquiring into any balances which appear to be in dispute, or old.

(v) Inspect the payables ledger balances for customers who are also suppliers and to whom the client owes money. Contra entries should be made to net off the two amounts to avoid overstating both assets and liabilities.

(vi) Review the individual accounts of major customers and those that appear unusual either by nature, composition or size of the balances or the transactions therein.

(vii) Review and test the year end cut-off procedures for sales, as dealt with in a previous chapter.

Analytical procedures

The auditor would typically perform the following analytical procedures in respect of receivables:

(i) A comparison of receivables days ratio

$$\frac{\text{receivables}}{\text{revenue}} \times 365$$

with budget and/or prior years. Separate computations may be appropriate to take into account different classes of business, varying credit terms and other factors.

(ii) A comparison of the proportion of the receivables in different age bands to prior years. This information should be available directly from the client.

A high or increasing incidence of old receivable balances may indicate either poor or deteriorating economic conditions or credit control. In such instances the work on irrecoverable receivables will become critical.

Irrecoverable receivables

This is one of the more subjective areas involved in the audit of receivables balances.

Audit procedures to establish appropriate provisions for potentially irrecoverable balances include consideration of:

(i) the company's previous experiences

(ii) evidence from the receivables circularisation

(iii) aged analysis of receivables

(iv) post year-end events (see below and later chapters).

In light of this information the auditor will have to consider whether the provision made by management in the accounts is adequate.

Only specific provisions may be made. Specific provisions are made for those balances which are known to be doubtful.

Returns inwards and credit notes

There should be strict internal controls over returns inwards and credit notes issued, to prevent the fraudulent cancellation of a company receivable.

From an audit point of view the major problem is likely to be the issue of a substantial volume of credit notes after the year end to cancel false sales made before the year end. This is known as 'window dressing' – recording a sale and the resulting receivable in the current period and then issuing a credit note to reverse the transaction in the following period (it could be seen as another example of a cut-off problem). For this reason, both the system, and post-year-end events, should be carefully examined to detect any possible misstatement of annual profits resulting from this procedure.

Prepayments

These are often disclosed in the financial statements under the general heading of receivables and similar audit considerations apply. However, prepayments are typically immaterial in amount and in this connection may attract relatively little audit attention. On the other hand, this is an area where subjective accounting estimates will often be required. Analytical procedures – comparing one period with another and seeking an explanation for major differences – are often extensively used in this area.

Prepayments are commonly made for rent, gas, electricity and telephone standing charges and other items where the expenditure has been paid for in the current period, but relates to the next period.

Audit evidence may include:

(i) considering the client's own system, if any, for accounting for prepayments

(ii) obtaining a schedule of prepayments, ensuring that it is cast correctly and comparing it with prior year prepayments and performing other analytical procedures

(iii) checking a sample of prepayments for correct calculation, referring to supporting documentation e.g. an invoice.

Audit verification work 4 – Receivables, cash and bank: **Chapter 8**

2 Direct circularisation procedures

2.1 Introduction

Circularisation is one of the most effective methods for confirming receivables balances. The auditor communicates directly with the customers of the client to seek direct confirmation of the amounts outstanding.

Replies to the circularisation will generally be considered to constitute reliable evidence as they arise outside the client under audit and they are in a written form.

The auditor must ask the client's permission before writing to the receivables, but, if the quality of the evidence is to be preserved, it is important that the process is under the auditor's control. So for example the replies should be sent direct to the auditors, not to the client to preserve their integrity as an item of audit evidence.

The circularisation of receivables satisfies a number of objectives:

(a) Reliable evidence is provided as to whether receivables are overstated – customers can usually be relied on to complain if the balance they are supposed to owe is too large. This in turn will help us gain some comfort over the existence of the balance.

(b) Evidence, albeit weaker, is provided as to whether receivables are understated – customers are less likely to complain if the balance is too small.

(c) Indirect evidence is generated of the accuracy of the sales figures.

(d) Evidence of the functioning of internal controls is generated – accurate receivables balances result from effective control procedures.

(e) Evidence is provided of the efficiency of the cut-off procedures if carried out at the year end.

(f) Evidence of the collectability of receivables is generated. If a customer maintains that the client's balance on their account is overstated, this may represent a receivable recorded by the client which requires to be written off or provided for.

It does not however give evidence as to recoverability. Our receivable may agree that the money is owed; this does not guarantee that they will pay us!

2.2 Timing and form of circularisation

Ideally the circularisation should be carried out at the year end, as this provides direct evidence of the statement of financial position figures. In practice, pressures to complete the audit by a deadline may mean that the circularisation is often carried out one or two months before the year end, and balances are then 'rolled forward' to the year end.

In the latter case movements on the control accounts should be reviewed in the period between the circularisation and the year end for reasonableness.

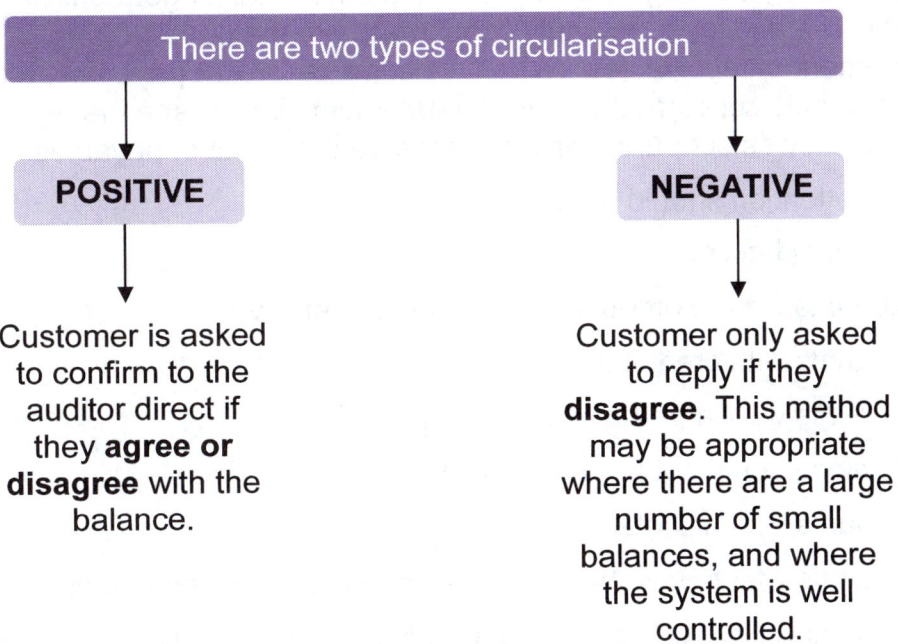

Positive circularisations are now generally used as these provide better quality evidence. A non-reply to a negative circularisation request will be taken by the auditor indicating agreement – but in fact the communication may never have been received by the customer or the customer may have taken a decision simply not to reply.

Examples of communications used in the two types of methods are shown later in this chapter.

2.3 Control of circularisation

As stated earlier it is important that in all cases the circularisation must be controlled by the auditor if the reliability of the audit evidence generated is to be preserved and maximised. This control by the auditor should be reflected at all the key stages in the circularisation process, as indicated below:

Selection

Customers to be circularised should be selected by the auditor from a receivables ledger listing which agrees to the nominal ledger control accounts. The auditor is primarily concerned with the possible overstatement of receivables. When we come to look at payables, where we are primarily concerned with understatement, we will see that we will not necessarily select our sample from the year-end list of payables.

Particular attention should be given to:

(i) old unpaid accounts

(ii) accounts written off during the period under review

(iii) accounts with credit balances

(iv) accounts with large balances.

The following should not be overlooked:

(i) accounts with nil balances

(ii) accounts which have been paid by the date of the examination.

If a client is unwilling to circularise a particular balance because, say, there are delicate negotiations in progress, the auditor should establish that the reason is a genuine one (and not an attempt to cover up a problem balance), and then perform alternative procedures such as those noted below.

Despatch of letters

The letters should be checked for accuracy by the auditor once they have been prepared and should be kept under the control of the auditor until they are sent. In checking the letter, particular attention should be paid to the client's contact details and to the account balance circularised. The letter is sent from the client on their letter headed paper.

The auditor's working papers should contain a control schedule recording all relevant details of the circularisation.

Response

Responses should be sent directly to the auditor. The auditor should check the replies against their schedule. A reminder should be sent if no replies are received.

2.4 Replies and non-replies

The audit work on the response to the circularisation will typically involve the following:

REPLIES	NON REPLIES

Agreed replies
• If the reply agrees with the balance circularised, the auditor should check that the letter has been signed and dated by a responsible official of the company and that the reply gives no cause for suspicion on the part of the auditor.
• If the auditor is happy the reply is filed.
Disagreed but reconciled
• If the reply indicates that the customer disagrees with the balance circularised, the auditor, or the client on behalf of the auditor, should attempt to reconcile the two balances.
• Reconciling items may be timing differences e.g. as goods or cash in transit or credit notes not yet recorded. These must be checked carefully. For example, the timing of the despatch of goods in transit must be agreed to delivery records to prove that the customer owed that amount at the confirmation date.
Once the auditor is happy with the reconciling items, these can be filed and treated as agreed replies.
	• Send a second letter
	• Email customer
	• Telephone customer
	• Cash received
	• Check receivable is genuine, look for evidence of:
	   – Signed order
	   – Signed GRN.
	Consider overall existence of receivable if insufficient evidence – discuss with client possible provision/adjustment.

Disagreed – not reconciled

- Disagreement of balances may result from more serious problems, indicating errors in the client's receivables balances or possibly weaknesses in the accounting and control systems e.g. sales invoices posted twice, cash received not recorded or disputes relating to prices charged or the availability of settlement discounts.

These replies should be reviewed carefully by the auditor and discussed with client management.

2.5 Evaluation of the results of the circularisation

After the completion of the circularisation it will form a key part of the evidence in relation to the receivables figure.

The auditor will summarise the results of the circularisation in the current audit file and will need to evaluate the results in terms of:

(a) percentage response

(b) number of disagreements

(c) outcome of follow-up of disagreements

(d) the materiality of the amounts involved.

2.6 Examples of receivables circularisation letters

(a) **Positive method**

> **Example**
>
> Swallow Limited
> Bird Estate
> Highcity
> Beds
>
> 30 April 20XX
>
> Hugh Allen Limited
> Brow Estate
> Lowtown
> Beds
>
> Dear Sir/Madam
>
> **CONFIRMATION OF INDEBTEDNESS**
>
> 1. In accordance with the request of our auditors, ABC & Co, we shall be obliged if you will confirm directly to them your indebtedness to us at 31 March 20XX which, according to our records, amounted to £1,457.67, as shown by the enclosed statement.
>
> 2. If you are in agreement with the balance shown, please sign this letter in the space provided below and return it intact DIRECTLY TO OUR AUDITORS in the enclosed reply paid envelope.
>
> 3. If you disagree with the balance, please notify our auditors, giving full details of the difference.
>
> PLEASE NOTE THAT THIS IS NOT A REQUEST FOR PAYMENT.
>
> We thank you for your co-operation in the above matter.
>
> Yours faithfully
>
> Swallow Limited

Audit verification work 4 – Receivables, cash and bank: Chapter 8

                                              Reply to: ABC & Co
                                                                                          Certified Accountants
                                                                                                                      2 Low Close
                                                                                                                      Downtown
                                                                                                                      Beds

The balance shown above is correct/incorrect*

Signature   Position:
Date:

Details of difference: (If relevant)

*Please delete as appropriate.

(b) **Negative method**

 Example

Dear Sirs

CONFIRMATION OF INDEBTEDNESS

In accordance with the request of our auditors, ABC & Co, we shall be obliged if you will confirm directly to them your indebtedness to us at 31 March 20XX which, according to our records, amounted to £1,457.67, as shown by the enclosed statement.
If you disagree with the balance, please inform our AUDITORS DIRECTLY, giving full details of the difference by completing the form below . . . .

Yours faithfully

The balance shown above is incorrect.

Signature: Position:
Date:
Details of difference:

2.7 Example of a circularisation summary

The results of a receivables circularisation exercise are summarised as follows to facilitate evaluation.

Example

HASTINGS & WARWICK
Receivables circularisation summary

CLIENT	PREPARED BY	DATE
	REVIEWED BY	DATE
	(Audit senior in charge)	
PERIOD	REVIEWED BY	DATE
	(Manager)	

	No of accounts	% of total accounts	Value £	% of total value	Ref to supporting schedules
Population total		100.0	£	100.0	
Sample for confirmation					
Statistical selections					
Additional selections					
Total sample					
Results of confirmation			£		

Confirmed by:
(a) Letter
(b) Email
(c) Telephone

Replies reconciled

Non-replies agreed by alternative procedures

Audit verification work 4 – Receivables, cash and bank: Chapter 8

Total balances agreed

Balances in dispute

Total sample £

Date initial circularisation letter despatched

Percentage reply on initial circularisation

Date of follow-up letter

2.8 Audit programme: receivables and prepayments

The following is a detailed example of a typical audit programme for receivables and prepayments.

> **Example**
>
> Audit programme
> # HASTINGS & WARWICK
> AUDIT PROGRAMME
>
> Sch Ref
>
> CLIENT _____ PREPARED BY _____ DATE _____
>
> REVIEWED BY _____ DATE _____
> (Audit senior in charge)
>
> PERIOD _____ REVIEWED BY _____ DATE _____
> (Manager)
>
> **AUDIT AREA – RECEIVABLES AND PREPAYMENTS**
>
> | The purpose of the auditing procedures set out in this section of the programme is to obtain reasonable assurance that receivables and prepayments are not materially misstated. | Work performed by | Ref to supporting working paper |
> |---|---|---|
> | **RELIANCE ON INTERNAL CONTROL PROCEDURES** | | |
> | 1   Where we have placed reliance on the client's internal control procedures, test that the controls on which we are relying have been complied with, and record the details of such tests in the working papers. | | |

AUDIT AND ASSURANCE

TESTS OF DETAIL

CONFIRMING THE EXISTENCE OF TRADE RECEIVABLES

Note: Receivables may be confirmed at the year-end date or at an interim date. If an interim date is chosen the follow-up procedures set out in paragraph 9 of this AP must also be applied.

2   Obtain a list of trade receivables at the confirmation date and test these receivables for overstatement by carrying out the audit procedures set out in paragraphs 3, 4 and 5 below.

3   Test the list as follows:

    (a) Agree or reconcile the total of the list with the receivables control account in the general ledger.

    (b) Test the casts of the list for overstatement.

    (c) Test the individual items on the list for overstatement, by applying the procedures set out below:

        (1) Select either debit balances from the list of receivables or invoices outstanding by use of sub-sampling techniques.

        (2) In respect of the selected balances, send out positive confirmation requests.

        (3) Where the receivable will not confirm the balance in writing, try (with the client's permission) to obtain confirmation by telephone.

        (4) Review each reply that we receive. In cases where the receivable disputes the balance, request the client to investigate the reasons for all differences. Establish the validity of the differences and prepare a schedule of the differences and their subsequent disposal.

        Note: It is important to investigate thoroughly any instances where the receivable disputes the amount paid or the date on which the client's records indicate payment was received. Factors such as these may indicate 'teeming and lading.'

4   Where we are unable to obtain confirmation of a receivable's balance, obtain evidence by applying appropriate procedures that the balance was a bona fide receivable of the client at the confirmation date. The appropriate alternative procedures consist of:

    (a) Checking the opening balance of the account with the list of balances at the previous year end, testing the casts of the account during the year and agreeing the balance.

(b) Testing the outstanding items with independent evidence of validity – including customers' orders, despatch records and subsequent payments (where these can be substantiated by remittance advices or other independent means).

(c) Testing for the understatement of payments etc. by discussing the outstanding items with a responsible official who is independent of the cash receiving function.

The purpose of the auditing procedures set out in this section of the programme is to obtain reasonable assurance that receivables are not materially misstated.

5 Where confirmation procedures are not applied, select individual balances from the list of receivables and carry out the procedures listed in paragraph 4 above.

6 Prepare a summary of the confirmation procedures applied under paragraphs 2 to 5 previously and of our conclusions.

TESTING THE VALUATION OF TRADE RECEIVABLES

7 Test trade receivables for collectability and for understatement of the provision as follows:

(a) Obtain reasonable assurance that the client's listing of overdue accounts has been correctly prepared by checking it with the sample selected in procedure 3 (c) (1). Check the casts of each column and agree the total with the receivables control account.

(b) Select overdue items from the client's listing of overdue accounts and check and investigate the extent to which they are collectable by reviewing credit reports, correspondence and other independent evidence.

(c) Establish the reasonableness of formulae used to calculate general provisions. Review generally the client's irrecoverable receivable experience for the current and recent financial years and establish the reasons for significant differences. Check the calculations on which the provision is based.

8 Test the receivable balances written off against the provision during the year for overstatement by selecting balances written off and checking them with such independent evidence of validity as correspondence with solicitors, debt collection agencies, etc.

FOLLOWING UP AN INTERIM CONFIRMATION OF TRADE RECEIVABLES

9 Where the procedures in paragraphs 2 to 8 previously were applied to a date other than the year-end date, apply the following additional procedures:

(a) Test for overstatement of trade receivables at the year-end date by examining the transactions in the intervening period from the confirmation date to the year-end date, as set out below:

(1) Test the credit sales in the intervening period for overstatement as follows. Select debit entries from the receivables control account and compare these with the final sales records. Select individual transactions by sub-sampling these final records and the related intermediate and initial sales records. Check these transactions with independent evidence of validity, such as customer orders, delivery notes signed by the receivables, despatch records etc.

(2) Test the sales returns and allowances in the intervening period for understatement, as follows. Examine the evidence of sales returns and allowances (such as goods returned records, correspondence with customers, and the relevant sales invoices). Trace major items in these records to the credit notes and (via the accounting records) to the credit of the receivables control account. In doing this ensure that these sales returns were recorded in the correct financial year.

(3) Test the receipts from receivables in the intervening period for understatement, as follows. Examine customers' remittance advices, and any other available independent evidence. Trace major items in these records (via the accounting records) to the credit of the receivables control account. In doing this, ensure that these receipts were recorded in the correct financial year.

(b) Review and summarise the movements on the receivables control account from the confirmation date to the year-end date and establish the reasons for all unusual fluctuations. Compare the individual balances which were selected for confirmation at the interim date with the corresponding balances at the year-end date, and investigate major differences.

Audit verification work 4 – Receivables, cash and bank: Chapter 8

TESTING THE CUT-OFF OF RECEIVABLES

10 Test for any overstatement of receivables as at the year-end date that has arisen from recording transactions in the wrong financial year. Do this by testing for overstatement of sales and for understatement of sales returns and receipts, in the following manner:

(a) Test for overstatement of credit sales in the period immediately preceding the year end, as follows: Compare major billings as recorded in the receivables control account in the last few days of the year, with evidence of the date on which goods were despatched or services were rendered. In doing this, ensure that the billings are for sales made during the financial year under review. The evidence of despatch should preferably comprise the customer's acknowledgement of delivery or service (such as signed delivery notes) or, failing that, the client's despatch records.

(b) Test for understatement of sales returns and allowances in the period immediately preceding the year end, as follows:

(1) Examine the evidence of sales returns and allowances (such as goods returned records, correspondence with customers, and the relevant sales invoices) for the last few days of the year and the first few weeks after the year end. Trace major items in these records to the relevant credit notes and (via the accounting records) to the credit of the receivables control account. In doing this, ensure that the sales returns and allowances have been recorded in the correct financial year or, alternatively, that adequate provision for sales returns and allowances has been made as at the year end.

(2) Compare major sales credit notes in the first few weeks after the year end with the relevant supporting evidence (such as goods returned records, correspondence with customers, and the relevant sales invoices). In doing this, ensure that these credit notes have been recorded in the correct financial year or, alternatively, that adequate provision for sales returns and allowances has been made as at the year end.

(c) Test for understatement of receipts from receivables in the last few weeks of the year, as follows. Examine customers' remittance advices, listings of remittances, and any other independent evidence. Trace major items in these records (via the accounting records) to the credit of the receivables control account. In doing this, ensure that these receipts were recorded in the correct financial year.

REVIEWING THE TRADE RECEIVABLES

11 Review generally the list of balances as at the year-end date. Compute trade receivables as a percentage of sales and as the number of days sales outstanding. Compare these ratios with those of preceding years and obtain satisfactory explanations for any significant differences.

Determine that the balances have been correctly classified for statement of financial position purposes and in particular that:

(a) Material credit balances have not been deducted from receivables (except where there is a right to set-off).

(b) Inter-group balances have been classified correctly.

(c) Balances due from any person or company which is in any way connected with the client arise from bona fide transactions on an arm's length basis.

TESTING OF OTHER RECEIVABLES AND PREPAYMENTS

12 Obtain a list of other receivables as at the year-end date or, where appropriate, at an interim date. Test this for overstatement, as follows:

(a) Agree the list with the balances on the relevant accounts in the general ledger.

(b) Test the casts of the list for overstatement.

(c) Determine the nature and bona fides of all significant receivables, paying particular attention to amounts due from any person or company which is in any way connected with the client.

13. Obtain a list of prepayments as at the year-end date or, where appropriate, at an interim date. Test this for overstatement, as follows:

    (a) Agree the list with the balances on the relevant accounts in the general ledger.

    (b) Test the casts of the list for overstatement.

    (c) Select prepayments from the list and test them for overstatement by comparing them with supporting independent documentation and with the corresponding amounts in prior years.

LOANS TO DIRECTORS OR EMPLOYEES

14. Identify loans made to, or balances due by either directors, or employees, and consider the disclosure of such loans in the financial statements.

3 The audit of bank and cash balances

3.1 Introduction

Because of their liquidity, these assets represent the most vulnerable of all the company's assets. On the other hand, they are amongst the most easily verified, because they are objective in nature and they lend themselves to being confirmed directly by third parties or by physical counts.

3.2 Internal controls over bank and cash

Due to the vulnerability of liquid assets, internal controls are usually very tight in order to eliminate, or minimise, the possibility of fraud. The objectives of cash internal controls are as follows.

(a) All sums are received and subsequently accounted for.

(b) No payments are made which should not be made.

(c) All receipts and payments are promptly and accurately recorded.

3.3 Verification – bank accounts

There are two aspects to the verification work on a client's bank balances:

- Direct confirmation from the bank or other financial institution, of the account balance. This gives the auditor written external evidence from a very reliable source.

- Examination of the bank reconciliation.

Each of these is now dealt with in more detail.

3.4 Direct bank confirmation – bank confirmation letter

This is achieved via a **bank confirmation letter** (also known as a bank certificate or bank letter).

Definition

A **bank certificate** is a standard request letter sent by the auditor to the bank requesting details of the client's financial arrangements managed by the bank.

The auditor should obtain a bank certificate as part of every audit. A standard request letter has been agreed with the clearing banks; this is shown below, together with the standard procedure followed by auditors.

Standard procedure

(a) The standard letter should be sent in duplicate on each occasion by the auditors on their own note paper to the manager of each bank branch with which it is known that the client holds an account or has dealt with since the end of the previous accounting period.

(b) Auditors should ensure that the bank receives the client's authority to permit disclosure. The clearing banks state that this authority must be evidenced by either:

　(i) the client's countersignature to the standard letter

　(ii) a specific authority contained in an accompanying letter, or

　(iii) a reference in the standard letter to a standing written authority given on a specified earlier date, which remains in force.

(c) Wherever possible, the letter should reach the branch manager at least two weeks in advance of the date of the client's financial year end. Special arrangements should be made with the bank if, because of time constraints, a reply is needed within a few days.

(d) In reviewing the bank's reply it is important for auditors to check that the bank has answered all questions in full.

3.5 Example of a standard letter

> **Example**
>
> **STANDARD LETTER OF REQUEST FOR BANK REPORT FOR AUDIT PURPOSES**
>
> (i) The form of the letter should not be amended by the auditor.
>
> (ii) Sufficient space should be left for the bank's replies.
>
> The Manager,
> .... (Bank)
>
> .... (Branch)
>
> Dear Sir,
> .... (Name of customer)
>
> STANDARD REQUEST FOR BANK REPORT FOR AUDIT PURPOSES FOR THE YEAR ENDED ....
>
> In accordance with your above-named customer's instructions given
>
> (1) hereon)
> (2) in the attached authority) Delete as
> (3) in the authority dated ....already held by you) appropriate
>
> Please send to us, as auditors of your customer for the purposes of our business, without entering into any contractual relationship with us, the following information relating to their affairs at your branch as at the close of business on..........and in the case of items 2, 4 and 10 during the period since .... For each item, please state any factors which may limit the completeness of your reply; if there is nothing to report, state 'none'.
>
> We enclose an additional copy of this letter, and it would be particularly helpful if your reply could be given on the copy letter in the space provided (supported by an additional schedule stamped and signed by the bank where space is insufficient). If you find it necessary to provide the information in another form, please return the copy letter with your reply.
>
> It is understood that any replies are in strict confidence.

Information requested	Reply
Bank accounts	
(1) Please give full titles of all accounts whether in sterling or in any other currency together with the account numbers and balances thereon, including NIL balances:	
(a) where your customer's name is the sole name in the title	
(b) where your customer's name is joined with that of other parties	
(c) where the account is in a trade name.	
(2) Full titles and dates of closure of all accounts closed during the period.	
(3) The separate amounts accrued but not charged or credited at the above date, of:	
(a) provisional charges (including commitment fees), and	
(b) interest.	
(4) The amount of interest charged during the period if not specified separately in the bank statement.	
(5) Particulars (e.g. date, type of document and accounts covered) of any written acknowledgement of set-off, either by specific letter of set-off, or incorporated in some other document or security.	
(6) Details of:	
(a) overdrafts and loans repayable on demand, specifying dates of review and agreed facilities	
(b) other loans specifying dates of review and repayment.	

Customer's assets held as security

(7) Please give details of any such assets whether or not formally charged to the bank.

Customer's other assets held

(8) Please give full details of the customer's other assets held, including share certificates, documents of title, deed boxes and any other items listed in your Registers maintained for the purpose of recording assets held.

Contingent liabilities

(9) All contingent liabilities.

Other information

(10) A list of other banks, or branches of your bank, or associated companies where you are aware that a relationship has been established during the period.

Yours faithfully

Disclosure authorised

For and on behalf of

(Official stamp of bank)

(Name of customer)

(Authorised signatory)

(Signed in accordance with the mandate for the conduct of the customer's bank account)

(Position)

(Date)

The authority to release such information must be obtained from the client and this is generally done by asking the client to communicate with the bank directly.

Important factors

The following matters are important:

- The standard form of the letter (reproduced above) should not be amended by the auditor.

- Where the style of letter is used for non-statutory engagements (e.g. the presentation of accounts of a sole trader) any reference to 'audit' should be deleted.

- The standard letter should be sent in duplicate by the auditor, on the headed paper of his or her firm, to each bank branch where the client is known to have an account.

- The letter should reach the relevant branch at least two weeks in advance of the date of the client's year-end.

- If it is necessary to request supplementary information from the bank, this request should be sent at the same time as the standard request.

- The authority to disclose may be granted by the client counter-signature on the letter or by a written request. Joint account holders must all give their consent when authorising a bank to disclose information to the auditor.

- In reviewing the bank's reply, the auditor must check that the letter has been answered in full.

> **Syllabus note**
>
> For the purposes of the Audit and Assurance assessment you do not need to know the precise wording of the letter, just be familiar with the information that the auditor is requesting!

3.6 Examination of the bank reconciliation

You should be very familiar with the bank reconciliation process from your basic accountancy studies. From the point of view of audit verification work, the auditor needs to check the reconciliation between the cash book figure, which will appear in the financial statements and the bank statement figure which has been the subject of direct confirmation by the bank. This stage is of great importance to the auditor.

The reconciliation should establish that:

(i) differences between the bank and the client's records can be specifically identified

(ii) the differences are differences of timing which should clear in the post year-end period

Audit verification work 4 – Receivables, cash and bank: Chapter 8

(iii) no very old differences are outstanding

(iv) any differences other than timing differences (e.g. errors or omissions by the bank or the client) are advised to the bank or adjusted in the client's accounting records.

Audit procedures on the reconciliation

Reconciliations usually start with the balance per the cash book and reconcile this to the balance per the bank statement, although the reverse is also acceptable. A simple example might show:

Example

Bank reconciliation as at 31 July 20X4

	£
Balance per cash book	12,345.22
Add: Un-presented cheques	223.46
Less: Outstanding lodgements	(16.34)
Difference	1.34
Balance per bank statement	12,553.68

- **Reconciling items** are usually due to timing delays. Cheques will have been sent to suppliers on the last day of the period but the suppliers will not have had a chance to bank the cheques. These cheques are '**un-presented**'.

- **Outstanding lodgements** are cheques received by the company and paid into the bank, but not yet credited by the bank i.e. there is usually a delay of two to three days for the cheques to be cleared.

- All un-presented cheques and outstanding lodgements should be checked to ensure that they do clear shortly after the period end by reviewing bank statements just after the period end. Any old items should be considered carefully. If a cheque has not been presented to the bank after six months, it may be that the supplier has lost it or has gone out of business. In any case the cheque will be out of date and the bank will not honour it even if it is presented. The auditor should consider the need for the payable to be reinstated and a new cheque issued, or the need for the cheque to be written back as income.

Differences, even small differences, must be investigated as they may represent large errors in both directions that net each other off. If there are known errors or omissions affecting the cash book, the normal procedure is to adjust the cash book for these items and then reconcile the adjusted cash book figure with the bank statement figure. For example:

> **Example**
>
> | | £ |
> |---|---|
> | Draft balance per cash book as at 31 July 20X4 | 12,153.32 |
> | Add: sundry receipts per bank statement not in cash book | 123.45 |
> | Less: direct debits per bank statement not in cash book | (21.55) |
> | Add error in addition of cash book | 90.00 |
> | Adjusted balance per cash book as at 31 July 20X4 | 12,345.22 |

Again, all of the adjusting items need to be checked to their source. As these are cash book errors and the cash book forms part of the double entry system, there is likely to be a double entry effect of these adjustments which the auditor should establish has been correctly dealt with.

Reconciliations are normally performed on a monthly basis and should show evidence of review i.e. who reviewed it and on what date. The auditor should check that they are cast correctly.

3.7 Verification – cash balances

The amount of audit verification work that the auditor will carry out on cash balances will be very much dependent on their materiality. If, for example, the only cash balance held in a large company is a small petty cash float where controls are strong, the auditor may carry out no substantive work at all. However, in situations where cash balances are more material, for example a cash based business, standard audit procedures would include:

- attendance at a cash count at the year-end date

- if cash is held at more than one location, all cash at all locations should be counted simultaneously

- if the auditor counts the cash, the auditor should do so in the presence of two or more officers of the company and obtain a signed receipt when the cash is handed back to the client

- the auditor should agree the balance on hand with the figure in the accounting records and check the validity of any reconciling items.

Audit verification work 4 – Receivables, cash and bank: **Chapter 8**

3.8 Audit programme: cash and bank balances

The following is an example of a detailed cash and bank audit programme.

> **Example**
>
> Audit programme for cash and bank balances
>
> **HASTINGS & WARWICK**
> AUDIT PROGRAMME
>
> Sch Ref
>
> CLIENT _____   PREPARED BY _____   DATE _____
>
> REVIEWED BY _____   DATE _____
> (Audit senior in charge)
>
> PERIOD _____   REVIEWED BY _____   DATE _____
> (Manager)
>
> **AUDIT AREA – BANK AND CASH BALANCES**
>
> | The purpose of the auditing procedures set out in this section of the programme is to obtain reasonable assurance that bank and cash is not materially misstated. | Work performed by | Ref to supporting working paper |
> |---|---|---|
> | **RELIANCE ON INTERNAL CONTROL PROCEDURES**
1 Where we have placed reliance on the client's internal control procedures, test that the controls on which we are relying have been complied with, and record the details of such tests in the working papers. | | |
> | **TESTS OF DETAIL**
CONFIRMING BANK BALANCES
2 Obtain or prepare a list of all bank accounts that were open at any time during the year. Send out requests for confirmation to the banks concerned at least two weeks before the confirmation date, usually the year end.
3 Obtain, and retain, a copy of the client's bank reconciliations as at the confirmation date. Test the reconciliations as follows:
(a) Check the casts of the reconciliations and agree the balances with the general ledger (or where appropriate with the cash books) and with bank statements. | | |

(b) Obtain bank statements for a sufficient period (usually ten working days) immediately subsequent to the confirmation date. (If there are any suspicious circumstances, obtain these statements direct from the bank). Carry out the following procedures:

(1) Test for understatement of outstanding cheques and other items which decrease the cash book balance as follows. Select from payments recorded by the bank in the subsequent period and comparing these with the payment records to ensure that they were recorded in the correct accounting period. Compare the cheques recorded prior to the confirmation date with the reconciliation.

(2) Check for overstatement of any unbanked receipts and other items which increase the balance at the bank. Do this by selecting from the list of unbanked receipts and comparing with paying-in slips and with bank statements. Investigate the reasons for any delay in banking receipts.

(3) Test for worthless cheques deposited to cover shortages by scrutinising the bank statements for dishonoured cheques in the first ten working days after the year end.

4 Agree bank certificates with the balances shown on the reconciliations as being due to or from the banks. Also check that all other information given on the certificates agrees with the client's records and is properly reflected in the accounts.

FOLLOWING UP AN INTERIM CONFIRMATION OF BANK BALANCES

5 Where the confirmation date differs from the year-end date:

(a) Review the client's reconciliations as at the year-end date. Obtain certificates from banks, agree the reconciliations with the ledger balances and the bank certificates, check any unusual reconciling items, and test the casts of the reconciliations. Check that all other information given on the certificates agrees with the client's records and is properly reflected in the accounts.

(b) Review the changes in the bank balances from the confirmation date to the year-end date and establish the reasons for all unusual fluctuations.

WINDOW DRESSING

6 Test for window dressing by reviewing material payments and receipts in the last month of the year and for a sufficient period immediately after the year-end date.

SETTING-OFF OF BALANCES

7 Ensure that:

    (a) A legal right of set-off exists where bank balances have been set-off.

    (b) The client has made all known material set-offs in the accounts.

CONFIRMING CASH BALANCES

8 Obtain or prepare a list of all petty cash funds, undeposited receipts, unclaimed wages and other items. Include, where appropriate, negotiable instruments, title deeds, share certificates, etc. Agree this list with the general ledger accounts or other appropriate records.

9 Where cash balances are material, count them (on the date chosen for the confirmation of bank balances) as follows:

    (a) Count and list notes, coins and cheques, vouchers and any negotiable instruments. Control all funds and other items to ensure that there can be no substitution. Carry out the count in the presence of the custodian of the funds and do not, at any time, assume sole custody of these funds. Where there is a significant difference between the book records and the count, consult the client's officials immediately.

    (b) In respect of cheques:

        (1) Ensure that these have been entered correctly in the receipt records. If they have not yet been entered, obtain a copy of the client's paying-in slip which records them and, subsequently, check that they have been properly recorded.

        (2) Ensure that these items are lodged in the bank promptly. Also check that there are no undeposited receipts on hand at the date of our count.

        (3) Where cashed cheques are part of petty cash funds, ensure that these are controlled, that they are not post-dated and that they are banked promptly. Review with an appropriate official of the client any cheques which are for a relatively large amount or are signed by the custodian or are in any way suspicious.

(c) In respect of vouchers:

(1) Inspect these for approval, for authenticity and for date.

(2) Ensure that the vouchers have been recorded in the cash fund records. If they have not been recorded, prepare a list of the items in sufficient detail to enable this check to be carried out at a subsequent date.

(3) Examine the cash fund records to ensure that those vouchers that have been used to support a cash fund balance do not also support previous payments.

FOLLOWING UP AN INTERIM CONFIRMATION OF CASH BALANCES

10 Where the confirmation date differs from the year-end date:

(a) Review all movements from the confirmation date to the year-end date and establish the reasons for all unusual fluctuations.

(b) Prepare a working paper which reconciles the balances at the confirmation date with those at the year-end date and which shows the totals of payments and receipts. Agree the receipts with the main cash book and the payments with the monthly ledger posting.

Test your understanding 1

During the external audit of Peppa Co, the audit junior sent out receivables confirmations. Several of the balances do not agree due to cash in transit and goods in transit. The audit junior is unsure how to deal with these items.

For each of the following, select whether they should be added on or deducted from the balance on Peppa Co's receivables ledger:

(a) Cash in transit should be ....?

(b) Goods in transit should be ....?

Audit verification work 4 – Receivables, cash and bank: Chapter 8

 Test your understanding 2

During the external audit of Perch Plc, the audit junior was requested to add up 10 pages of the cash book from throughout the year. 9 pages added up correctly but one page had a transposition error leading it to be under cast by £69.

The turnover of Perch was £3.5m for the year and the profit was £469,000.

In respect of this matter, select whether the audit junior should take no further action or refer to the supervisor.

 Summary

Receivables may be a major asset of the company and therefore may require significant audit attention.

The principal audit verification procedure involves the circularisation of a sample of receivables which generates high quality, written, external evidence for the auditor. The auditor must control the circularisation and carefully analyse the replies received.

Bank balances are readily verifiable with a third party through the use of bank confirmation letters. These should be in a standard format and used by the auditor in accordance with a standard procedure agreed with the banking industry. The bank letter can also be used to ask other questions such as about bank guarantees. The other major aspect of the auditor's work on bank balances is a careful examination of the bank reconciliation statement.

The amount of audit work on cash balances will depend on the materiality of the amounts involved – it will revolve primarily around the auditor attendance at cash counts.

Test your understanding answers

 Test your understanding 1

(a) Deducted from.
(b) Deducted from.

 Test your understanding 2

No further action as it is immaterial and is clearly due to human error.

AUDIT AND ASSURANCE

Audit verification work 5 – Liabilities, shareholders' funds and statutory books

Introduction

This chapter introduces liabilities and how we may go about verifying them. We will look at an audit programme for payables, accruals and provisions and then we will consider auditing share capital.

ASSESSMENT CRITERIA
Methods used to obtain audit evidence (4.1)
Audit approach (4.4)
Audit assertions (4.5)

CONTENTS
1   An introduction to liabilities: the audit approach
2   Provisions and contingencies
3   The audit approach to share capital
4   Auditing reserves

Audit verification work 5 – Liabilities, shareholders' funds and statutory books: Chapter 9

1 An introduction to liabilities: the audit approach

1.1 Introduction

The usual testing procedures can be used to cover the financial statement assertions. However, there is likely to be a change in the emphasis of the audit work when dealing with liabilities as compared with assets. In the case of assets, the view is that clients are more likely to overstate the figures than to understate – hence audit emphasis is usually on existence. The auditor will want to ensure that all the assets which the company assert that they have, do actually exist. By contrast, any deliberate misstatement of liabilities is likely to understate the figures as this will present a better picture of financial performance. So, much of the audit evidence relating to liabilities focuses on completeness – the auditor will want to ensure that all liabilities that exist are recorded in the financial statements.

For this reason many auditors find reaching a conclusion on liabilities more difficult than reaching a conclusion on assets balances. In the case of assets, you are starting from a figure given by the client and setting out to verify that the assets representing that figure exist. In the case of liabilities, the auditor is looking for items that are not listed – the auditor is searching for unrecorded liabilities.

In addition to dealing with all significant categories of liabilities, this chapter also covers shareholders' funds and a company's statutory books and records.

1.2 Classification

Liabilities can be classified as follows:

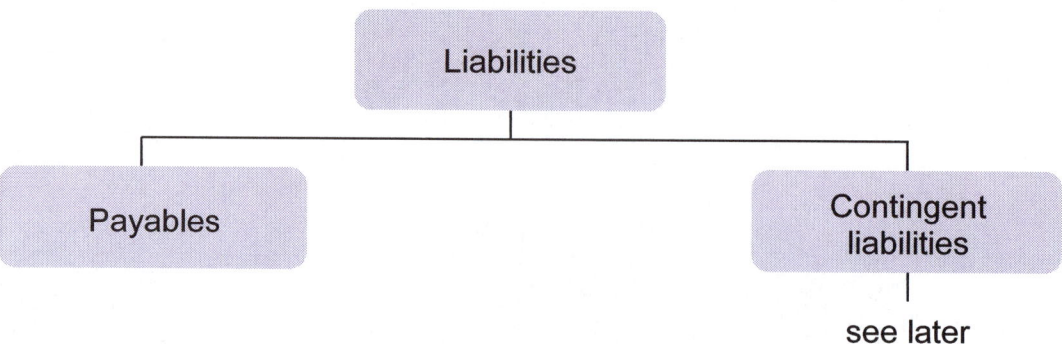

- Trade payables.
- Accruals and deferred income.
- Debenture loans.
- Bank loans and overdrafts.
- Payments received on account.
- Amounts owed to group undertakings.
- Other payables including taxation and social security.

Amounts falling due within one year **(current)** must be shown separately in the financial statements from amounts falling due after more than one year **(non-current)** for each item.

1.3 Current liabilities

Of the types of payable in the above listing, the item requiring most work will be trade payables. Many companies will have a large number of trade payable accounts so the audit approach to this will therefore usually involve sampling.

The other items are likely to be checked in detail, where material. Some of the items are not included in your assessment as they require accounting knowledge which has not been covered. The items that are relevant are covered below.

1.4 Internal controls over trade payables

Internal controls over trade payables are designed to ensure that:

(a) purchased goods/services are ordered under proper authorities and procedures

(b) purchased goods/services are only ordered as necessary for the proper conduct of the business operations and are ordered from suitable suppliers

(c) goods/services received are effectively inspected for quality and quantity

(d) invoices and related documentation are properly checked and approved as being valid before being entered as trade payables

(e) all valid transactions relating to trade payables (suppliers' invoices, credit notes and adjustments), and only those transactions, should be accurately recorded in the accounting records.

1.5 Trade payables – substantive procedures

Always bear in mind that the audit emphasis here will be on completeness – have all liabilities that exist been fully recorded in the financial statements? The main verification procedures are as follows.

(a) Obtain a schedule of the trade payables with appropriate age analysis and compare this with the control account and the payables ledger.

(b) Debit and credit balances should be separated, debit balances being included in receivables.

(c) Review the individual accounts with the largest throughput of transactions during the period (not necessarily the largest balances at the year-end).

(d) Review the year-end cut-off procedures for purchases.

The following should be considered during the tests of individual balances:

(i) Is the balance made up of specific items outstanding for a reasonable period?

(ii) Does the amount agree or can it be reconciled with payables statements? This is an important step – the auditor is using written, external evidence as a source for verification. It is also a means whereby the auditor may detect possible unrecorded amounts.

(iii) Consider the need to perform a payables circularisation. As external evidence exists in the case of payables, in the form of supplier statements, auditors do not always undertake a payable circularisation. However, if controls are weak or suppliers statements are unavailable or considered to be unreliable, a circularisation of a sample of payable balances may be appropriate.

(iv) Reconcile payments to payables just after the year end.

(e) Review the internal control over the purchases system which ensures that all goods received are properly recognised as liabilities of the company.

(f) Perform analytical procedures on payables, comparing age analysis with previous periods and payable days

$$\frac{\text{payables}}{\text{cost of sales}} \times 365$$

This again may help the auditor to detect possible unrecorded liabilities – any major changes in the ratio over time should be investigated in the light of this possibility.

(g) A general review for unrecorded liabilities should be carried out. In addition to analytical procedures, the auditor's knowledge of the business can be very helpful here. For example, if the auditor knows that X plc is a major supplier of inventory items to the client, but the amount shown as owing to X plc is zero at the year-end date, this would warrant some investigation by the auditor.

Test your understanding 1

Trade payables usually form the major component of a company's liabilities, and as such will therefore require a substantial amount of audit work.

Tasks

(a) Explain why a company should ensure that there is a satisfactory system of internal control over payables.

(b) State what the auditor should consider when testing individual balances.

1.6 Bank overdrafts

Bank overdrafts are shown under current liabilities even though there may be balances on other accounts which are shown as assets the only exception being if there is a legal right of set-off.

Verification of bank overdrafts is in other respects identical to the verification of bank balances as dealt with in the previous chapter.

1.7 Accruals

Accruals, like prepayments, are commonly made for rent, gas, electricity, telephone and other items where the expenditure has been incurred in the current period but where no invoice has yet been paid. Accruals are often immaterial and reliance is often placed on analytical procedures. Nevertheless, as year-end adjustments, there are rarely any controls over accruals and any errors are likely to be those of understatement.

Audit procedures, similar to those applied to prepayments, will include:

(i) Considering the client's own system (if any) for identifying and recording accruals.

(ii) Obtaining a schedule of accruals, ensuring that it is cast correctly. It should be compared with prior year accruals subject to other analytical procedures. Again, the auditor should use their knowledge of the business to identify possible unrecorded accrued liabilities. Areas that companies often miss in establishing year-end accruals include employee and directors' bonuses, sales staff commission and employee holiday pay.

(iii) Reviewing a sample of accruals for correct calculation, referring to supporting invoices received in the next period.

(iv) Include confirmation of the completeness of accruals in the management representation letter.

(v) Reviewing invoices received post year-end and ensuring costs are accrued if they relate to the previous period.

1.8 Long-term bank loans

The audit procedures are the same as for a similar item under current liabilities. It should also be appreciated that if all or part of the loan has a due date of payment within one year of the year-end date, then that loan (or the part payable within one year) must be disclosed under current liabilities.

Particular points to note in respect of these items include:

- Circularisation might be advisable if amounts are particularly material or controls are considered to be weak.

- Evidence relating to bank loans can be obtained from the standard bank confirmation letter already dealt with.

- In addition to verifying the amount outstanding on the loan itself, the auditor should consider the adequacy of any accrual for unpaid interest.

- The auditor can recalculate the interest paid on the loan based on the loan agreements and check this to the actual amounts.

Definition

A **debenture loan** is a written acknowledgement by a company, usually under seal, of a loan made to it, containing provisions as to payment of interest and repayment of capital.

1.9 Debenture loans

(a) **Issue**

The auditor should refer to the client's Memorandum and Articles to ascertain the borrowing powers of the company as although a trading company has implied power to borrow up to any amount, it is possible that such power may be restricted by the Memorandum or Articles. Legal difficulties may arise if the company exceeds its borrowing powers.

When a new issue of debentures takes place in the year it is necessary to disclose the class of debentures issued, the amount issued for each class and the consideration received. The auditor should ensure that the cash proceeds are received and properly recorded by the company. Any discounts or costs of the issue should be properly recorded. However, this can now be a complex issue under financial reporting practice and is beyond the scope of this unit.

(b) **Redemption**

Debentures may be redeemable according to the terms of the issue, at specified dates, by annual or other drawings (a process for selecting which debentures are to be redeemed that year), or at the option of the company, after due notice has been given of intention to repay. The auditor should examine the provisions of the debenture deed or the debenture bonds relating to the redemption, and ascertain that they are duly complied with.

The auditor's principal duties with regard to the redemption are to:

(i) examine the debenture deed as to the terms of the redemption, and note that these have been complied with

(ii) review the payment of cash to the debenture holders

(iii) inspect the cancelled bonds.

Audit verification work 5 – Liabilities, shareholders' funds and statutory books: Chapter 9

2 Provisions and contingencies

2.1 Provisions and contingencies

A provision is a liability of uncertain timing or amount. In other words, it is a liability where the entity is unsure of the amount of cash required to settle it, or when the cash payment will be required. For example, the company might have sold goods and given customers a warranty against break downs. The company knows that it is very likely to have to make some payments under the terms of the warranty but the exact amount cannot be predicted.

A contingency may be defined as a condition which exists at the year-end date where the ultimate outcome (gain or loss) will only be confirmed by the occurrence or non-occurrence of one or more uncertain future events. For example, a pending court case against the company might result in it paying damages, but the case has yet to be heard.

IAS 37 *Provisions, Contingent Liabilities and Contingent Assets* sets out the requirements for recognising and measuring provisions and contingencies. See Chapter 17 Financial Reporting Topics for help with the key requirements of IAS 37, should you need it.

2.2 Sources of audit evidence

We have already stressed the point that the auditor needs to search for the possibility of unrecorded liabilities. This aspect of the audit work is particularly relevant to the area of contingencies, as the client may have failed to recognise the existence of these items in the draft financial statements.

There are a wide range of sources of information available to the auditor which can be used in a search for possible contingencies. The major sources are set out below:

(a) Standard letter of request to the bank

This is likely to provide the necessary evidence in respect of any guarantees. This letter is considered in an earlier chapter as the primary method of verifying bank balances.

(b) Pending legal matters

Pending lawsuits and other actions against the company often present problems to the auditors. The following steps should be taken:

(i) Review the client's system of recording claims including the procedure for bringing them to the attention of management.

(ii) Discuss with the client's legal department or company secretary the procedures for instructing solicitors.

(iii) Inspect board or management minutes for indications of possible claims.

(iv) Inspect correspondence with solicitors, including bills rendered.

(v) Obtain a list of matters referred to solicitors with the company's estimates of possible liabilities.

(vi) Obtain a letter of representation from the relevant director that the director is not aware of any other matters referred to solicitors.

The auditor may consider it useful to obtain the client's consent to send a letter requesting confirmation of specific matters to the client's solicitor. An example of such a letter is shown below.

> **Example**
>
> In connection with the presentation and audit of our accounts for the year ended ……. the directors have made estimates of the ultimate liabilities (including costs) which might be incurred, and which are regarded as material, in relation to the following matters on which you have been consulted. We should be obliged if you would confirm that in your opinion these estimates are reasonable.
>
> | Matter | Estimated liability including cost |
> |---|---|
> | Libel action against the company in connection with statements appearing in newspaper. | £25,000 |
>
> Signed ……………………………………
>
> Dated ……………………………………
>
> Etc.

(c) Letter of representation

   The knowledge of contingent liabilities may very well be confined to management and is therefore a suitable matter for inclusion in such a letter. In addition, it will remind the directors of their responsibility to disclose such matters to the auditor.

2.3 The audit of accounting estimates

ISA 540 *Auditing accounting estimates and related disclosures* requires that auditors obtain sufficient appropriate evidence of accounting estimates. Estimates include estimates of provisions for depreciation, deferred tax, write-downs to net realisable value, losses on long-term contracts, legal claims against the company, other contingent liabilities, and other areas in which a significant element of judgement is required.

Areas such as those described above are inherently more risky than non-judgmental items and control risk is usually higher as these are non-routine transactions. The auditor should pay special attention to such items and would perform the following steps:

(a) review and test the process used by management to develop the estimate

(b) use an independent estimate (generated by the auditor) to compare with management's estimate

(c) review subsequent events.

Where in the case of contingent liabilities, subsequent events crystallise the liability, there will be no need to review management's processes or use independent estimates.

The auditor will normally test the calculations of the estimate, assess the assumptions made (e.g. the court is 90% likely to find in our favour), compare estimates with those made in previous periods and ensure that the estimate is in accordance with the auditor's knowledge of the business and the other audit evidence obtained.

2.4 Audit programme: payables, accruals and provisions

The following is a detailed example of an audit programme for trade payables, accruals and provisions.

Example

Audit programme

HASTINGS & WARWICK

AUDIT PROGRAMME

CLIENT	PREPARED BY	DATE
	REVIEWED BY (Audit senior in charge)	DATE
PERIOD	REVIEWED BY (Manager)	DATE

Sch Ref

AUDIT AREA – PAYABLES, ACCRUALS AND PROVISIONS

The purpose of the auditing procedures set out in this section of the programme is to obtain reasonable assurance that payables, accruals and provisions are not materially misstated.	Work performed by	Ref to supporting working paper
RELIANCE ON INTERNAL CONTROL AND INTERNAL AUDIT PROCEDURES		
1 Where we have placed reliance on the client's internal control or internal audit procedures:		
(a) List the internal control or internal audit procedures that we consider are essential to the system of internal control or internal audit.		
(b) State whether each procedure is, or is not, documented in writing.		
(c) Test that the controls have been complied with, and record the details of our tests in the working papers.		

TESTS OF DETAIL

TESTING TRADE PAYABLES FOR UNDERSTATEMENT

Confirmation date

2. Obtain a list of payables at the confirmation date and apply the following procedures:

    (a) Agree or reconcile the total of the list with the general ledger accounts.

    (b) Cast the list.

    (c) Establish whether or not the list appears reasonable by reviewing it for payables which are obviously misstated, or which, clearly, have been omitted (e.g. by comparing the list with the balances at the beginning of the period and with the general ledger debit sample).

3. Test the subsidiary records of trade payables (normally the payables ledger or a listing of unpaid invoices) for understatement or omission of amounts due to suppliers at the confirmation date. Do this by selecting suppliers for confirmation as follows:

    (a) Determine the length of the average trade payables cycle by dividing the larger of the trade payables balances at the most recent month end or at the preceding year end (or the estimated current year-end balance if it is expected to be significantly larger) by the average monthly payments to trade payables.

    (b) Select suppliers' accounts for confirmation by selecting a sample for a period of two trade payables cycles (or three months if longer) prior to the examination date from either:

        (1) the cash payment records, or

        (2) the general ledger debits (i.e. in purchase and expense accounts).

4. For the period we used in 3 (b) above, do one of the following:

    (a) If we have sampled from the cash payment records, determine the total payments made in the period to each supplier we have selected.

    (b) If we have sampled from the ledger debits, determine the total purchases made in the period from each supplier we have selected.

    Note: The purpose of this step is to enable us to evaluate the results of the confirmation procedures.

5   Request each supplier selected in 3 (b) above to confirm their balance in writing. If we receive no reply send second requests or apply other procedures (e.g. telephone calls made under our control) that might be expected to produce a direct reply from the supplier.

6   (a) Reconcile each reply that we receive with the subsidiary records of trade payables and investigate any differences by examining supporting documents, direct contact with the supplier or other appropriate means.

   (b) Where we are unable to obtain a direct reply from the supplier, either:

   (1) Obtain a payables statement from the client, scrutinise it for evidence of alteration, and reconcile the balance at the examination date as in (a) above, or

   (2) If a statement is not available, examine purchase invoices and documents supporting cash payments to that supplier for a period of one trade payables cycle following the confirmation date to determine the adequacy of the liability recorded at that date. Sample also the debit entries to the payables' account and establish their validity by examining paid cheques, credit notes or other relevant evidence. Agree the opening payables balance on the account with the list of payables at the previous year end and test the casts of the account.

Note: For the purpose of 6 previously, our reconciliation with supporting documentation will include selecting purchase items on a judgement basis and tracing them to the goods received records and the inventory records.

7   Consider whether the extent of the errors we discover necessitates our extending the confirmation procedures.

Following up an interim confirmation of payables

Note: If trade payables have been confirmed at the year-end date omit procedures 8 to 10.

8   Test debit entries to the trade payables recorded between the confirmation date and the year-end date as follows:

   (a)   Select items from the cash payments records and examine supporting documents (including each related cancelled cheque) to determine whether a liability recorded at the confirmation date has been satisfied.

   (b)   Trace the selected items to the credits in the subsidiary records of trade payables.

   (c)   Review the level of purchase returns and allowances. If they are material, select a sample of purchase returns and allowances from the debit entries to the payables control account and ensure that they are both valid and recorded in the correct accounting period by comparing them with supporting evidence (such as goods returned records, inspection records, correspondence with suppliers and the relevant credit note).

9   Review and summarise the movements on the payables control account from the confirmation date to the year-end date, and establish the reasons for any unusual movements.

10 Compare the individual balances which we selected for confirmation at the confirmation date with the corresponding balances at the year-end date, and investigate any major differences.

Year-end date

11 Select a sample of items from the cash payments records for one trade payables cycle, or (if shorter) the period between the year-end date and the approximate date of completion of fieldwork.

12 Where the completion of fieldwork occurs later than one trade payables cycle from the year-end date, select all further top stratum payments until the date of completion of fieldwork.

13 Test the items selected in 11 and 12 above with supporting documents and determine whether those payments that satisfied a liability at the year-end date satisfied a recorded liability at that same date.

14 Test for understatement of credit purchases in the period immediately preceding the year end by selecting items on a judgement basis from the purchase and expense records for the first few weeks after the year end, and ensuring that those purchases and expenses which relate to the period before the year-end were accrued as liabilities at the year end.

15 Enquire whether any old, disputed or questionable liabilities (either recorded or unrecorded) exist, and investigate as we deem appropriate.

16 Review the level of trade payables and its relationship to purchases. Compare with the previous year and investigate any significant changes in the composition of the trade payables between the opening balance and the balance at the year-end date. Record the results of the investigation in a working paper.

17 Evaluate the errors we discover during our work. If the revised monetary precision is unacceptable, apply any or all of the following procedures:

   (a) Extend the confirmation at the year-end date.

   (b) Extend the tests conducted in 8 to 14 above.

   (c) Request the client to re-check the recorded liabilities at the year-end date.

   (d) Request the client to record an acceptable adjustment based on the estimated population error in the evaluation for trade payables.

18 Review unpaid suppliers' invoices and unmatched receiving reports shortly before the completion of fieldwork. Identify any items that represent unrecorded liabilities at the year-end date.

TESTING ACCRUALS AND PROVISIONS

19 Test for omission and other understatement of accrued liabilities and provisions. Do this by examining documentation and by checking calculations to ensure that adequate (but not excessive) provision has been made for the items listed in (a) to (j) below. Where there is no independent evidence available concerning the amount of an accrual, test the debits to the accrual accounts by comparing with internal evidence of validity and with paid cheques, etc.

   (a) Periodic payments (e.g. rent, utilities, insurance, etc.).

   (b) Accrued salaries, wages and employer's social security contributions.

   (c) Accumulated holiday pay.

   (d) Accrued commissions and bonuses.

- (e) Payroll deductions (e.g. PAYE, NI, and pension scheme contributions).
- (f) Professional charges.
- (g) Directors' remuneration.
- (h) Royalties and similar charges.
- (i) Further expenditure for completed work and for after-sales service (e.g. warranties).
- (j) VAT.

20 In addition, test for omission of other accruals and provisions, by comparing with accruals and provisions in previous years, by comparing with expenses incurred during the year, by making enquiry, and by other appropriate methods. Ensure that the basis for recognising provisions conforms with IAS 37.

3 The audit approach to share capital

3.1 Statutory requirements relating to share capital

Shares issued by a company must have a nominal or par value which is determined by the company itself. The share capital account of the company must be maintained at the nominal value of the shares. It is unlawful for a company to issue shares for a price below their nominal value (i.e. at a discount). If shares are issued at a premium (i.e. above their nominal value), the excess must be recorded in a share premium account. This is then treated as part of the capital of the company (so, for example, a dividend cannot be paid out of the share premium account).

The statement of financial position of a company shows share capital as the nominal value of the called up share capital. Any called up share capital not paid at the year-end date is shown as part of receivables.

Definition

The **called up share capital** is the amount of nominal value of the shares which the company has asked the shareholders to pay as at the year-end date.

In the notes to the accounts, the issued share capital must be disclosed by class of share e.g. preference or ordinary shares.

 Definition

The **authorised share capital** is the total amount of shares which the company is allowed to issue under its Memorandum of Association.

The **issued share capital** is the total amount of the authorised share capital which has actually been issued.

In addition, full details must be given of any changes in the share capital during the year (e.g. new share issues).

3.2 Audit of share capital

As any change in share capital is likely to be a material transaction (by reference to its nature, even if not material by reference to its size) which is subject to special legal requirements, all changes should be subject to examination by the auditor. Sampling would not be appropriate except for an issue of shares for cash involving a substantial number of shareholders.

Appropriate procedures would be as follows:

(a) compare authorised capital limit to Memorandum and Articles

(b) inspect changes to issued capital in year and agree to board minutes

(c) trace all transactions involving cash to the cash book and bank statement

(d) ensure that appropriate returns have been made to the Registrar of Companies

(e) ensure that all transactions are legal and that premiums in particular have been accounted for in accordance with legislation.

It is also important that the auditor performs tests in respect of any dividends paid/proposed; these tests should include checks that the dividends do not contravene the distribution provisions of the Companies Act 2006.

4 Auditing reserves

4.1 Introduction

 Definition

A company's **reserves** represent the total net assets of a company in excess of its issued share capital (remember that total shareholder funds = share capital + reserves).

Possible categories of reserves include the following:

(a) share premium account, as referred to above

(b) revaluation reserve arising on a revaluation of non-current assets

(c) capital redemption reserve, a technical reserve which may arise if a company buys back from its shareholders or redeems part of its issued share capital

(d) reserves provided for by the Articles of association e.g. a capital reserve

(e) other reserves e.g. plant replacement reserve, designed to build up a pool of funds to finance the replacement of non-current assets at the end of their economic lives

(f) retained earnings.

Syllabus note

Some of these are highly specialised and beyond the scope of the Audit and Assurance paper. Those reserves which you need to be aware of are dealt with in more detail below.

4.2 Disclosure

Under the Companies Act disclosure rules, reserves must be presented under the headings shown in the previous section. In addition, the Companies Act requires that the movement for the period on each reserve should be disclosed in the financial statements. This movement will involve a detailed reconciliation of the differences between the opening and closing balances on each reserve.

4.3 Share premium

Definition

If a company issues shares for a consideration in excess of the nominal value of the shares, the excess is known as **share premium**.

Example

A company issues 10,000 shares at a price of £1.20 each; the nominal value of the shares is £1.00. The company would record the following amounts to the share capital and share premium accounts:

	£
Share capital (10,000 × £1.00)	10,000
Share premium (10,000 × £0.20)	2,000

The Companies Act imposes restrictions on the uses to which the balance on the share premium account should be put.

The auditor should confirm that share premium entries shown above are made correctly and that the provisions restricting the uses of the share premium account are complied with.

The principal permitted uses of the share premium account are as follows:

- providing for a fully paid issue of bonus shares
- writing off preliminary expenses (formation costs) of a new company
- writing off cost of share or debenture issues including discounts on issues
- writing off premiums on redemption of debentures and, in limited circumstances, premiums on redemption of shares.

4.4 Revaluation reserve

If a company measures property, plant and equipment using the revaluation model (rather than the cost model) then any gains arising on revaluation to fair value will be accumulated in a revaluation reserve.

The audit of the revaluation reserve will involve:

(a) assessment of the reason for the revaluation, the basis of valuation and its reasonableness in the light of the auditor's judgement.

(b) evaluation of the qualifications and experience of the valuer, which must be disclosed in the year in which the valuation takes place (the year of the valuation is given in subsequent years).

(c) ensuring that adequate disclosures are made and that any difference between market value and the recorded value is disclosed.

4.5 Capital reserve

The term capital reserve is not a reserve required by statute or any accounting standards. Nevertheless, on occasions, a company's Articles may require that certain profits of a capital nature (for example, profits on sale of property) be transferred to a capital reserve account.

The auditor must ensure, therefore, that the company has complied with the relevant rules contained in the articles.

4.6 Retained earnings

This represents accumulated retained profits of the business. The balance at the year-end consists of the balance brought forward from the previous year plus the retained profit for the current year.

Test your understanding 2

You are the audit senior for a client, Hasels Ltd and are about to commence the audit for the year end 31/1/X5. Hasels Ltd revalue their non-current assets annually. The land originally cost £10,000 on 31/1/X1 and has been subsequently revalued as follows:

 31/1/X2 £20,000
 31/1/X3 £30,000
 31/1/X4 £35,000

The revaluation reserve was £50,000 as at 31/1/X4. This includes £25,000 relating to the land and £25,000 relating to other revalued non-current assets. You are aware that there has been a recent slump in the property market which is not expected to recover and are concerned that the asset is overstated.

Following discussions with management they inform you that the land has fallen in value to £8,000 and they will be offsetting the £27,000 impairment loss against the revaluation reserve?

Tasks

(a) Explain whether this treatment is permissible.

(b) Outline the audit procedures that you would perform to verify the value of the reserve.

Test your understanding 3

During the year ended 31 December 20X2, Nerja Ltd acquired a fleet of 10 new lorries for distribution, at a cost of £7m payable in 3 annual instalments on a finance agreement at 8%.

Set out in a manner suitable for inclusion in the audit plan:

(i) the audit risks relating to the loan

(ii) the procedures to be undertaken in order to ensure that the loan is properly classified and disclosed in the financial statements.

5 Summary

This chapter completes your work on substantive audit procedures. The main area to focus on is the audit of liabilities. Bear in mind that the auditor's main area of interest here is completeness – have all liabilities that exist been recorded. This can make the audit of liabilities a more challenging area than the audit of assets.

The audit of share capital and reserves is an important area in practice but typically not a major area in Audit and Assurance assessments. The work here mainly consists of checking that the various legal requirements and disclosures have been complied with.

Test your understanding answers

 Test your understanding 1

(a) A company should ensure it has a proper system of internal control over its payables for the following reasons:

- to ensure all goods/services purchased are authorised
- to ensure goods/services purchased are only ordered for business purposes and from appropriate suppliers
- to ensure all goods/services received are inspected as to quality and quantity
- to ensure all invoices and supporting documentation are checked and approved to ensure their validity
- to ensure only valid transactions are accurately processed.

(b) When verifying individual payable balances, the auditor should consider the following factors:

- whether or not the balance comprises items outstanding within a reasonable timescale
- whether the outstanding items have been authorised for payment
- whether the amount can be reconciled to the payable's statements
- whether a payable's circularisation is required
- whether payments made to payables just after year end relate to specific outstanding items.

> **Test your understanding 2**
>
> (a) In respect of Hasels Ltd, the maximum amount that can be transferred is £25,000 (i.e. £35,000 – £10,000) even though the reserve is £50,000 as the remaining £25,000 relates to other assets. £2,000 of the total £27,000 will have to be recorded in the statement of profit or loss.
>
> (b) The audit procedures that should be performed are as follows:
>
> - enquire with management as to the reason for the revaluation
> - inspect the qualifications of the valuer
> - inspect the valuation report and assess the assumptions made
> - compare the valuation to similar properties in the surrounding area
> - inspect the disclosure note for accuracy.

Test your understanding 3

(i) **Risks**

Incorrect classification of the lorries within non-current assets.

Incorrect classification of the finance agreement within liabilities.

Incorrect calculation of the finance.

Inappropriate depreciation policy.

Incorrect calculation of depreciation.

Inaccurate cost figures used.

Incorrect calculation of the interest on the loan.

Incorrect disclosure of the loan terms and interest.

Recording purchase in the wrong period.

Failure to record new assets at all.

Failure to record loan payments.

(ii) **Procedures**

Check date of purchase to invoice.

Check amount capitalised to invoice.

Check recorded under motor vehicles in non-current assets note.

Agree accuracy of entry in non-current asset register.

Obtain depreciation policy and review for reasonableness.

Recalculate depreciation for the year on lorries.

Recalculate interest paid on loan.

Agree interest calculated to statement of profit or loss.

Calculate split of loan between less than one year by reference to the loan agreement.

Agree loan split to liabilities note.

Agree interest payment to bank statement and cash book.

Agree loan repayment to cash book and bank statement.

Audit verification work 6 – Statement of profit or loss

Introduction

This chapter discusses the statement of profit or loss and how we may go about auditing it.

ASSESSMENT CRITERIA	CONTENTS
Methods used to obtain audit evidence (4.1) Audit approach (4.4) Audit assertions (4.5)	1 An introduction to the profit and loss: the audit approach 2 Revenue 3 Payroll and other expenses

Audit verification work 6 – Statement of profit or loss: **Chapter 10**

1 An introduction to the profit and loss: the audit approach

1.1 Introduction

When auditing the statement of profit or loss, the auditor is testing the following financial statement assertions – occurrence, completeness, accuracy, cut-off, classification and presentation.

The auditor needs to consider whether the profit is likely to be understated or overstated. If a business is being sold, there is the risk that revenue may be overstated and expenses understated to show a healthier financial performance. On the other hand, if the company is trying to reduce their tax liability, revenue may be understated and expenses may be overstated.

The majority of transactions in the statement of profit or loss are audited indirectly through the direct tests performed on assets and liabilities in the statement of financial position. However, there will also be additional substantive procedures that need to be performed.

1.2 Internal controls over revenue and expenses

Internal controls over revenue and expenses are designed to ensure that:

(a) all revenue and expenses are included in the financial statements

(b) revenue and expenses are recorded at the correct amounts

(c) revenue and expenses are recorded in the correct period.

2 Revenue

2.1 Revenue – substantive procedures

IFRS 15 *Revenue from Contracts with Customers* sets out the revenue recognition process in five steps. See Chapter 17 Financial Reporting Topics for help with the key requirements of IFRS 15, should you need it.

The main audit verification procedures for revenue are as follows.

(a) Select a sample of orders from customers and agree these to the Goods Despatch Notes (GDNs) and sales invoices and ensure the sale has been included in the receivables ledger. This tests completeness.

(b) Inspect a sample of GDNs just before and after the year end and ensure the revenue has been included in the correct period. This tests cut-off.

(c) Recalculate discounts and sales tax applied to a sample of invoices. This tests accuracy.

(d) Review credit notes issued just after the year end, trace to GDN and verify if they relate to a pre year end sale. This tests occurrence.

(e) Compare revenue against prior year and budgets and investigate any significant fluctuations. This tests occurrence, accuracy and completeness.

(f) Calculate the gross profit margin and compare to the prior year and investigate any significant fluctuations. This tests occurrence, accuracy and completeness.

3 Payroll and other expenses

3.1 Payroll and other expenses – substantive procedures

The main verification procedures are as follows.

(a) Agree the total payroll expense per the payroll records to the nominal ledger. This tests completeness.

(b) Recalculate net pay and deductions for a sample of employees. This tests accuracy.

(c) Agree the net pay per the payroll to the cash book and bank statements. This tests occurrence.

(d) Review Goods Received Notes (GRNs) just before and after the year end and ensure the expense has been included in the correct period. This tests cut-off.

(e) Select a sample of purchase orders and agree to GRN and corresponding invoice and ensure the purchase has been posted to the nominal ledger. This tests completeness.

(f) Compare the payroll figure for this year and last year and investigate any significant fluctuations. Also, calculate the average salary based on employee numbers and compare to last year. This tests completeness and accuracy.

(g) Compare expenses year on year and investigate any significant fluctuations. This tests accuracy, completeness and occurrence.

(h) Calculate the net profit margin and compare to the prior year and investigate any significant fluctuations. This tests occurrence, accuracy and completeness.

Test your understanding 1

Identify whether the following are tests of control or substantive procedures.

(a) Comparing payroll costs year on year and investigating significant fluctuations.

(b) Reviewing whether purchase orders have been correctly authorised.

Test your understanding 2

You are auditing the payroll and revenue system at a client. For each of the audit tests listed below, state what audit assertion is being tested.

Choose from: existence, occurrence, accuracy, cut-off, classification

(a) Recalculate a sample of payroll deductions.

(b) Review GDNs from just before and after the year end and trace to the nominal ledger.

4 Summary

This chapter completes your work on substantive audit procedures. The statement of profit or loss is an important area of the financial statements and careful consideration has to be given to audit procedures.

Test your understanding answers

Test your understanding 1
(a) Substantive procedure
(b) Test of control

Test your understanding 2
(a) Accuracy
(b) Cut-off

AUDIT AND ASSURANCE

Completion stages of an audit

Introduction

In this chapter we assume that we are coming to the end of the audit assignment and we consider the various steps that must be taken before the auditor is ready to submit an audit opinion, including feeling satisfied that the company can continue in business for the foreseeable future.

ASSESSMENT CRITERIA
The role of audit working papers (3.4)
External audit opinion (5.2)
Report audit findings to management (5.3)

CONTENTS
1 The completion stages
2 Review of audit working papers
3 Compliance with accounting standards and statute
4 Written representations to auditors
5 The going concern basis in financial statements

Completion stages of an audit: **Chapter 11**

1 The completion stages

1.1 Introduction

The completion stages of any audit will primarily be concerned with a detailed review of both the audit working papers and the financial statements. Such procedures are aimed at providing the auditor with final assurance on the following matters:

- That the evidence which has been gathered and recorded is sufficient to support the opinion which is to be given in the auditor's report.

- That the financial statements comply with accounting standards, statute and any other regulations.

- That the accounting policies selected and disclosure given in the financial statements are such that they render the statements as a whole true and fair.

- That the financial statements are free from material misstatement.

2 Review of audit working papers

The work performed by each member of the audit team must be reviewed by a more senior member to:

- ensure that the work has been adequately performed
- confirm that the results support the audit conclusions reached.

2.1 Audit functions at final review

The audit functions fulfilled by the final review are as follows:

- The figures in the draft accounts are consistent with the audit evidence.

- The impact of any unadjusted errors is assessed and the decision to press for further adjustments taken.

- All appropriate disclosure and other requirements are complied with in the accounts.

- There is sufficient, relevant and reliable audit evidence to support the audit opinion.

- Recommendations to be made to the client in the management letter are considered.
- To assist next year's audit, a schedule of relevant points forward is prepared and the permanent audit file is left up to date.

2.2 Audit senior

The audit senior's principal responsibilities may be to:

- review in detail the work of all juniors
- check that all current and permanent file working papers are complete
- prepare interim notes linking interim and final visits (see below)
- update the results of the overall analytical procedures
- prepare a summary of unadjusted errors
- prepare or review the tax computations
- draft the representation letter (see later in this chapter)
- complete a disclosure checklist (see later in this chapter)
- review post year-end events
- prepare a list of points for partner (see below)
- draft the audit opinion (see Chapter 12)
- prepare the management letter (see Chapter 12)
- complete staff evaluations for audit juniors
- prepare a schedule of points forward to the next audit (see overleaf) and update permanent file.

2.3 Interim notes

If a separate interim audit visit is made, it is usual to complete all work on internal controls at this time. Any unfinished work must be documented by the senior with brief details of what needs to be done at the final visit. The interim notes should also summarise results to date and any implications for materiality and risk. For example, if controls are stronger than expected (i.e. control risk is lower) less detailed testing may be proposed.

2.4 Points for partner

This schedule should be restricted to material points and include brief explanations of the following:

- the results and financial position as shown by the draft accounts, and any changes from prior years, budget and expectations
- any audit problems including areas where major judgements have been exercised
- outstanding work which has proved impossible to complete
- variances from budget on the costs to date (and estimated costs to completion).

2.5 Points forward

The purpose of this schedule is to provide a link between this year's final visit and next year's planning. Points may include the following:

- recommendations to reduce audit work in specific areas
- recommendations to use alternative procedures to overcome difficulties encountered
- client's future plans for changes in the accounting systems and internal controls
- major changes in the business (e.g. new products, factory closures)
- changes in legislation and accounting standards
- proposals for improvements in timetabling and staffing arrangements.

2.6 Audit manager

The audit manager's principal responsibilities may be to:

- review the working papers in the context of the audit plan and later facts emerging
- ensure there is sufficient appropriate evidence to support the audit opinion
- at the end of the interim visit, review interim notes and take appropriate action
- consider results of analytical procedures
- review unadjusted errors and make recommendations for further adjustment/audit opinion
- review tax computations

- review the management representation letter
- review draft accounts for compliance with requirements
- review and edit the points for partner and recommend action thereon
- review the management letter to ensure it is commercially realistic and professionally sound
- review time costs summary, variances from budget and staff evaluations
- review points forward and ensure permanent file updated
- before the audit opinion is to be signed, ensure all evidence documented and post year-end event review updated.

2.7 Audit partner

At the completion stage of the audit, the audit partner will usually:

- review audit files in sufficient detail to be assured that the audit has been done satisfactorily
- take decisions on the points for partner
- clear all material outstanding points (meet with client/consult with another partner)
- approve the final management letter for submission to the client
- approve the form and content of the accounts
- review and approve the representation letter
- agree wording of the auditor's report.

The partner should also:

- approve the final accounts
- sign and date the auditor's report.

Completion stages of an audit: **Chapter 11**

3 Compliance with accounting standards and statute

3.1 Introduction

For the majority of audit assignments, the auditor will need to consider whether the financial statements comply with:

- International Financial Reporting Standards (IFRS® Standards) and International Accounting Standards (IAS® Standards), and
- the Companies Act 2006.

These are both concerned with accounting policies and disclosure.

The Companies Act 2006 also prescribes formats for both statement of financial position and statement of profit or loss.

3.2 Accounting policies

For each audit area:

- establish the accounting policy
- consider whether the stated policy has been complied with
- consider whether the stated policy is appropriate and complies with any relevant IFRS® Standards or IAS® Standards or statutory provision.

3.3 Disclosure

The auditor will need to be satisfied that:

- all matters that should be disclosed have been disclosed, and
- the information which has been disclosed is correct.

The first objective is best achieved by the use of a detailed disclosure checklist.

The second objective can be achieved in most cases by referring back to audit work already performed. For instance, the figure disclosed as depreciation charge should have been audited as part of the non-current asset work.

However, certain items may need further validation, as follows.

3.4 Directors' loans and transactions

Directors have several areas of potential conflict of interest with the company. It is important that the members are made aware of any such conflict in order for the accounts to give a true and fair view and, in some cases, in order for the members to vote on the directors' proposed actions.

The areas of potential conflict include:

- remuneration, and
- loans, quasi-loans and credit transactions from the company to the directors or their connected persons (e.g. spouse).

Consequently there are a number of statutory regulations concerning the legality and the disclosure in the financial statements of such transactions.

3.5 Directors' remuneration

The Companies Act 2006 requires that the remuneration received by the directors and chairman must be accurately disclosed in the financial statements. This is a particularly sensitive area and the auditor will need to ensure that disclosure is correct – the concept of materiality is thus applied in a different manner to this area of the financial statements (material by nature).

The figure which is included in the financial statements may be verified by referring to:

- Articles of Association
- Board minutes
- P11Ds
- Letters of confirmation of emoluments.

3.6 Directors' loans

The Companies Act 2006 (s197) states there is a requirement for shareholder consent to be obtained prior to a company entering into a loan to a director or a quasi-loan agreement with a director.

If any company enters such a transaction, the details have to be disclosed in the financial statements (irrespective of the amount). A quasi-loan is thus an indirect loan. Examples of quasi-loans are where a company settles a liability owed by a director or buys goods on his or her behalf.

Definition

Quasi-loans: Where a company pays or promises to pay a third party on behalf of a director (or connected person), and the director (or connected person) undertakes to repay the company in due course.

3.7 Credit transactions

The Companies Act 2006 (s201) states that a company may not enter into a credit transaction as creditor for the benefit of a director or give a guarantee or provide security in connection with a credit transaction entered into by any person for the benefit of such a director unless the credit transaction has been approved by a resolution of the members of the company.

Definition

Credit transactions: Where goods or services are supplied and payment is deferred or paid by instalments (e.g. leases, hire-purchase transactions or normal trade credit).

3.8 Disclosure

When auditing a relevant company it can be seen from the above regulations that there are potentially far more transactions which the auditor must ensure are disclosed in the financial statements. The details to be disclosed for loans, quasi-loans and credit transactions are:

- the name of the director (or connected person)
- the amount of the loan outstanding at the beginning and end of the year
- the maximum amount outstanding at any point in the year
- any provisions made by the company against non-payment of interest or capital.

3.9 Audit work

- Establish clients' procedures for ensuring all disclosable transactions are identified and recorded.
- Inspect board minutes and records of transactions with directors.

- Inspect agreements and contracts involving directors and check details to source documentation.
- Check whether transactions are on commercial terms. Consider:
  - whether amounts due are recoverable – the legality of these transactions
  - the effect of post year-end events (e.g. receipt of after-date cash).
- Obtain a statement from the directors confirming the details of disclosable transactions.

4 Written representations to auditors

4.1 Introduction

During an audit many representations are made to the auditors, either unsolicited or in response to specific enquiries. The auditors may consider certain of these representations to be critical to obtaining sufficient appropriate audit evidence on which to base their audit opinion. The auditors may also require representations on general matters, for example that the directors have made all accounting records available to the auditors.

The possibility of misunderstandings between auditors and management is reduced when oral representations are confirmed in writing. Written confirmation of representations may take the form of:

- a representation letter from management, or
- a letter from the auditors outlining their understanding of management's representations, duly acknowledged and confirmed in writing by management, or
- minutes of meetings of the board of directors, or similar body, at which such representations are approved.

Auditors must obtain written confirmation of appropriate representations from management before their report is issued.

4.2 Procedures

It is advisable for auditors to discuss such matters with those responsible for giving the written confirmation before they sign it to ensure that they understand what it is that they are being asked to confirm.

When representations to the auditors relate to matters which are material to the financial statements, they must:

- seek corroborative audit evidence

- evaluate whether the representations made by management appear reasonable and are consistent with other audit evidence obtained, including other representations, and

- consider whether the individuals making the representations can be expected to be well-informed on the particular matters.

Representations by management cannot be a substitute for other audit evidence that auditors expect to be available.

If auditors are unable to obtain sufficient appropriate audit evidence regarding a matter which has, or may have, a material effect on the financial statements and such audit evidence is expected to be available, this constitutes a limitation on the scope of the audit, even if a representation from management has been received on the matter. In these circumstances it may be necessary for them to consider the implications for their report (see Chapter 12).

4.3 Written representations many be the only audit evidence available

In certain instances, such as where knowledge of the facts is confined to management (e.g. when the facts are a matter of management intentions), or when the matter is principally one of judgment or opinion (e.g. on the trading position of a particular customer), written representations may be the only audit evidence available. In some exceptional cases, the matter may be of such significance that the auditors refer to the representations in their report as being relevant to a proper understanding of the basis of their opinion.

4.4 Contradiction between written representation and other audit evidence

If a representation appears to be contradicted by other audit evidence, the auditors should investigate the circumstances to resolve the matter and consider whether it casts doubt on the reliability of other representations.

The investigation of apparently contradictory audit evidence regarding a representation received usually begins with further enquiries of management, to ascertain whether the representation has been misunderstood or whether the other audit evidence has been misinterpreted, followed by corroboration of management's responses. If management is unable to provide an explanation or if the explanation is not considered adequate, further audit procedures may be required to resolve the matter.

4.5 Basic elements of a management representation letter

Addressee

When requesting a management representation letter, auditors request that it be addressed to them, that it contain specified information and that it be appropriately dated and approved by those with specific knowledge of the relevant matters.

Board approval

Auditors usually request that the management representation letter be discussed and agreed by the board of directors or similar body, and signed on their behalf by the chairperson and secretary, before they approve the financial statements, to ensure that the board as a whole is aware of the representations on which the auditors intend to rely in expressing their opinion on those financial statements. The auditors may also wish to consider whether to take the opportunity to remind the directors that, under s501 of the Companies Act 2006, it is an offence to mislead the auditors.

Date

A management representation letter is normally dated on the day the financial statements are approved. If there is any significant delay between the date of the management representation letter and the date of the auditor's report, the auditors may consider it necessary to obtain further representations regarding the intervening period.

Test your understanding 1

State whether the following statements are true or false in respect of matters for which auditors would normally obtain written representations:

1. Confirmation that the directors believe the company to be a going concern for the foreseeable future.

2. Confirmation that all books, records, information and explanations have been supplied to the auditors.

3. Explanation of reasons why errors passed on by the auditors have not been adjusted.

4.6 Action if management refuses to provide written confirmation of representations

If management refuses to provide written confirmation of a representation that the auditors consider necessary, the auditors should consider the implications of this scope limitation for their report. In such circumstances, it may no longer be appropriate for the auditors to place reliance on other representations made by management during the course of the audit.

4.7 Illustration

Set out below is an example of a letter of representation based on the Appendix to the ISA 580 *Written representations*. It is not intended to be a standard letter because representations by management can be expected to vary not only from one enterprise to another, but also from one year to another in the case of the same audit client.

Example

(To Auditor) (Date)

This representation letter is provided in connection with your audit of the financial statements of ABC Company for the year ended 31 December 20X1 for the purpose of expressing an opinion as to whether the financial statements give a true and fair view of the financial position of ABC Company as of 31 December 20X1 and of the results of its operations and its cash flows for the year then ended in accordance with the Companies Act 2006.

We acknowledge our responsibility for the fair presentation of the financial statements in accordance with (indicate applicable financial reporting framework).

We confirm, to the best of our knowledge and belief, the following representations:

- There have been no irregularities involving management or employees who have a significant role in internal control or that could have a material effect on the financial statements.

- We have made available to you all books of account and supporting documentation and all minutes of meetings of shareholders and the Board of Directors.

- We confirm the completeness of the information provided regarding the identification of related parties.

- The financial statements are free of material misstatements, including omissions and obscurements.

- The Company has complied with all aspects of contractual agreements that could have a material effect on the financial statements in the event of noncompliance. There has been no noncompliance with requirements of regulatory authorities that could have a material effect on the financial statements in the event of noncompliance.

- The following have been properly recorded and, when appropriate, adequately disclosed in the financial statements:

    (a) the identity of, and balances and transactions with, related parties

    (b) losses arising from sale and purchase commitments

    (c) agreements and options to buy back assets previously sold

    (d) assets pledged as collateral.

- We have no plans or intentions that may materially alter the carrying value or classification of assets and liabilities reflected in the financial statements.

- We have no plans to abandon lines of product or other plans or intentions that will result in any excess or obsolete inventory, and no inventory is stated at an amount in excess of net realisable value.

- The company has satisfactory title to all assets and there are no liens or encumbrances on the company's assets.

- We have recorded or disclosed, as appropriate, all liabilities, both actual and contingent, and have disclosed in Note X to the financial statements all guarantees that we have given to third parties.

- Other than . . . described in Note X to the financial statements, there have been no events subsequent to period end which require adjustment of or disclosure in the financial statements or Notes thereto.

- The ...claim by XYZ Company has been settled for the total sum of XXX which has been properly accrued in the financial statements. No other claims in connection with litigation have been or are expected to be received.

- There are no formal or informal compensating balance arrangements with any of our cash and investment accounts. Except as disclosed in Note X to the financial statements, we have no other line of credit arrangements.

....

Senior Executive Officer Senior Financial Officer

5 The going concern basis in financial statements

5.1 Accounting requirements

IAS 1 *Presentation of financial statements* requires that an entity should prepare its financial statements on a going concern basis unless:

- it intends to liquidate, or
- the directors have no realistic alternative but to liquidate the entity or to cease trading.

In such circumstances the financial statements can be prepared on another basis, other than the going concern basis.

When preparing the financial statements, the directors should assess whether there are any significant doubts about an entity's ability to continue as a going concern.

5.2 Impact on financial statements

If the going concern basis is inappropriate, this affects the manner in which assets and liabilities are shown in the financial statements:

- amounts recorded in respect of assets may not be recovered (through use/realisation)
- amounts and dates of maturities of liabilities may change
- further liabilities may need to be recognised, e.g. redundancy costs/contract severance charges.

If there are any material uncertainties that may cast significant doubt upon the ability to continue as a going concern, the financial statements should include note disclosures about the matters giving rise to the concern.

5.3 Impact on audit

When forming an opinion as to whether financial statements give a true and fair view, auditors should consider a company's ability to continue as a going concern and any relevant disclosures.

UK auditor's reports must always include a section on going concern. The precise details are tailored to the engagement in question. For reports with unmodified opinions, the section is headed 'Conclusions Relating to Going Concern' and it provides a summary of the auditor's conclusions on this area (see later sections for further detail).

5.4 Audit evidence

Auditors should assess the adequacy of the means by which the directors have satisfied themselves that the going concern basis is appropriate (with any necessary disclosures). For this purpose the auditor should:

- make enquiries of directors and examine appropriate available information

- plan and perform procedures to identify material matters which could indicate concern about the entity's ability to continue as a going concern.

5.5 Sources of information

When the auditor is assessing the adequacy of the going concern basis, there are a number of sources of information they would look to:

- Client's system for timely identification of warnings of risks and uncertainties.

- Budgets, forecast information, etc.

- Obligations, undertakings, guarantees with lenders, suppliers, group companies for giving or receiving support. The auditor might want to check that these guarantees are still relevant.

- Bank borrowing facilities and suppliers' credit, e.g. the company might be losing their borrowing facility.

5.6 Matters to consider

There are a number of issues an auditor would be on the lookout for when assessing the going concern assumption and these are as follows:

- Liabilities exceed assets/net current liabilities.

- Necessary borrowing facilities not agreed.

- Breach of loan agreement/covenants.

- Normal trade credit terms refused by suppliers.

- Fundamental market/technological changes.

- Loss of key management/suppliers/customers/product.

- Major litigation.

> **Test your understanding 2**
>
> You are responsible for the audit of a company that assembles computers from components purchased from South East Asia and sells them to major retailers and to individuals and businesses.
>
> By stating true or false, indicate which of the following can be considered as an indication that your client is facing going concern problems:
>
> 1 Fall in sales due to recession and stiff competition.
>
> 2 Fall in gross profit margin and trading loss.
>
> 3 Certain computers may be obsolete.

5.7 Procedures

The extent of audit procedures is influenced primarily by how far there is an excess of financial resources available over the financial resources required in the foreseeable future. For a stable business with uncomplicated circumstances, discussions with the directors may suffice. Cash budgets, management accounts, etc. are not required as a matter of course.

The auditor would usually review forecasts in order to see if management's assumptions are in line with their going concern assumption.

5.8 Examination of borrowing facilities

It may be necessary for the auditor to:

- obtain confirmation of existence and terms of bank facilities, and
- make their own assessment of the bankers' intentions.

5.9 Written representations

Written representations may be needed regarding:

- the directors' assessment of the entity as a going concern
- any relevant disclosures in the financial statements.

If the auditor is unable to obtain these representations, the auditor must consider whether there is a limitation on the scope of the audit, requiring modification to the auditor's report (see next chapter).

5.10 Assessing disclosures

When forming an opinion on whether the financial statements show a true and fair view, the auditor should consider:

- the entity's ability to continue as a going concern, and
- any relevant disclosures made in the financial statements.

If the going concern basis is inappropriate or significantly uncertain, and the financial statements do not give disclosure, the audit opinion may need to be modified on the grounds of disagreement with disclosure.

5.11 Reporting on financial statements

Going concern is a crucial issue in the audit and, as a result, it is always mentioned in the UK auditor's report. Auditors must decide what sort of disclosure should be made for the situation at hand.

Auditors are in agreement with the basis upon which the financial statements have been prepared

- Where the going concern assumption is appropriate, the auditor's report would include a section headed 'Conclusions Relating to Going Concern'. It provides a summary of the auditor's conclusions on this area.

- In rare circumstances, in order to give a true and fair view, directors may prepare the financial statements on a basis other than going concern. This is the break up basis. Under the break up basis, all assets are restated at their realisable values and everything is reclassified as current in the financial statements.

    If the financial statements have been prepared on an alternative basis (e.g. the break up basis), and the auditor is in agreement, then the auditor would include an emphasis of matter paragraph in their auditor's report to emphasise the importance of this. In this situation, the auditor would not include a 'Conclusions Relating to Going Concern' section.

    It is important to note that the inclusion of an emphasis of matter paragraph does not affect the audit opinion. These paragraphs simply draw the readers' attention to a matter that is fundamental to the readers' understanding of the financial statements.

Please see below for an example paragraph:

Emphasis of matter

In forming our opinion, we have considered the adequacy of the disclosures made in note 1 of the financial statements concerning the uncertainty as to the continuation and renewal of the company's bank overdraft facility. In view of the significance of this uncertainty we consider that it should be drawn to your attention but our opinion is not modified in this respect.

Opinion should not be modified on these grounds alone, provided disclosures are adequate. The disclosures required are as follows:

- statement that the financial statements are prepared on the going concern basis
- statement of pertinent facts
- nature of concern
- statement of directors' assumptions (must be clearly distinguishable from facts)
- details of any relevant actions by directors.

If disclosure is inadequate in any material respect, the audit opinion will be modified (see Chapter 12).

5.12 Material uncertainty related to going concern

Where the going concern assumption is appropriate but there is a material uncertainty in relation to it, then the financial statements should disclose this uncertainty. The auditor then highlights the importance of this disclosure by including a 'Material Uncertainty Related to Going Concern' section in the auditor's report.

If the disclosure in the financial statements is not appropriate, then there is a material misstatement; the auditor must then express a qualified or adverse opinion.

In this situation, the auditor would not include a 'Conclusions Relating to Going Concern' section.

5.13 Adverse opinion

Where the going concern assumption is inappropriate but the financial statements have been prepared on the going concern basis, then this is a material and pervasive misstatement that would give rise to an adverse auditor's opinion.

In this situation, the auditor would not include a 'Conclusions Relating to Going Concern' section.

5.14 Disclaimer

If the auditor concludes that the directors have not taken adequate steps to satisfy themselves that the going concern basis is appropriate then the auditor will not be satisfied that they have obtained sufficient appropriate evidence and a disclaimer of opinion may be appropriate.

In this situation, the auditor would not include a 'Conclusions Relating to Going Concern' section.

Test your understanding 3

State whether the following statements are true or false:

1. Auditors assess the company's ability to continue as going concern and directors satisfy themselves that the use of the going concern basis of accounting is reasonable and disclosures made adequate.

2. There are no disclosure implications if the company is a going concern.

3. If there are going concern problems, the basis on which the financial statements have been prepared have to be disclosed.

6 Summary

You should now appreciate that the completion stages of an audit are particularly important and have an understanding of some of the issues which must be considered at this stage, including:

- whether the financial statements comply with IFRS® Standards, IAS® Standards and relevant legislation

- whether there is proper disclosure of all relevant directors' loans and transactions in the financial statements

- the need for written representations

- whether the business is a going concern.

As well as appreciating the issues, you should also understand how they are likely to be addressed in practice.

Test your understanding answers

Test your understanding 1
1. True.
2. True.
3. True.

Test your understanding 2
1. True.
2. True.
3. True.

Test your understanding 3
1. False.
2. True.
3. True.

AUDIT AND ASSURANCE

The reporting function

Introduction

Having gathered sufficient and appropriate evidence, the auditor must now draft reports to management. This chapter examines the management letter and the statutory audit opinion that is submitted at the end of the audit assignment. We will consider both unmodified and modified opinions and, in addition, auditor's reports where additional paragraphs are required.

ASSESSMENT CRITERIA
The regulatory environment (1.2)
External audit opinion (5.2)
Report audit findings to management (5.3)

CONTENTS	
1	Reports to directors or management
2	Evaluation of misstatements
3	Statutory auditors' reports
4	Modified opinion
5	Additional paragraphs

1 Reports to directors or management

1.1 Introduction

It is common practice for all auditors to report to management. However, for external auditors, reports to management are a by-product of the statutory audit rather than a main objective.

The auditor's report to the shareholders on the financial statements is the principal objective of the entire external audit procedure.

The principal purpose of reports to directors or management are for auditors to communicate points that have come to their attention during the audit:

- on the design and operation of the accounting system and system of internal control and to make suggestions for their improvement
- of other constructive advice, for example comments on potential economies or improvements in efficiency, and
- on other matters, for example comments on adjusted and unadjusted errors in the financial statements or on particular accounting policies and practices.

1.2 Material deficiencies in the accounting system and system of internal control

When material deficiencies in the accounting system and system of internal control are identified during the audit, auditors should report them in writing to the directors, the audit committee or an appropriate level of management on a timely basis.

Definition

A material deficiency in the accounting system and system of internal control is a condition which may result in a material misstatement in the financial statements.

If the directors or management have detected a material deficiency and, in the view of the auditors, have taken appropriate corrective action, the auditors do not need to report to directors or management on the matter. In these circumstances they normally document the considerations which resulted in their conclusion that no report to directors or management in respect of this matter is needed.

1.3 Form of report

Usually, material deficiencies in the accounting system and system of internal control are communicated to directors or management in a written report issued by the auditors. In some circumstances it may be appropriate for the relevant matters to be raised orally with directors or management, followed by a file note circulated to those attending the meeting to provide a record of the auditors' observations and any responses of the directors or management.

When no material deficiencies in the accounting system and system of internal control are identified during the audit, the auditors may choose not to issue a report to directors or management. When auditors do not intend to issue a report to directors or management they may consider it appropriate to inform them that no report is to be issued.

1.4 Other matters

In the course of the audit, the auditors may identify deficiencies in the accounting system and system of internal control other than material deficiencies, or other matters which they consider appropriate to bring to the attention of directors or management.

Usually these matters are included in a report to directors or management, together with details of any material deficiencies, although they may be issued in a separate report. The auditors may consider it appropriate to raise these matters orally with directors or management and in these circumstances they normally prepare a file note to provide a record of their observations.

1.5 Disclaimer

In any report to directors or management, auditors explain that the report is not a comprehensive statement of all deficiencies which exist or of all improvements which may be made, but that it documents only those matters which have come to their attention as a result of the audit procedures performed.

1.6 Timing

To be effective, a report to directors or management is best made as soon as possible after completion of the audit procedures giving rise to comment. Where the audit work is performed on more than one visit, it is often appropriate to report to directors or management after the interim visit as well as after the final audit visit, but making clear that the overall audit work is only partially complete and further matters may still arise. Where an interim report details serious deficiencies, the auditor will review corrective action taken by management during the final audit.

1.7 Management's response

Normally, auditors ask for a reply to the points raised in a report to directors or management, indicating the actions that the directors or management intend to take as a result of the comments made in the report.

1.8 Disclosure to third parties

Auditors normally state in their report to directors or management that:

- the report has been prepared for the sole use of the entity
- it must not be disclosed to a third party, or quoted or referred to, without the written consent of the auditors, and
- no responsibility is assumed by the auditors to any other person.

An express disclaimer of liability normally provides protection against an unforeseen liability to a third party.

1.9 Structure of the report

The letter should be as clear, concise and constructive as possible. To achieve this, the comments are presented to management using the following standard structure, usually in a tabular format.

Explanation

The nature of each deficiency is described. The description is concise but specific, and the extent of the error quantified if possible.

Consequence

This points out to management the possible consequences of the deficiency in terms of the financial statements (e.g. they could contain errors), and/or the business's assets (e.g. financial loss may result).

Recommendation

For every deficiency a recommendation is made as to how the problem could be overcome. Such recommendations are as practical and cost-effective as possible in order to encourage management to adopt them.

If a recommendation is not adopted, and the same deficiency still exists in the following year, reference to this would be made in the following year's management letter. However, the consequence or recommendation may need to be revised to get the deficiency resolved.

The management letter usually deals with the most serious deficiencies first in order to lend weight to the report as a whole.

> **Test your understanding 1**
>
> During the audit of Media Co, a film production company, it was discovered that although the company maintained a non-current asset register to record the details of its cameras and other equipment, no checking procedures other than reconciliation with the nominal ledger are undertaken.
>
> Prepare extracts suitable for inclusion in a report to management of Media Co, which set out:
>
> (i) The possible consequences; and
>
> (ii) The recommendations you would make in respect of this matter.

2 Evaluation of misstatements

In accordance with ISA 450 *Evaluation of misstatements identified during the audit*, all misstatements should be communicated to management on a timely basis, unless they are clearly trivial. Management should be asked to correct all misstatements identified during the audit.

If management refuses to adjust the identified misstatements, the auditor should:

- try and obtain an understanding of management's reasons for refusing to adjust

- determine whether uncorrected misstatements are material in aggregate or individually, and

- consider the potential impact on their audit report of material misstatements.

Prior to evaluating the significance of uncorrected misstatements the auditor should reassess materiality to confirm whether it remains appropriate to the financial statements.

Finally, the auditor should obtain a written representation from management and those charged with governance that they believe the effect of the uncorrected misstatements is immaterial, individually and in aggregate.

Once these procedures have been completed the auditor should consider the impact of uncorrected misstatements on their reporting. This is considered in more detail.

3 Statutory auditors' reports

3.1 Legal background

The external auditor's principal purpose in performing the work described in the preceding chapters is to produce a report to the members of the company. The auditor is obliged to produce such a report by the Companies Act 2006.

The auditor's report will be included, together with the financial statements, in the annual report which is laid before the members at the Annual General Meeting.

3.2 Unmodified opinions

The following is the text of an audit report provided in accordance with ISA 700 (Revised) *Forming an opinion and reporting on financial statements*:

Example

INDEPENDENT AUDITOR'S REPORT TO THE MEMBERS OF XYZ CO

Opinion

We have audited the financial statements of XYZ Company (the Company), which comprise the statement of financial position as at December 31, 20X1, and the statement of comprehensive income, statement of changes in equity and statement of cash flows for the year then ended, and notes to the financial statements, including a summary of significant accounting policies.

In our opinion, the financial statements:

- give a true and fair view of the state of the company's affairs as at……..and its profit (or loss) for the year then ended

- have been properly prepared in accordance with United Kingdom Generally Accepted Accounting Practice; and

- have been prepared in accordance with the requirements of the Companies Act 2006.

Basis for opinion

We conducted our audit in accordance with International Standards on Auditing (UK) ISAs and applicable law. Our responsibilities under those standards are further described in the Auditor's Responsibilities for the Audit of the Financial Statements section of our report. We are independent of the Company in accordance with the ethical requirements that are relevant to our audit of the financial statements in the UK, including the FRC's Ethical Standard, and have fulfilled our other ethical responsibilities in accordance with these requirements. We believe that the audit evidence we have obtained is sufficient and appropriate to provide a basis for our opinion.

Responsibilities of Directors

As explained more fully in the directors' responsibilities statement [set out on page …], the directors are responsible for the preparation of the financial statements and for being satisfied that they give a true and fair view, and for such internal control as the directors determine is necessary to enable the preparation of financial statements that are free from material misstatement, whether due to fraud or error. In preparing the financial statements, the directors are responsible for assessing the company's ability to continue as a going concern, disclosing, where applicable, matters related to going concern and using the going concern basis of accounting unless the directors either intend to liquidate the company or cease operations, or have no realistic alternative but to do so.

Auditor's Responsibilities for the Audit of the Financial Statements

Our objectives are to obtain reasonable assurance about whether the financial statements as a whole are free from material misstatement, whether due to fraud or error, and to issue an auditor's report that includes our opinion. Reasonable assurance is a high level of assurance, but is not a guarantee that an audit conducted in accordance with ISAs (UK) will always detect a material misstatement when it exists. Misstatements can arise from fraud or error and are considered material if, individually or in the aggregate, they could reasonably be expected to influence the economic decisions of users taken on the basis of these financial statements.

Registered auditors

Date   *Address*

3.3 Opinions

The report is addressed to the shareholders of the company, and gives an indication of the scope of the auditor's work (i.e. that work has been done in accordance with ISAs). The auditor must give an opinion on the following matters:

- whether the financial statements give a true and fair view of the profit or loss of the company for the period and its state of affairs at the year end, and

- whether the financial statements have been properly prepared in accordance with the applicable financial reporting framework and with the Companies Act 2006.

These are known as the auditor's express opinions.

There are, however, further matters upon which Companies Act 2006 requires to be reported on by exception. These are known as the implied opinions:

- proper records of account have been kept by the company
- the accounts agree with the underlying records
- returns from branches not visited by the auditor are adequate for audit purposes
- all information and explanations necessary for audit purposes have been obtained
- the information given in the director's report is not inconsistent with the accounts.

It is a requirement that these points are to be included in UK auditor's reports (even if there are no problems) to aid the users' understanding of what the audit entails.

In addition, if matters relating to directors' emoluments and other transactions are not properly disclosed in the accounts, they will be included in the auditors' report and disclosed there. The audit opinion will be modified on the grounds that the financial statements have not been properly prepared in accordance with the Companies Act.

3.4 The meaning of the term 'true and fair'

Although it is difficult to define the term exactly, as you saw in Chapter 1, in practice, if the auditor states that in their opinion the 'financial statements show a true and fair view', this generally implies that:

- IFRS® Standards and IAS® Standards have been complied with as necessary, or
- if an IFRS® Standard or IAS® Standard has not been complied with, the non-compliance was necessary in order to give a true and fair view
- the financial statements have been otherwise drawn up using acceptable bases and conventions.

3.5 The meaning of the term 'financial statements'

In the context of the auditor's report, the 'financial statements' that are within the scope of the auditor's examination are:

- Statement of profit or loss
- Statement of financial position
- Statements of cash flows and changes in equity
- the related notes.

3.6 Date and signature of the auditors' report

The date of the auditor's report is the date on which the auditors sign (in manuscript) their report expressing an opinion on the financial statements for distribution with those statements. This will be following:

- receipt of the financial statements and accompanying documents in the form approved by the directors for release
- review of all documents which they are required to consider in addition to the financial statements (for example the directors' report, chairman's statement or other review of an entity's affairs which will accompany the financial statements), and
- completion of all procedures necessary to form an opinion on the financial statements (and any other opinions required by law or regulation) including a review of post year-end events.

The report may be signed in the name of the auditors' firm, the personal name of the auditor, or both, as appropriate. The signature is normally that of the firm because the firm as a whole assumes responsibility for the audit. To assist identification, the report normally includes the location of the auditors' office. Where appropriate, their status as registered auditors is also stated.

4 Modified opinion

4.1 Introduction

A modified opinion is issued when either of the following circumstances exist:

- the financial statements as a whole are not free from material misstatements, or
- the auditor has been unable to obtain sufficient appropriate evidence to conclude that the financial statements as a whole are free from material misstatement.

If the auditor believes that the matter is material they will modify the wording of the opinion. If the auditor considers the matter to be pervasive to the financial statements, then this must also be incorporated in to the audit opinion.

Pervasive means that the matter is:

- not confined to specific elements of the financial statements
- if confined, represents a substantial proportion of the financial statements; or
- fundamental to users understanding of the financial statements.

The effects on the audit opinion can be summarised in the table below:

	Auditor's judgement	
Nature of matter	**Material but not pervasive**	**Material and pervasive**
Financial statements are materially misstated.	Qualified opinion	Adverse opinion
Inability to obtain sufficient appropriate evidence.	Qualified opinion	Disclaimer of opinion

When the auditor modifies the opinion they include a basis for modification paragraph in the audit report that describes the matter. This paragraph is included after the opinion paragraph.

4.2 Qualified opinion

With a qualified opinion, the auditor is stating that whilst there are material misstatements, they are confined to a specific element of the financial statements but the remainder may be relied upon. Therefore, the opinion usually states that "except for the matters described in the Basis for Qualified Opinion paragraph, the financial statements present fairly....."

The text which follows is based on ISA 705 (Revised) *Modifications to the opinion in the independent auditor's report*.

We have audited ... (remaining words are the same as illustrated in the specimen report above).

We conducted our audit in accordance with ... (remaining words are the same as illustrated in the specimen report above).

As discussed in Note X to the financial statements, no depreciation has been provided in the financial statements which, in our opinion, is not in accordance with International Accounting Standards. The provision for the year ended 31 December 20X1, should be xxx based on the straight-line method of depreciation using annual rates of 5% for the building and 20% for the equipment. Accordingly, the non-current assets should be reduced by accumulated depreciation of xxx and the loss for the year and accumulated deficit should be increased by xxx and xxx, respectively.

In our opinion, except for the effects of the matter described in the Basis for Qualified Opinion paragraph, the financial statements present fairly, in all material respects, (or give a true and fair view of) the financial position of XYZ Co as at.... (remaining words are the same as illustrated in the specimen report above).

4.3 Adverse opinion

If the auditor concludes that the matter is pervasive, they are claiming that the financial statements cannot be relied upon in any part. The opinion will be reworded to state that the financial statements "do not present fairly...."

The text which follows is based on ISA 705 (Revised).

We have audited ... (remaining words are the same as illustrated in the specimen report above).

We conducted our audit in accordance with ... (remaining words are the same as illustrated in the specimen report above).

The reporting function: Chapter 12

In our opinion, because of the significance of the matter discussed in the Basis for Adverse Opinion paragraph, the financial statements do not present fairly (or do not give a true and fair view of) the financial position of XYZ Co as at 31 December 20X1, and of their financial performance and their cash flows for the year then ended in accordance with United Kingdom Generally Accepted Accounting Practice and do not comply with the Companies Act 2006.

Note that the adverse opinion is an extreme form of modification. It effectively recommends that the shareholders should not make any use of the financial statements.

4.4 Disclaimer of opinion

If the auditor gives a disclaimer of opinion they will state that they "do not express an opinion on the financial statements."

The text which follows is based on ISA 705 (Revised).

We were engaged to audit the accompanying statement of financial position of the XYZ Co as of 31 December 20X1, and the related statement of profit and loss and statement of cash flows for the year then ended. These financial statements are the responsibility of the Company's management. (Omit the sentence stating the responsibility of the auditor).

(The paragraph discussing the scope of the audit would either be omitted or amended according to the circumstances).

We were not able to observe all physical inventories and confirm accounts receivable due to limitations placed on the scope of our work by the company.

Because of the significance of the matters discussed in the Basis for Disclaimer of Opinion paragraph, we have not been able to obtain sufficient appropriate audit evidence to provide a basis for an audit opinion. Accordingly, we do not express an opinion on the financial statements.

As with the adverse opinion, this is such an extreme form of modification that it should be avoided unless the situation is so extreme that only a disclaimer would suffice.

> **Test your understanding 2**
>
> For each of the following situations which have arisen in two unrelated audit clients, select whether or not the audit opinion on the financial statements would be modified.
>
> (i) Alpha Co capitalised costs of £150,000 in respect of repairs and maintenance and included these costs in non-current assets. The amount capitalised represents 30% of Alpha Co's profit before tax. The directors refuse to make any adjustments in respect of this matter.
>
> (ii) There is a significant uncertainty about Beta Co's ability to continue as a going concern. The directors of Beta Co have prepared the financial statements on a going concern basis and have fully disclosed the uncertainty in the notes to the financial statements.

5 Additional paragraphs

Having formed their opinion, there are circumstances where the auditor must draw the reader's attention to additional matters. These are categorised as follows:

- matters already disclosed in the financial statements that are fundamental to understanding the financial statements. These are presented in Emphasis of Matter paragraphs; and
- other matters relevant to either understanding the audit, the auditor's responsibilities or the audit report. These are presented in Other Matter paragraphs.

We will also discuss the potential need for a Material Uncertainty Related to Going Concern paragraph and what this would entail.

5.1 Emphasis of matter paragraphs

These paragraphs draw the reader's attention to a note already disclosed in the financial statements. The matters referred to have to be fundamental to the readers' understanding of the financial statements. They are included immediately after the opinion paragraph. It is important to note that they do not affect the audit opinion.

Examples of where it may be necessary to include an Emphasis of Matter paragraph are as follows:

- an uncertainty relating to the future outcome of exceptional litigation
- early application of new accounting standards that has a pervasive effect on the financial statements
- a major catastrophe that has had a significant effect on the entity's financial position.

The text which follows is based on ISA 706 (Revised) *Emphasis of matter paragraphs* and other matter paragraphs in the independent auditor's report.

In our opinion ... (remaining words are the same as illustrated in the specimen unmodified report above).

Without qualifying our opinion we draw attention to Note X to the financial statements. The Company is the defendant in a lawsuit alleging infringement of certain patent rights and claiming royalties and punitive damages. The Company has filed a counter action, and preliminary hearings and discovery proceedings on both actions are in progress. The ultimate outcome of the matter cannot presently be determined, and no provision for any liability that may result has been made in the financial statements.

5.2 Material Uncertainty Related to Going Concern

Under ISA 570 (Revised), where there is a material uncertainty regarding the going concern status of the entity, which the directors have adequately disclosed in the financial statements, the auditor will continue to express an unmodified opinion, but must include a separate section under the heading 'Material Uncertainty Related to Going Concern'. This section will:

- draw attention to the note in the financial statements that discloses the matters giving rise to the material uncertainty, and
- state that these events or conditions indicate that a material uncertainty exists which may cast significant doubt on the entity's ability to continue as a going concern and that the auditor's opinion is not modified in respect of the matter.

The section headed 'Material Uncertainty Related to Going Concern' is included immediately after the Basis for Opinion paragraph. It should be noted that where the uncertainty is not adequately disclosed in the financial statements the auditor would modify the opinion.

AUDIT AND ASSURANCE

5.3 Other matter paragraphs

Circumstances where these may be included are as follows:

- When national regulations require the auditor to elaborate on their responsibilities.

- When there is an inability to obtain sufficient appropriate evidence imposed by management but the auditor cannot withdraw from the engagement due to legal restrictions.

- When the financial statements of the prior period have been audited by a predecessor auditor or were not audited.

> **Test your understanding 3**
>
> Described below are situations which have arisen in separate audits. For each situation describe the effect on the audit report.
>
> 1. A fire in the warehouse of Oak Co destroyed the inventory sheets which were the only record of the company's inventory at the year-end. The company has included an estimated inventory figure of £780,000. The pre-tax profits for the year were £1.1 million and total assets were £6.5 million.
>
> 2. Elm Co has included a note in the financial statements explaining that 90% of its revenue is derived from a national retailer with whom it has a three year renewable contract. This contract is due for renewal in September. However, the directors require the audit report to be signed on 31 May.
>
> 3. Ben and Holly Co has included a provision for doubtful debts of £100,000 in the year end accounts. Obviously the provision cannot be estimated with complete accuracy but the reporting partner believes it should be materially higher.

6 Summary

It is important that you understand the following matters:

- the matters to be included in reports to management
- the matters to be included in the auditors' report:
    - in all cases, and
    - by exception only
- the meaning of the term 'financial statements' in the context of the auditors' report
- the factual matters required by statute to be included in the auditors' report if they are not included in the financial statements
- the contents of the ISA on auditors' opinions and in particular:
    - the distinction between disagreement, scope limitation and inherent uncertainty
    - the circumstances giving rise to uncertainties and disagreement
    - the format and wording of an unmodified opinion
    - the auditors' report wording associated with the various forms of modification.

Test your understanding answers

Test your understanding 1

(i) **Consequences**

Equipment recorded in the register may not exist or may have been stolen.

Equipment in existence, acquisitions or disposals may not be recorded.

Equipment may be fully written down but still in use.

Equipment may be impaired and consequently overvalued.

Depreciation charges on the equipment may be inappropriate.

(ii) **Recommendations**

Periodic reconciliation of physical equipment to register to ensure completeness of recording.

Periodic reconciliation of entries in the register to physical equipment to ensure existence and in good condition.

Reconciliation to be performed independent of custodian.

Differences to be reported and investigated.

Monitoring of procedures to ensure checks are undertaken.

Test your understanding 2

(i) Modified.
(ii) Unmodified.

> **Test your understanding 3**
>
> 1. The issue here is an inability to obtain sufficient appropriate audit evidence. Due to the loss of the physical inventory count records the auditor will not be able to perform normal audit procedures in this area.
>
>   The inventory balance is clearly material to the accounts as it represents 70% of profit and 12% of total assets. However in this instance the issue is the extent to which the inventory balance quoted is incorrect. As the inability to obtain evidence leads to uncertainty, it is not possible to quantify exactly the size of any adjustment.
>
>   Assuming the inability to obtain evidence is material but not so material or pervasive the audit opinion would be modified as we would give a qualified opinion.
>
> 2. There is a significant uncertainty at the year-end in respect of whether or not the company is a going concern. This is dependent on the renewal of the contract which is significant to the viability of the company. The auditor needs to establish the likelihood of renewal. If the company is not a going concern then the accounts should be prepared on the break-up basis.
>
>   No information has been provided to quantify the adjustments but these are likely to be material.
>
>   There are a few possible impacts on the audit report as follows:
>
>   (i) Assuming the accounts are prepared on a going concern basis and if the auditor agrees and is satisfied that the disclosure is appropriate, an unmodified audit opinion would be given but the audit report would include a section for Material Uncertainty Related to Going Concern to explain the significant uncertainty.
>
>   (ii) Assuming the accounts are prepared on a going concern basis but the auditor disagrees then an adverse opinion would be given as this is likely to be deemed so material or pervasive.
>
> 3. A qualified opinion will be given based on disagreement. As the reporting partner disagrees with the size of the provision necessary.

AUDIT AND ASSURANCE

The legal and professional framework

Introduction

In this chapter, we will discuss the legal requirements of auditors according to the Companies Act 2006 and how an auditor is appointed and removed from their position. We will also consider the rights and duties of both auditors and directors.

ASSESSMENT CRITERIA	CONTENTS
The role of corporate governance in the audit and assurance process (1.3)	1 Legal requirements
The role of internal audit (1.4)	2 Eligibility and ineligibility of auditors
	3 Appointment of auditors
	4 Vacation of office
	5 Duties and rights of auditors
	6 Duties of directors in accounting and reporting matters
	7 Corporate governance

The legal and professional framework: **Chapter 13**

1 Legal requirements

1.1 The legal and professional framework

The Companies Act 2006 (CA 2006) provides the legal framework within which the auditor operates. Although the law relating to auditors is quite detailed, the subject matter is not essentially difficult.

The auditor carries out their role in accordance with the profession's ethical guidance and regulations.

Regulations are bound by professional bodies to ensure that their members:

- are independent
- are competent, and
- conduct their affairs in a professional manner.

The regulations of the **Institute of Chartered Accountants in England and Wales (ICAEW)** take the form of guidelines on professional ethics, backed up by a disciplinary system which investigates allegations of professional misconduct. The **Association of Chartered Certified Accountants (ACCA)** issues Rules of Professional Conduct. The **AAT** has a Code of Professional Ethics which its members must adhere to.

1.2 Legal rules

Most external audit work is concerned with companies registered under the Companies Act 2006. This Act also regulates the auditors of such companies.

The legislation relating to the auditor is designed to:

- ensure the competence of auditors by requiring them to be professionally qualified
- ensure the auditor's independence by disqualifying certain people from eligibility for appointment and by controlling the manner of their removal or resignation
- ensure the auditor's integrity by requiring the auditor to be a member of a body which upholds and enforces high ethical standards
- define the auditor's duties and the matters covered by their report, and
- give the auditor the rights needed to carry out their defined duties.

1.3 Statutory requirement for an audit

A company registered under the Companies Act can be limited by shares (public or private), limited by guarantee or unlimited (private).

Companies Act 2006 s485 requires registered companies to appoint an auditor.

There are two exceptions (subject to specified criteria being met):

- dormant companies (s480)
- companies with at least 2 of the following: an annual turnover of no more than £10.2 million; assets worth no more than £5.1 million; 50 or fewer employees on average.

1.4 The auditor's function

CA 2006 requires the auditor to report on the annual accounts laid before the members at the Annual General Meeting (AGM) during their term of office.

The auditor holds office from the conclusion of the general meeting at which the auditor is appointed until the end of the next general meeting when accounts are presented to the members.

CA 2006 requires the auditor to carry out such investigations as will enable the auditor to form their opinion.

Note that the Companies Act does not say (in as many words) that a company's accounts or financial statements must be audited. But taken together, the following requirements mean that this is the case:

- Auditor's report to be annexed to accounts.
- Duty of auditors to report to members and to carry out any investigations necessary.
- Requirement for companies to appoint auditors.

1.5 Unincorporated businesses

There is no overall statutory requirement for unincorporated businesses to have an audit; any regulations in this respect would depend on legislation peculiar to a specific type of business (e.g. the Financial Services Act 2012), or on the terms of the engagement as agreed between auditor and client.

The legal and professional framework: Chapter 13

2 Eligibility and ineligibility of auditors

2.1 Who can be an auditor?

To be an auditor a person or firm (a body corporate or partnership) must fulfil certain criteria (CA 2006). They must be a member of a recognised supervisory body and have an approved qualification.

2.2 Members of a Recognised Supervisory Body (RSB)

RSBs are currently:

- Institute of Chartered Accountants in England and Wales (ICAEW)
- Institute of Chartered Accountants of Scotland (ICAS)
- Institute of Chartered Accountants in Ireland (ICAI)
- Association of Chartered Certified Accountants (ACCA).

2.3 Appropriate qualification

The auditor must be a person appropriately qualified or a firm controlled by persons who are appropriately qualified i.e. either:

- a member of one of the bodies listed above
- a holder of a qualification from a Recognised Qualifying Body (RQB), or
- a holder of a similar non-UK qualification.

All four chartered bodies mentioned above have RSB and RQB status.

2.4 Who may not be an auditor?

The following persons are ineligible for appointment as auditor (CA 2006):

- an officer or employee of the company (or any associated undertaking), or
- a partner or employee of an officer or employee of the company.

The officers of a company are generally agreed to be the directors and the company secretary.

2.5 Effect of ineligibility

If an existing auditor becomes disqualified the auditor should:

- resign immediately, and
- give notice to the company.

The penalty for failing to do so is a fine (CA 2006).

If the company auditor was ineligible for any part of the period during which the audit was conducted, the Secretary of State can direct the company to retain a person who is eligible to:

- carry out a second audit
- review the first audit and report, giving reasons why a second audit is needed (CA 2006).

3 Appointment of auditors

3.1 Introduction

The main statutory provisions for the appointment of auditors are contained in the CA 2006 and are summarised below.

3.2 Appointment by members

When

- At AGM (or any other meeting with ordinary resolution) when annual accounts are presented:
  - to reappoint retiring auditor
  - to appoint an auditor other than the retiring auditor
  - to reappoint an auditor appointed by the directors.

How

- Ordinary resolution.

- Ordinary resolution with special notice (28 days).

The legal and professional framework: **Chapter 13**

When

- Private companies only. No AGM necessary to reappoint retiring auditor (automatic annual reappointment for as long as election remains in force).

- To fill a casual vacancy if the directors do not make an appointment.

How

- Elective (100%) resolution with ordinary notice. Revoked by ordinary resolution.

- Ordinary resolution with special notice.

3.3 Appointment by directors

When

- To fill a casual vacancy.
- To appoint first auditors, between the date of incorporation and the first AGM.

How

- Reappointment must be by members at next AGM, by ordinary resolution with special notice.

3.4 Appointment by Secretary of State

When

- If at the conclusion of the AGM no auditor is appointed.

How

- Company must inform the Secretary of State within one week.

The members do not 'ratify' an audit appointment made by the directors. Where the directors are empowered to make an appointment they may do so without the approval or consent of the members. When the term of office of an auditor appointed by the directors expires, the members may choose to:

- reappoint the retiring auditor, or
- make a new appointment.

The auditor's remuneration is fixed by those who appoint the auditor. In practice, this task is usually delegated to the directors.

AUDIT AND ASSURANCE

 Test your understanding 1

In relation to the appointment of auditors, when will appointment by the Secretary of State take place?

(a) To fill a casual vacancy.

(b) If at the conclusion of the AGM, no auditor is appointed.

(c) To appoint the first auditors on incorporation.

4 Vacation of office

4.1 Vacation

The main statutory provisions for the vacation of the office of auditor are contained in the CA 2006 and are summarised as follows:

4.2 Removal (before expiry of term of office)

Method

- Ordinary resolution with special notice (28 days).
- Notice of resolution to state if auditor has made representations.

Auditor's rights

- To have written representations of a reasonable length circulated to all members.
- To receive notice of, attend and be heard at the meetings at which:
  - their term of office would have expired, and
  - it is proposed to appoint a new auditor.

The legal and professional framework: Chapter 13

4.3 Resignation method

Method

- Auditor must submit written notice to the company.
- Company must notify:
  - the registrar of companies, and
  - all parties entitled to receive copies of accounts.

Auditor's rights

- To requisition an Extraordinary General Meeting to consider reasons for resignation.
- To require the company to circulate a statement in advance of the meeting:
  - at which their term of office would have expired
  - to appoint a new auditor.

4.4 Statement by person ceasing to hold office as auditor

Whenever an auditor ceases to hold office (for whatever reason) the auditor must deposit at the registered office of the company either:

- a statement that there are no circumstances connected with their ceasing to hold office which the auditor considers should be brought to the attention of the members or payables, or
- a statement of any such circumstances.

A notice of resignation is not effective unless accompanied by either statement. In the case of failure to seek reappointment, the statement is required at least 14 days before the next auditors are appointed. In any other case, this statement must be deposited within 14 days of ceasing to hold office.

Reason for vacation

- Resignation
- With notice of resignation
- Other

When deposited

- Failure to seek reappointment
- At least 14 days before next auditor appointed (usually AGM)
- Within 14 days of ceasing to hold office.

If there are circumstances to be brought to the attention of members or payables the company must send a copy to every person entitled to receive a copy of the accounts.

The purpose of these provisions is to ensure that the members are made aware of any important circumstances surrounding the removal or resignation, such as disagreement over an accounting policy which may be the reason for directors wanting to remove the auditor.

Note that the auditor may not use their rights to secure publicity for defamatory material about the client's directors or anyone else. The Court has the power, on application by the company or any other aggrieved person, to order that the representations not be circulated or read out, on the grounds that it is defamatory.

5 Duties and rights of auditors

5.1 Primary duty

The primary duty of an auditor is set out in the CA 2006, which requires the auditor to report to the company's members on every set of accounts (i.e. statement of financial position, statement of profit or loss, etc. and accompanying notes) of which a copy is laid before the members in respect of an accounting reference period.

The auditor's report must be read to the members at the general meeting (normally the AGM) and must be available for their inspection.

The report must state whether in the auditor's opinion:

- the accounts have been properly prepared in accordance with the CA 2006, and

- a true and fair view is given of the state of affairs of the company at the end of its financial year, and of the profit or loss for that year.

5.2 Other duties

In preparing their report an auditor is required by the CA 2006 to carry out such investigations as will enable the auditor to form an opinion as to whether:

- proper accounting records have been kept by the company

- proper returns, adequate for audit purposes, have been received from any branches not visited by the auditor, and

- the accounts are in agreement with the records and returns.

If the auditor forms the opinion that any of these are not the case the auditor must say so in their report.

Also, if either of the following situations arises the auditor should state the fact in their report:

- if the auditor has been unable to obtain all the information and explanations necessary for their audit, and
- if there is any inconsistency between the accounts and the directors' report.

The following mnemonic may help you to remember these requirements:

R eturns from branches

A greement with records and returns

P roper accounting records

I nformation and explanations

D irectors' report consistent.

CA 2006 also requires that if the accounts do not contain the necessary information on the director's emoluments, loans and transactions, then the omitted information must be disclosed in the auditor's report.

5.3 Rights of auditors

The following rights are given to the auditor of a company by the CA 2006 to enable the auditor to carry out their duties effectively and to make their report to the members:

- to have access at all times to the books, accounts and vouchers of the company
- to require from the officers of the company any information and explanations which the auditor thinks necessary for the purposes of their audit
- to receive notice of and attend any general meeting of members, and to be heard at any general meeting on business which concerns the auditor.

CA 2006 extends the right to require information and explanations from the company's officers. It is the duty of subsidiary companies and their auditors to make any information available to the holding company's auditors to enable them to carry out their duties.

In addition, the auditor has important rights specified in other sections already dealt with – in particular the rights associated with their removal or resignation.

6 Duties of directors in accounting and reporting matters

6.1 Introduction

A director can be described as an agent having a fiduciary relationship with a principal, i.e. the employing company. A fiduciary relationship is one of trust.

6.2 Duties in respect of company accounts (CA 2006)

- To keep books of accounts and proper accounting records.
- To produce a statement of profit or loss and statement of financial position in such a fashion as to show a true and fair view.
- To produce a directors' report which is consistent with the financial statements and contains certain specified information.

6.3 Special matters affecting directors' transactions with the company

The directors are obliged to:

- disclose any loans or credit arrangements permitted under CA 2006
- disclose all emoluments received by them in respect of their office and any payments received as compensation for loss of office (these sums must be approved by the company at a general meeting)
- ensure that the financial statements give, to the best of their knowledge and belief, all the statutory information required by the Act
- ensure they do not to give misleading or reckless information to the company auditors (a criminal offence for directors or officers under CA 2006).

7 Corporate governance

7.1 Introduction

Corporate governance is the system of rules, practices and processes by which a company is directed and controlled. Corporate governance refers to the way in which companies are governed and to what purpose. It identifies who has power and accountability, and who make decisions.

7.2 Principles of good corporate governance

Definition

Corporate governance is the means by which a company is operated and controlled.

The aim of corporate governance is to ensure that companies are run well in the interests of their shareholders, employees and other key stakeholders such as the wider community.

The aim is to try and prevent company directors from abusing their power which may adversely affect these stakeholder groups. For example, the directors may pay themselves large salaries and bonuses whilst claiming they have no money to pay a dividend to shareholders. Similarly, they may be making large numbers of staff redundant but awarding themselves a pay rise.

In response to major scandals (e.g. Enron), regulators sought to change the rules surrounding the governance of companies, particularly publicly owned ones.

In the US, the Sarbanes Oxley Act (2002) introduced a set of rigorous corporate governance laws. The UK Corporate Governance Code introduced a set of best practice corporate governance initiatives into the UK.

Advantages of a company following good corporate governance principles:

- Greater transparency
- Greater accountability
- Efficiency of operations
- Better able to respond to risks
- Less likely to be mismanaged.

AUDIT AND ASSURANCE

The UK Corporate Governance Code is particularly important for publicly traded companies because large amounts of money are invested in them, either by 'small' shareholders, or from pension schemes and other financial institutions. The wealth of these companies significantly affects the health of the economies where their shares are traded.

7.3 The comply or explain principle

The listing rules for the London Stock Exchange require that public listed companies disclose how they have complied with the code and explain, in their Annual Report, where they have not applied the code. This is referred to as the 'comply or explain' principle.

The aim of the comply or explain principle is to empower shareholders to make an informed evaluation as to whether non-compliance is justified, given the company's circumstances.

Private companies are also encouraged to conform, however there is no requirement for disclosure of compliance in private company accounts.

7.3.1 The UK Corporate Governance Code (2018)

The Financial Reporting Council's (FRC) mission is to promote transparency and integrity in business, by setting the UK Corporate Governance Code.

The first version of the Code was published in 1992. It defined corporate governance as 'the system by which companies are directed and controlled. Boards of directors are responsible for the governance of their companies. The shareholders' role in governance is to appoint the directors and the auditors and to satisfy themselves that an appropriate governance structure is in place.' This remains true today, but the environment in which companies, their shareholders and wider stakeholders operate continues to develop rapidly.

At the heart of the Code is a set of Principles that emphasise the value of good corporate governance to long-term sustainable success. By applying the Principles, following the more detailed Provisions and using the associated guidance, companies can demonstrate throughout their reporting how the governance of the company contributes to its long-term sustainable success and achieves wider objectives.

Board leadership and company purpose

Principles

- A successful company is led by an effective and entrepreneurial board, whose role is to promote the long-term sustainable success of the company, generating value for shareholders and contributing to wider society.

- The board should establish the company's purpose, values and strategy, and satisfy itself that these and its culture are aligned. All directors must act with integrity, lead by example and promote the desired culture.

- The board should ensure that the necessary resources are in place for the company to meet its objectives and measure performance against them. The board should also establish a framework of prudent and effective controls, which enable risk to be assessed and managed.

- In order for the company to meet its responsibilities to shareholders and stakeholders, the board should ensure effective engagement with, and encourage participation from, these parties.

- The board should ensure that workforce policies and practices are consistent with the company's values and support its long-term sustainable success. The workforce should be able to raise any matters of concern.

Division of responsibilities

Principles

- The chair leads the board and is responsible for its overall effectiveness in directing the company. They should demonstrate objective judgement throughout their tenure and promote a culture of openness and debate. In addition, the chair facilitates constructive board relations and the effective contribution of all non-executive directors, and ensures that directors receive accurate, timely and clear information.

- The board should include an appropriate combination of executive and non-executive (and, in particular, independent non-executive) directors, such that no one individual or small group of individuals dominates the board's decision-making. There should be a clear division of responsibilities between the leadership of the board and the executive leadership of the company's business.

AUDIT AND ASSURANCE

- Non-executive directors should have sufficient time to meet their board responsibilities. They should provide constructive challenge, strategic guidance, offer specialist advice and hold management to account.
- The board, supported by the company secretary, should ensure that it has the policies, processes, information, time and resources it needs in order to function effectively and efficiently.

Audit, risk and internal control

Principles

- The board should establish formal and transparent policies and procedures to ensure the independence and effectiveness of internal and external audit functions and satisfy itself on the integrity of financial and narrative statements.
- The board should present a fair, balanced and understandable assessment of the company's position and prospects.
- The board should establish procedures to manage risk, oversee the internal control framework, and determine the nature and extent of the principal risks the company is willing to take in order to achieve its long-term strategic objectives.

7.4 The importance of an effective audit committee

```
                        The audit
                        committee
        ┌──────────────────┼──────────────────┐
   Composition         Objectives          Function
        │                  │                  │
   Minimum of       Increase public        Financial
   3 non-execs         confidence          statements
        │                  │                  │
   At least 1 with   Financial awareness    Controls
   financial expertise  of non-execs           │
                          │              Internal audit
                      Liaison with             │
                    external auditors     External audit
                                               │
                                         Whistleblowing
```

The Code recommends audit committees be comprised of at least three members, all of whom should be independent non-executive directors and one of whom should have recent and relevant financial experience.

The objectives of the audit committee include:

- Increasing public confidence in the credibility and objectivity of published financial information (including unaudited interim statements).

- Assisting directors (particularly executive directors) in meeting their responsibilities in respect of financial reporting.

- Strengthening the independent position of a company's external auditor by providing an additional channel of communication.

Benefits of an audit committee include:

- Improved credibility of the financial statements through an impartial review of the financial statements and discussion of significant issues with the external auditors.

- Increased public confidence in the audit opinion as the audit committee will monitor the independence of the external auditors.

- Stronger control environment as the audit committee help to create a culture of compliance and control.

- The skills, knowledge and experience (and independence) of the audit committee members can be an invaluable resource for a business.

- It may be easier and cheaper to arrange finance, as the presence of an audit committee can give a perception of good corporate governance.

- It will be less of a burden to meet listing requirements if an audit committee (which is usually a listing requirement) is already established.

- The internal audit function will report to the audit committee increasing their independence and adding weight to their recommendations.

7.5 Internal audit and corporate governance

Internal audit has an important role to play in assisting the board, and audit committee, fulfil their corporate governance responsibilities.

Internal auditors will work closely with the audit committee. The audit committee will:

- Ensure that the internal auditor has direct access to the board chair and to the audit committee and is accountable to the audit committee.

- Review and assess the annual internal audit work plan.

- Receive periodic reports on the results of internal audit work.

- Review and monitor management's responsiveness to the internal auditor's findings and recommendations.

- Meet with the head of internal audit at least once a year without the presence of management.

- Monitor and assess the effectiveness of internal audit in the overall context of the company's risk management system.

The roles and functions of internal audit are covered in Chapter 16.

Test your understanding 2

Which two of the following are functions of audit committees?

(a) Planning the annual external audit.

(b) Reviewing the effectiveness of internal financial controls.

(c) Reviewing and monitoring the external auditor's independence.

Test your understanding 3

Which of the following statements best defines Corporate Governance?

(a) Corporate governance refers to the importance a company attaches to systems and controls.

(b) Corporate governance is the means by which a company is operated and controlled.

(c) Corporate governance is the extent to which a company is audited, both internally and externally.

(d) Corporate governance is an appraisal activity as a service to the entity.

8 Summary

The legal provisions are an essential part of the framework within which the external auditor operates. You should ensure that you are familiar with the:

- requirement for an audit and the position of dormant and small companies
- rules governing eligibility and ineligibility
- rules governing the appointment, removal and resignation of auditors
- duties and rights of the auditor
- duties of directors in accounting and reporting matters, including the need to maintain proper accounting records.

Corporate governance

- Principles of good corporate governance.
- Audit committees – importance and objectives.
- Internal audit and corporate governance.

Test your understanding answers

Test your understanding 1

Answer (b)

If at the conclusion of the AGM no auditor has been appointed then the Secretary of State will step in. This is very rare.

Test your understanding 2

Answer (b) and (c)

Test your understanding 3

Answer (b)

AUDIT AND ASSURANCE

Professional ethics

Introduction

In this chapter, we will introduce the concept of auditor independence and discuss the five fundamental principles. We will also consider the threats to auditor independence and discuss safeguards that can be put in place to mitigate or eliminate these threats, allowing the auditor to continue with their engagement.

ASSESSMENT CRITERIA

The principles and characteristics of ethical codes and the implications for the auditor (2.1)

Threats to the independence of auditors (2.2)

Safeguards to eliminate or reduce threats to the independence of auditors (2.3)

The fundamental ethical principles in relation to internal and external audit (2.4)

CONTENTS

1. Independence of auditors
2. Fundamental ethical principles
3. Confidentiality and conflicts of interest
4. Threats to auditor independence
5. Data security

1 Independence of auditors

1.1 Introduction

Assurance providers should be, and be seen to be independent.

> **Definition**
>
> **Independence** – a state of mind that permits the expression of a conclusion without being affected by influences that compromise professional judgement.

Without doubt, the most important professional attribute of auditors (whether external or internal) is their independence. Unless they are totally independent so that their ability to express an opinion is never subordinated to the will of a client's management, the objectivity, and thus the value of the report to the client's members or proprietors, is lost. The AAT Code of Professional Ethics requires auditors to consider whether their independence might be questioned by external parties because of:

- business relationships
- personal relationships
- long association with the client
- fee dependence; and
- non-audit services provided.

Where there is a lack of independence in the external auditor, shareholders' interests can be at risk from:

- auditors and directors colluding to produce financial statements containing wrong or misleading information or suppressing information, and
- auditors yielding to directors on matters of principle in order to preserve their appointment.

1.2 Opportunities for directors to overrule auditors

Where the directors are in a position to exert influence over the members

In many cases where shareholders are not involved with the day-to-day running of a company, and especially where no one member or group of members holds a sizeable proportion of the share capital, it is not easy for them to oppose moves made by directors without making common cause at an annual general meeting. Thus if a director or directors (acting as members) propose a change of auditors, they stand a good chance of approving the proposals despite any representations made by the existing auditors.

There are, of course, very many companies, whose directors hold all or a majority of the shares, and where the auditor's position is potentially even weaker.

Where the auditor is in any way dependent on the client

For example, where:

- a substantial part of their fee income derives from that client
- the auditor is in some way personally involved with the client, or
- the auditor receives preferential treatment from their client (e.g. substantial discounts on the client's products).

In such cases, an auditor is more likely to capitulate when a disagreement arises between the auditor and a client's directors. The ultimate sanction (of qualification of the auditor's report) may not be invoked if the resulting loss of the audit would have a material effect on the auditor and/or their firm.

In practice, the majority of firms have their own rules preventing involvement with their clients, and the guidelines for professional ethics published by each of the professional bodies advises against most of the above mentioned situations, but the efficiency of this safeguard obviously depends greatly on the integrity of the auditor.

1.3 Objectivity

Objectivity is a state of mind, but in certain roles the preservation of objectivity needs to be protected and demonstrated by the maintenance of an auditor's independence from influences which could affect his or her objectivity.

An auditor's objectivity must be beyond question. That objectivity can only be assured if the auditor is, and is seen to be, independent.

1.4 Areas of risk regarding an auditor's objectivity

- Objectivity may be threatened or appear to be threatened by undue dependence on any audit client or group of connected clients regarding fees.

- An auditor's objectivity may be threatened or appear to be threatened as a consequence of a family or other close personal or business relationship.

- A member's objectivity may be threatened or appear to be threatened where the auditor holds a beneficial interest in the shares or other forms of investment in a company upon which the practice reports. Where a partner or member of staff holds shares in any capacity in a company which is an audit client of the practice they should not be voted on at any general meeting of the company in relation to the appointment, removal or remuneration of auditors.

- Objectivity may be threatened or appear to be threatened by a loan to or from an audit client.

- The existence of significant overdue fees from an audit client or group of connected clients can be a threat or appear to be a threat to objectivity akin to that of a loan.

- Objectivity may be threatened or appear to be threatened by acceptance of goods, services or hospitality from an audit client.

- There are occasions where objectivity may be threatened or appear to be threatened by the provision to an audit client of services other than the audit.

We will review these threats in more detail below and also consider the safeguards that can be applied to mitigate against the risks.

1.5 Review procedures

To guard against loss of independence, every audit firm should establish review procedures, including an annual review, to:

- satisfy itself that each engagement may be accepted/continued, and
- identify situations where independence may be at risk so that appropriate safeguards can be applied.

Wherever the review procedures indicate that an audit assignment should be accepted or continued only with additional safeguards against loss of independence, the engagement partner's decision and the range of safeguards appropriate to the assignment should be subject to an independence review by a partner unconnected with the engagement.

Safeguards against loss of independence should include the following, according to the size and circumstances of the practice and the size and circumstances of the clients:

- the inclusion of a manager or other qualified employee in the audit team
- rotation of the engagement partner, and
- rotation of senior members of staff.

AUDIT AND ASSURANCE

2 Fundamental ethical principles

2.1 Principles based or rules based guidance

There are two main approaches to ethical guidance.

Principles based	Rules based
Encourages the accountant to use judgement	May be easier to follow because it is objective
Requires compliance with the spirit of the guidance	Needs frequent updating to ensure the guidance applies to new situations
Flexible, so can be applied to new, unusual or rapidly changing situations	May encourage accounts to interpret requirements narrowly in order to get round the spirit of the requirements
Can still incorporate rules where necessary	

A principles based approach is taken by the AAT.

2.2 AAT Code of Professional Ethics

Under the AAT Code of Professional Ethics, auditors must comply with five fundamental ethical principles as follows:

- **Integrity**

    Auditors should be straightforward and honest in al professional/ business relationships.

- **Objectivity**

    Auditors do not allow bias or conflict of interest in business judgements.

- **Professional competence and due care**

    Auditors have a duty to maintain their professional knowledge and ensure all their work is planned and completed to a high standard.

- **Confidentiality**

    Information on clients must not be disclosed without appropriate authority, or used for personal advantage.

- **Professional behaviour**

    Auditors must not act in such a way that could bring the accountancy profession in to disrepute.

Professional ethics: Chapter 14

> **Test your understanding 1**
>
> Which of the following is not one of the stated fundamental principles in the AAT Code of Professional Ethics?
>
> (a) Integrity
> (b) Courtesy
> (c) Objectivity
> (d) Confidentiality

3 Confidentiality and conflicts of interest

3.1 Confidentiality – improper disclosure

Information confidential to a client or employer acquired in the course of professional work should not be disclosed except where consent has been obtained from the client, employer or other proper source, or where there is a legal right or duty to disclose.

Right to disclose	Duty to disclose
Client permission obtained	If ordered to disclose by a court
Where disclosure is in the public interest	If required by a regulator e.g. Financial Conduct Authority, Charity Commission
To defend the firm in a negligence claim	Suspicions of money laundering should be reported to the National Crime Agency
	Suspicions of terrorist activity should be reported to the police

Where a member is in doubt as to whether the auditor has a right or duty to disclose the auditor should, if appropriate, initially discuss the matter fully within their firm or organisation. If that is not appropriate, or if it fails to resolve the problem, the auditor should consider taking legal advice and/or consult their Recognised Supervisory Body.

3.2 Improper use of information

A member acquiring or receiving confidential information in the course of his or her professional work should neither use nor appear to use that information for their personal advantage or for the advantage of a third party.

When a member changes their firm or employment, the auditor is entitled to use experience gained in the previous firm or employment but not confidential information acquired there.

3.3 Acting for competing clients

There is nothing improper about an accountant having two clients whose interests are in conflict. Indeed, many accountancy firms use their expertise in a particular industry sector as a selling point, which increases the chances of them having clients who are in competition with each other.

It is important that the firm can demonstrate that their work on one client will not adversely affect another client.

The accountant must notify the relevant clients of the situation and seek their consent to continue to act for both parties.

If the firm continues to act for two clients whose interests are in conflict then safeguards should be implemented to preserve confidentiality:

- Separate teams
- Information barriers
- Ensure no overlap between different teams
- Physical separation of teams
- Procedures for maintaining security of paper and electronic records
- Confidentiality agreements signed by employees and partners
- Review of the application of safeguards by an independent partner.

If adequate safeguards cannot be implemented, the firm may have to cease to act for one or both of the clients.

Professional ethics: **Chapter 14**

4 Threats to auditor independence

4.1 Threats to objectivity

The AAT Code sets out the approach that accountants should take to independence issues:

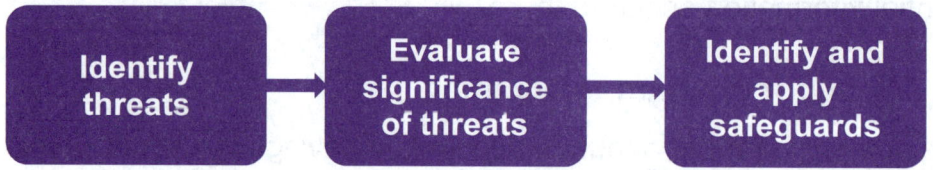

Safeguards are steps that the accountant can take to eliminate the threats, or reduce it to an acceptable level.

If no safeguards are available, the accountant should:

- Eliminate the interest or activities causing the threat
- If this is not possible, decline or discontinue the engagement.

4.2 Threats to objectivity

There are five threats to objectivity that you need to be aware of.

We will now review the threats in more detail and consider the safeguards that can be applied to mitigate the risks.

4.2.1 Self-interest threat

A self-interest threat arises where the auditor has a financial or non-financial interest in a client that could influence their judgement or behaviour.

Threats	Safeguards
Fee dependency Over-dependence on an audit client could lead to the auditor making decisions to ensure they do not upset the client.	Listed clients: Fees for audit and non-audit services shall not exceed 10% of the firm's fee income. Where fees amount to 5%–10%, this fact needs to be disclosed to the ethics partner and those charged with governance at the client and appropriate safeguards adopted where necessary. Non-listed clients: Fees for audit and non-audit services shall not exceed 15% of the firm's fee income. Where fees amount to 10%–15%, this fact needs to be disclosed to the ethics partner and those charged with governance at the client and appropriate safeguards adopted where necessary.
Share ownership The auditor may want to maximise their return and therefore overlook adjustments that would affect the value of their investment.	Owning shares in the audit client is prohibited.
Gifts and hospitality Acceptance of gifts and hospitality from audit clients can create a self-interest threat as the auditor may feel indebted to the client.	Only minor gifts of trivial and inconsequential value should be accepted. If in doubt, refer to the firm's ethics partner.
Personal relationships The auditor may have a personal interest in how successful the client is.	Remove individual with the relationship from audit team.

Employment with client The employee will not wish to do anything that could affect their potential future employment.	Ensure employees notify the audit firm straight away about their impending employment. Remove individual from audit team. Independent review of individual's work on that audit client.
Overdue fees The overdue fees may be regarded as a loan and loans are not permitted to an audit client.	Do not perform any more work until payment arrangement in place. If fees remain unpaid for a significant period of time, consider whether this constitutes a loan and whether it is appropriate to continue/seek reappointment.

4.2.2 Self-review threat

A self-review threat arises where there is a risk of the auditor reviewing their own work that could influence their judgement.

Threats	Safeguards
Provision of non-audit services Providing non-audit services e.g. accountancy services, taxation calculation, internal audit, may mean that the auditor is unlikely to admit errors in their own work. Also, the auditor may place too much reliance on their own work.	Before accepting non-audit work, the auditor must consider whether a reasonable and informed third party would regard the non-audit work as impairing the firm's objectivity and independence. General safeguards for non-audit work include: • Separate teams for the audit and non-audit work • Engagement quality review of the work and conclusions of the audit team in relation to the non-audit service. Some non-audit services are explicitly prohibited for listed clients, for example preparation of tax forms, payroll services, valuation services and legal services.
Client staff joins audit firm If the employee was involved in the production of financial statements, they may not make independent decisions.	Such individuals should not be assigned to the audit if that person would be evaluating elements of the financial statements for which they had prepared accounting records. They should not be involved in the audit of that client for 2 years.

4.2.3 Familiarity threat

A familiarity threat arises due to a long or close relationship with a client. The auditor may become too sympathetic to the client's interests or too accepting of the client's work.

Threats	Safeguards
Long association of senior staff The auditor may become too trusting of the client.	Listed clients: Engagement partner rotation after 5 years (can extend by 2 years if necessary to safeguard audit quality). Engagement quality reviewer rotation after 7 years. Non-listed clients: Audit firms should have a mechanism in place for monitoring the length of time that key team members have been associated with recurring engagements.
Personal relationships A familiarity threat may arise where a member of the audit team has a personal relationship with someone at the client who can exert significant influence over the financial statements.	Remove individual from audit team.
Audit staff join the client A threat arises if the audit staff member can exert significant influence over the audit team.	Where a partner (Engagement partner or Quality review partner) leaves the firm to become a director/key management at the client, the firm must resign as auditor and cannot accept reappointment for 2 years. Any other member of the audit team: the firm shall consider the composition of the audit team.

4.2.4 Advocacy threat

An advocacy threat arises where an auditor promotes a client's interest of position to the point where the auditor's independence is compromised.

Threats	Safeguards
Representing or promoting the client The audit firm could be seen as 'taking sides' with the client.	These services should always be declined.

4.2.5 Intimidation threat

An intimidation threat arises where an auditor is deterred from acting objectively due to perceived or actual threatening behaviour from the client.

Threats	Safeguards
Overpowering client An overpowering client could put undue pressure or exert too much influence on the auditor.	Consider composition of audit team.

Test your understanding 2

Which of the threats to objectivity is affected by the following statement?

The client has requested that the auditor assist them with the selection of a new accounting package.

(a) Self-interest

(b) Familiarity

(c) Self-review

5 Data security

5.1 The importance of data security

Accountants are required to keep client information confidential. This is an important aspect of the trust between client and accountant as, to do their job, accountants require access to information about their business that clients would not want made public externally to the business and, in some cases, such as where it relates to pay or future intentions of the directors, internally to the business either.

In practice, this means that an accountant should not discuss client matters with anyone outside the firm of accountants and, in cases where there is a conflict of interest with another audit client, with anyone outside of the team assigned to that client.

There is a risk of information passing outside the business if assurance providers work on a different client's file at another client's premises, or by losing or leaving files unprotected (for example, in a car which might be stolen) or through lack of electronic controls (for example, by computer hacking).

Security procedures are recommended to prevent accidental disclosure of information, such as:

- Not discussing client matters with any party outside of the accountancy firm (for example, friends and family, even in a general way).
- Not discussing client matters with colleagues in a public place.
- Not leaving audit files unattended in unsecured premises (at a client's premises or elsewhere).
- Not removing working papers from the office, unless strictly necessary.
- Not working on electronic working papers on systems that do not have the requisite protection.

Safeguarding data from corruption and unauthorized access by internal or external people can protect the auditor and/or client from financial loss and reputation damage.

Actions an audit firm can take against cyber-attacks include:

- Establishing strong passwords
- Setting up firewalls
- Antivirus protection
- Scheduling backups of data
- Educating employees about the importance of data security.

6 Summary

Professional ethics is quite a detailed topic. It is important that you appreciate the spirit of the guidance. We have covered the following key areas:

Fundamental ethical principles

- Integrity
- Objectivity
- Professional competence and due care
- Confidentiality
- Professional behaviour

Threats to independence

- Self-interest threat
- Self-review threat
- Familiarity threat
- Advocacy threat
- Intimidation threat

Integrity, objectivity and independence

Areas of risk are:

- undue dependence on an audit client
- family and other personal relationships
- beneficial interests in shares and other investments voting on audit appointments
- loans
- overdue fees
- goods and services: hospitality
- provision of other services to audit clients.

Review procedures are an important safeguard.

Confidentiality

- Improper disclosure.
- Improper use of information.

Test your understanding answers

Test your understanding 1

Answer (b)

The fundamental principles stated in the AAT Code of Professional Ethics are integrity, objectivity, professional competence and due care, confidentiality, and professional behaviour.

Test your understanding 2

Answer (c)

This causes a self-review threat as the auditor will have to review the client's systems as part of the statutory audit.

AUDIT AND ASSURANCE

Responsibilities and liabilities of the auditor

Introduction

This chapter examines auditor's liability to third parties and focuses on the importance of quality management procedures within an audit firm. We will finish with discussing the role of auditors with relation to fraud.

ASSESSMENT CRITERIA
The regulatory environment (1.2)
The role of corporate governance in the audit and assurance process (1.3)

CONTENTS
1 The auditor's liability in contract and tort
2 Quality management
3 Review procedures
4 Fraud and the role of the auditor

1 The auditor's liability in contract and tort

1.1 Introduction

The responsibilities and resulting liabilities of an auditor arise in both statute and common law. The auditor's statutory responsibilities are set out principally in the Companies Act 2006 and are not considered further in this chapter, as they were covered in Chapters 1 and 13.

Under common law the auditor has a contractual relationship with their client – negligent auditing may lead to an auditor being sued for breach of contract.

The auditor also has a common law duty of care towards third parties under the law of tort. This aspect of the auditor's liability is the subject of recent case law and has given rise to much debate (both within and outside the accountancy profession).

1.2 Reasonable skill and care

There is a contractual relationship between an external auditor and their client, and an implied term of the contract is that the auditor will carry out their work with reasonable skill and care. The IESBA Code of Ethics tells auditors that they must act with professional competence and due care.

This term cannot be precisely defined, and ultimately its meaning will be decided by the courts in view of the facts of each particular case. However, the following points are relevant in determining what is a reasonable standard of care:

- applying the most up-to-date accounting and auditing standards
- adhering to all standards of ethical behaviour laid down by the relevant professional bodies
- being aware of the terms and conditions of the appointment as set out in the engagement letter and as implied by law
- employing competent staff who are adequately trained and supervised in carrying out instructions.

Failure to exercise reasonable skill and care constitutes a breach of contract and also may lead to a claim of negligence by the client if the company has suffered financial loss. This type of claim usually arises when an auditor has failed to discover a fraud during the audit. The remedy is usually damages.

An auditor can reduce the risk of exposure to claims for damages with Professional Indemnity Insurance.

Professional Indemnity Insurance (PII): Audit firms must take out PII. PII provides cover for the financial consequences of professional negligence, following a breach of professional duty by way of neglect or error.

1.3 Liability to third parties

It has also been argued that as well as being potentially liable to their client, the auditor might also incur liability to third parties. External auditors can limit their liability to third parties if they include a disclaimer in their auditor's report. This is referred to as Bannerman paragraph and would include a statement that the 'report is intended solely for the company's members.'

1.4 General duty of care

The case **Hedley Byrne v Heller and Partners** established that a professional person may owe a general duty of care to third parties, where:

- the professional person acted negligently
- the professional person knew or ought to have known that their statement would be relied upon by third parties, and
- the third party suffered financial loss as a result of relying on the professional's statement.

2 Quality management

2.1 Introduction

The following methods of quality management are used in the auditing profession:

- professional regulations issued by RSBs (Recognised Supervisory Bodies)
- the guidance given in the International Standards on Quality Management (ISQM 1 and ISQM 2) and ISA 220 (Revised) *Quality management for an audit of financial statements*
- review procedures
- audit committees (committees of non-executive directors who liaise with the auditors).

In addition, the law goes some way towards ensuring that auditors are competent and independent.

2.2 Professional regulations

The professional bodies expect their members to keep up to date by engaging in Continuing Professional Development (CPD). The bodies discipline individual members under the Joint Disciplinary Scheme.

Under the Companies Act 2006 there is a statutory requirement for the professional bodies to implement and enforce such regulations in order to retain recognition as an RSB.

2.3 Auditing Standards

Quality control policies and procedures should be implemented both at the level of the audit firm and on individual audits.

2.4 Audit firm

Audit firms should establish and monitor quality management policies and procedures designed to ensure that all audits are conducted in accordance with Auditing Standards and should communicate those policies and procedures to their personnel in a manner designed to provide reasonable assurance that the policies and procedures are understood and implemented.

The quality management policies to be adopted by auditors usually incorporate the following:

- **Professional requirements** – personnel adhere to the principles of independence, integrity, objectivity, confidentiality and professional behaviour.

- **Skills and competence** – personnel have attained and maintain the technical standards and professional competence required to enable them to fulfil their responsibilities with due care.

- **Acceptance and retention of clients** – prospective clients are evaluated and existing clients are reviewed on an ongoing basis. In making a decision to accept or retain a client, the auditors' independence and ability to serve the client properly and the integrity of the client's management are considered.

- **Assignment** – audit work is assigned to personnel who have the degree of technical training and proficiency required in the circumstances.

- **Delegation** – sufficient direction, supervision and review of work at all levels is carried out in order to provide confidence that the work performed meets appropriate standards of quality.

- **Consultation** – consultation, whenever necessary, within or outside the audit firm occurs with those who have appropriate expertise.
- **Monitoring** – the continued adequacy and operational effectiveness of quality management policies and procedures are monitored.

2.5 Individual audits

Any work delegated to assistants should be directed, supervised and reviewed in a manner which provides reasonable assurance that such work is performed competently.

The audit engagement partner and personnel with supervisory responsibilities consider the professional competence of assistants performing work delegated to them when deciding the extent of direction, supervision and review appropriate for each assistant.

2.6 Direction

Appropriate direction of assistants to whom work is delegated involves informing them of their responsibilities and the objectives of the procedures they are to perform. It also involves informing them of matters such as the nature of the entity's business and possible accounting or auditing problems which may affect the nature, timing and extent of audit procedures with which they are involved. Means of communicating audit directions, in addition to briefing meetings and informal oral communications, include audit manuals and checklists as well as the audit programme and the overall audit plan.

2.7 Supervision

Supervision is closely related to both direction and review and may involve elements of both. Personnel with supervisory responsibilities perform the following functions during the audit:

- monitor the progress of the audit to consider whether:
  - assistants have the necessary skills and competence to carry out their assigned tasks
  - assistants understand the audit directions
  - the work is being carried out in accordance with the overall audit plan and the audit programme.
- become informed of and address significant accounting and auditing questions raised during the audit, by assessing their significance and modifying the overall audit plan and the audit programme as appropriate
- resolve any differences of professional judgment between personnel and consider the level of consultation that is appropriate.

2.8 Review

Work performed by each assistant is reviewed by personnel of appropriate experience to consider whether:

- the work has been performed in accordance with the audit programme
- the work performed and the results obtained have been adequately documented
- any significant audit matters have been resolved or are reflected in audit conclusions
- the objectives of the audit procedures have been achieved, and
- the conclusions expressed are consistent with the results of the work performed and support the audit opinion.

3 Review procedures

3.1 Introduction

The standards on quality management do not give details of how monitoring reviews should be carried out. The most common methods are described below.

3.2 Review within the firm

Most common are methods of review within the audit firm.

3.3 Audit review panel

This will comprise a small number of partners and/or technical senior managers. Prior to issuing the auditor's report they will consider:

- conflicts of interest
- proposed qualifications
- interpretation of law and accounting standards
- contentious matters (e.g. an apparent change of view from one year's audit to the next).

3.4 Second partner review

The second partner should be as independent as possible but should have knowledge of the client. The second partner will:

- comprehensively review all audit files
- form their own opinion based on the work and evidence and compare it to the first partner's opinion. Any conflict must be resolved before the auditor's report is issued.

This is a more in-depth review, and is therefore more time-consuming and expensive. For this reason, it is sometimes limited to high risk and public interest audits.

3.5 Hot review

Performed by a review department before the auditor's report is issued. Reviewers will:

- check that work done conforms to the firm's standards
- ensure that all review points have been satisfactorily cleared
- confirm that legal requirements and accounting standards have been complied with
- review the report to management in the light of the audit files
- check that the letter of engagement has been complied with
- ensure that the letter of management representation covers all relevant points.

The depth of review undertaken is between that of a second partner review and an audit panel review.

3.6 Post-audit review (cold review)

Checks the extent of compliance with the firm's standards and policies in areas such as:

- auditing procedures
- accounting and reporting principles
- working paper preparation and presentation.

The cold review:

- determines whether the audit evidence obtained is sufficient, relevant and reliable enough to support the audit opinion
- reviews the performance of audit staff and assists them in improving

- identifies areas of weakness in the firm's procedures or in their application, and makes recommendations for improvement
- ensures that unnecessary work is eliminated and efficiency improved.

Cold reviews are performed by senior staff or partners from other offices, after the auditor's report has been issued. It is therefore independent of the staff involved in the audit work. Because of the time involved, cold reviews are undertaken on a rotational basis for selected audits, covering all audit partners and managers.

The review will concentrate on problem audits, for example high risk clients and loss-making assignments.

Test your understanding 1

State whether the following statements are true or false:

1. Compliance with quality management policies and procedures will constitute a good defence against allegations that the audit firm has been negligent.

2. Audit partners should ensure that commercial considerations do not override the quality of work performed.

3.7 External review – peer review

This involves the review of a firm by another firm of auditors or a committee of external experts. This practice is much used in the USA. The review will consider the adequacy of the firm's policies and procedures and the extent to which they are complied with.

3.8 Audit committees

An audit committee is a group of (usually) non-executive directors within the audit client who are able to view a company's affairs in a detached and objective manner and to liaise between the main Board of Directors and the external auditor.

It is argued that they assist in:

- increasing public confidence in the credibility and objectivity of financial statements
- enabling directors to meet their responsibilities in respect of financial reporting

- strengthening the independence of the company's external auditor – the committee can advise on the appointment of the external auditor and provide a channel of communication to the main board

- increasing the non-executive directors' understanding of the financial statements, and all directors' understanding of the nature and scope of the statutory audit.

As yet there is no legal requirement for a UK company to have an audit committee. Supporters of proposals for legislation suggest that audit committees should be required for all companies in which there is a public interest. However, most public companies have set up audit committees in response to pressure from the Stock Exchange following the Cadbury and Greenbury reports into corporate governance.

 4 Fraud and the role of the auditor

4.1 Introduction

An auditor has no statutory duty to detect fraud as an end in itself. However, a material fraud may affect the truth and fairness of the financial statements and the auditor should therefore design their work to have a reasonable expectation of detecting material fraud.

This has been a controversial area of audit regulation. The public wish to be reassured that fraud, particularly fraud committed by senior management, is being prevented and detected by the audit. Auditors are reluctant to accept such a responsibility because fraud can be so carefully concealed that it becomes almost impossible to detect. ISA 240 *The auditor's responsibilities relating to fraud in an audit of financial statements* deals with this issue.

4.2 Fraud and error

It is for the court to determine in a particular instance whether fraud has occurred. Auditors need to be alert to conduct which may be dishonest before considering whether it may be fraudulent. Fraud comprises both the use of deception to obtain an unjust or illegal financial advantage and intentional misrepresentations affecting the financial statements by one or more individuals among management, employees, or third parties.

Fraud may involve:

- falsification or alteration of accounting records or other documents, misappropriation of assets, or theft
- suppression or omission of the effects of transactions from records or documents
- recording of transactions without substance
- intentional misapplication of accounting policies
- wilful misrepresentations of transactions or of the entity's state of affairs
- money laundering.

Error refers simply to unintentional misstatements.

4.3 Responsibilities

Management is responsible for both the prevention and detection of fraud. Such responsibilities may be discharged by the installation of an effective accounting system and an appropriate system of internal controls, amongst others.

4.4 Audit approach

When planning the audit, the auditors should assess the risk that fraud or error may cause the financial statements to contain material misstatements.

Based on their risk assessment, the auditors should design audit procedures so as to have a reasonable expectation of detecting misstatements arising from fraud or error which are material to the financial statements.

4.5 Procedures where there is an indication that fraud or error may exist

When auditors become aware of information which indicates that fraud or error may exist, they should obtain an understanding of the nature of the event and the circumstances in which it has occurred, and sufficient other information to evaluate the possible effect on the financial statements. If the auditors believe that the indicated fraud or error could have a material effect on the financial statements, they should perform appropriate modified or additional procedures.

The auditors should as soon as practicable document their findings and communicate them to the appropriate level of management, the Board of Directors or the audit committee if:

- they suspect or discover fraud, even if the potential effect on the financial statements is immaterial, or
- material error is actually found to exist.

Test your understanding 2

State whether the following statements are true or false:

1. A misstatement can be material, whether caused by fraud or by error.
2. The auditor performs the audit with the aim of deterring fraud.

Test your understanding 3

An audit firm has been informed by its client, B Co, that it has discovered that a payroll fraud was in operation during the previous financial year, a year in respect of which the audit firm gave a 'true and fair' auditor's opinion.

B Co says that the audit firm was responsible for preventing the fraud. A review of the previous year's audit working papers shows that the audit firm failed to perform any procedures at all in relation to the payroll.

State whether the following statements are true or false:

1. The audit firm was responsible for preventing the fraud.
2. The audit firm failed to discharge its responsibilities as auditor.

4.6 Reporting to addressees of the auditor's report

Where the auditors conclude that the view given by the financial statements could be affected by a level of uncertainty concerning the consequences of a suspected or actual error or fraud which, in their opinion, is significant, they should include an explanatory paragraph referring to the matter in their report.

Where the auditors conclude that a suspected or actual instance of fraud or error has a material effect on the financial statements and they disagree with the accounting treatment or with the extent, or the lack of disclosure in the financial statements of the instance or of its consequences they should issue an adverse or qualified opinion. If the auditors are unable to determine whether fraud or error has occurred because of limitation in the scope of their work, they should issue a disclaimer or a qualified opinion.

Modifying the auditor's report or providing an explanatory paragraph provides the auditor with a solution to the dilemma created by knowing that fraud may have been committed. It is unsatisfactory to permit the matter to go unreported because the victims of the fraud will feel that the auditor has let them down. Reporting the fraud to a third party, such as the police, will breach the auditor's duty of confidentiality.

Another advantage of bringing matters to light through the auditor's report is that the auditor is protected against claims of defamation. If anyone claims to have been libelled in the auditor's report then the auditor merely has to prove that the auditor has acted in good faith. If the auditor makes a report to a third party and that party subsequently sues the auditor for damages then the auditor would have to prove that the fraud allegations were true, which could be difficult or even impossible given the standards of proof required in criminal cases.

4.7 Reporting to third parties

Where the auditors become aware of a suspected or actual instance of fraud they will normally be prevented from reporting this to a third party because of duties of professional confidentiality. The auditor could, however, have a duty to set this duty aside in order to best serve the public interest. This is a complex issue and the auditor should seek legal advice before doing anything.

The auditor might decide that it is necessary to resign in the light of the facts that have been uncovered. UK company law requires that the auditor file a report of any matters associated with the resignation that should be brought to the attention of the shareholders or payables. That might provide a further means by which the auditor's concerns can be brought to the attention of the company's members.

5 Summary

This chapter has covered:

- the circumstances in which an auditor may be found to be negligent
- the circumstances in which an auditor may be liable to clients and to third parties
- the persons to whom an auditor may be liable
- possible methods of excluding or limiting an auditor's liability (particularly quality management procedures)
- audit considerations regarding the detection and reporting of fraud.

Test your understanding answers

Test your understanding 1

1 True
2 True

Test your understanding 2

1 True
2 False

Although the deterrence of fraud may be a consequence of the audit, the auditor does not perform the audit with this aim – their aim is to obtain evidence regarding the truth and fairness of the financial statements.

Test your understanding 3

1 False
2 True

The prevention of fraud is the responsibility of management, not the auditor. However, the auditor is responsible for obtaining evidence to address the risks of material misstatement, which it failed to do in relation to payroll.

AUDIT AND ASSURANCE

Internal audit

16

Introduction

This chapter examines the role of internal audit. It starts by discussing the requirement for internal audit and moves on to set out the differences between external and internal audit. There are various roles of internal audit and different types of internal audit work that we will see in this chapter, along with the risks associated with a lack of independence.

ASSESSMENT CRITERIA
The role of internal audit (1.4)
Audit approach (4.4)

CONTENTS
1 The requirement for internal audit
2 Difference between internal and external audit
3 Roles of internal audit
4 Types of internal audit work
5 Risks associated with a lack of independence

Internal audit: Chapter 16

1 The requirement for internal audit

1.1 Introduction

A company must create a strong system of internal control in order to fulfil its responsibilities.

However, it is not sufficient to simply have mechanisms in place to manage a business, the effectiveness of those mechanisms must be regularly evaluated. All systems need some form of monitoring and feedback. This is the role of internal audit.

ISA 610 *Using the work of internal auditors* focuses on whether the external auditor can use the work of the internal audit function for purposes of audit.

1.2 The need for internal audit

Definition

Internal audit is an independent, objective and consulting activity designed to add value and improve an organisation's operations.

Having an internal audit department is generally considered to be best practice, but is not required by law. This allows flexibility in the way that internal audit is established to suit the needs of a business.

In small, or owner managed businesses, there is unlikely to be a need for internal audit because the owners are able to exercise more direct control over operations, and are accountable to fewer stakeholders.

The need for internal audit (IA) therefore will depend on:

- **Scale and diversity of activities.** In a larger, diversified organisation there is a risk that controls do not work as effectively because of the delegation of responsibility down the organisation. Internal audit can report back to the audit committees if controls are not as effective as they should be.

- **Complexity of operations.** The more complex the organisation is, the greater the benefit obtained from having an IA function as there is a greater risk of things going wrong. With larger organisations, the consequences of poor controls/risk management/corporate governance practices are likely to be greater.

- **Number of employees.** The greater the number of employees, the greater the risk of fraud.

- **Cost/benefit considerations.** It will be worthwhile establishing an IA function if the benefits outweigh the costs. For example, a company might be losing money as a result of fraud, not using the most cost effective of reliable suppliers, or incurring fines for non-compliance with laws and regulations. If these costs outweigh the cost of employing an IA function, it will be beneficial to the company to establish a department.

- **The desire of senior management to have assurance and advice on risk and control.** The directors may wish to have the comfort that there is ongoing monitoring of the organisation to help them discharge their responsibilities.

- **The current control environment and whether there is a history of fraud or control deficiencies.** If so, it will be beneficial for the company to establish an internal audit function to prevent and detect fraud.

2 Difference between internal and external audit

2.1 Introduction

An external audit is an audit carried out by an external, as opposed to an internal, auditor. Remember that the objective of an external auditor of financial statements is to enable auditors to express an opinion on whether the financial statements are prepared (in all material respects) in accordance with the applicable financial reporting framework.

2.2 Difference between internal and external audit

Contrast this with the definition of the internal audit function given at the beginning of this chapter. The external audit is focused on the financial statements, whereas the internal audit is focused on the operations of the entire business.

	External audit	Internal audit
Objective	Express an opinion on the truth and fairness of the financial statements in a written report.	Improve the company's operations by reviewing the efficiency and effectiveness of internal controls.
Reporting	Report to shareholders.	Reports to management of those charged with governance.
Availability of report	Publicly available.	Not publicly available. Usually only seen by management or those charged with governance.
Scope of work	Verifying the truth and fairness of the financial statements.	Wide in scope and dependent on management's requirements.
Appointment and removal	By the shareholders of the company.	By the audit committee or board of directors.
Relationship with company	Must be independent of the company.	May be employees (which limits independence) or an outsourced function (which enhances independence).

The table shows that although some of the procedures that the internal audit function undertake are very similar to those undertaken by the external auditors, **the whole basis and reasoning of their work is fundamentally different**.

Test your understanding 1

State whether the following statements are true or false:

(a) Internal auditors always report directly to shareholders.

(b) The internal auditor's work may be determined by management.

(c) There is no legal requirement for companies to have an internal audit department.

3 Roles of internal audit

3.1 Introduction

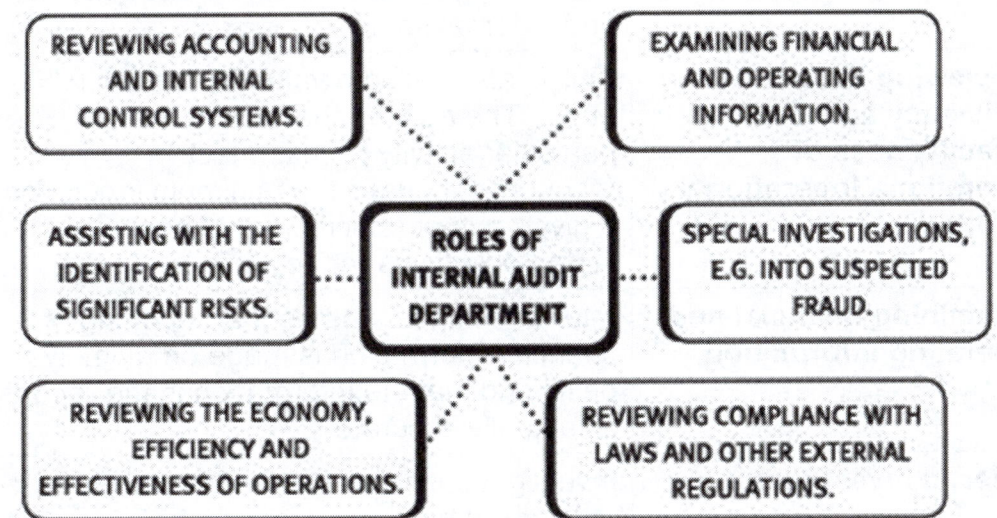

3.2 Roles of internal audit

	Comment
Reviewing accounting systems and systems of internal control (financial audit)	This is the traditional view of internal audit. The internal auditor checks the financial controls in the company, possibly assisting or sharing work with the external auditor. The internal auditor would comment on whether appropriate controls exist as well as whether they are working correctly. In this work, the internal auditor does not manage risk, but simply reports on controls.
Assisting with the identification of significant risks	In this function, the internal auditor focuses their attention on risks. The auditor may be asked to investigate areas of risk management, with specific reference on how the company identifies, assesses and controls significant risks from both internal and external sources.
Reviewing the economy, efficiency and effectiveness of operations (operational audit)	This is also called a value for money (VFM) audit. The auditor checks whether a particular activity is cost effective (economical), uses the minimum inputs for a given output (efficient) and meets its stated objectives (effective).
Examining financial and operating information	Internal auditors ensure that reporting of financial information is made on a timely basis and that the information in the reports is factually accurate.
Special investigations	Investigations into other areas of the company's business e.g. checking the cost estimates for a new factory.
Reviewing compliance with laws and other external regulations	This objective is particularly relevant regarding the Sarbanes Oxley Act where the internal auditor will be carrying out detailed work to ensure that systems of internal control and financial reports meet stock exchange requirements.

Test your understanding 2

Which of the following is NOT part of the role of internal audit?

(a) Risk identification and monitoring.

(b) Expression of opinion to the shareholders on whether the financial statements give a true and fair view.

(c) Assessing compliance with laws and regulations.

Test your understanding 3

Smarter Supermarkets operates a chain of fifteen supermarkets across the country. At head office, there is an internal audit department which carries out audits and investigations on the individual supermarkets in the chain.

Which TWO of the following could the internal audit department carry out and still operate effectively?

(a) Test of controls are Supermarket A as part of a routine internal audit cycle.

(b) Temporarily filling the role of the Supermarket B manager while he or she is on sick leave.

(c) Identification of risks at Supermarket X which is due to open next year.

Internal audit: **Chapter 16**

4 Types of internal audit work

4.1 Introduction

The internal audit function will carry out many different types of audit, as highlighted by the department's varied roles.

4.2 Financial audit

Financial auditing is traditionally the main area of work for the internal audit department. It embraces:

- the conventional tasks of examining records and evidence to support financial and management reporting in order to detect errors and prevent fraud

- analysing information, identifying trends and potentially significant variations from the norm.

4.3 Operational audit

Operational auditing covers:

- examination and review of a business operation

- the effectiveness of controls

- identification of areas for improvement in efficiency and performance including improving operational economy, efficiency and effectiveness – the three Es of value for money auditing.

There are four main areas where such an approach is commonly used:

- procurement

- marketing

- treasury

- human resources.

4.4 Project auditing

Best value and IT assignments are really about looking at processes within the organisation and asking:

- were things done well?

- did the organisation achieve value for money?

Project auditing is about looking at a specific project, for example commissioning a new factory or implementing new IT systems, and asking:

- were the objectives achieved?
- was the project implemented efficiently?
- what lessons can be learnt from any mistakes made?

4.5 Value for money audit

An area that internal auditors have become increasingly involved in is the value for money audits. These are sometimes referred to as 'best value' audits.

The auditor assesses three main areas:

- **Economy.** The economy of a business is assessed by looking at the inputs to the business (or process), and deciding whether these are the most economical that are available at an acceptable quality level. For example, if assessing the economy of a commercial company the inputs would be capital (plant and machinery, buildings etc.), raw materials, the workforce and any administrative function required to run the business.

- **Efficiency.** The efficiency of an operation is assessed by considering how well the operation converts inputs into outputs. In a manufacturing company this might involve looking at wastage in production or quality control failures for example.

- **Effectiveness.** The effectiveness of an organisation is assessed by examining whether the organisation is achieving its objectives. To assess effectiveness there must be clear objectives for the organisation that can be examined. In some organisations, particularly not for profit and public service organisations, deciding suitable objectives can be one of the most difficult parts of the value for money exercise.

4.6 Social and environment audit

An environment audit is defined as:

'A management tool comprising systematic, documented, periodic and objective evaluation of how well organisations, management and equipment are performing, with the aim of contributing to safeguarding the environment by facilitating management control of environmental practices, and assessing compliance with company policies, which would include meeting regulatory requirements and standards applicable.'

The social audit would look at the company's contribution to society and the community. The contributions made could be through:

- Donations
- Sponsorship
- Employment practices
- Education
- Health and safety
- Ethical investments, etc.

A social audit could either confirm statements made by the directors, or make recommendations for social policies that the company should perform.

4.7 Management audit

A management audit it defined as 'an objective and independent appraisal of the effectiveness of managers and the corporate structure in the achievement of the entities' objectives and policies. Its aim is to identify existing and potential management weaknesses and recommend ways to rectify them.'

Test your understanding 4

Fraud and error present risks to an entity. Both internal and external auditors are required to deal with risks to the entity. However, the responsibilities of internal and external auditors in relation to the risk of fraud and error differ.

Required:

Explain how the internal audit function helps an entity deal with the risks of fraud and error.

Test your understanding 5

Internal auditors perform many different types of assignment including value for money audits.

Required:

Briefly explain the three 'Es' which are reviewed as part of a value for money audit.

5 Risks associated with a lack of independence

5.1 Introduction

Internal auditors should be objective in performing their work. Internal auditor independence is the freedom from conditions that threaten the ability of the internal audit function to carry out internal audit responsibilities in an unbiased manner.

5.2 Limitations of internal audit

Internal auditors may be employees of the company they are reporting on and therefore may not wish to raise issues in case they lose their job.

In smaller organisations in particular, internal audit may be managed as part of the finance function. They will therefore have to report upon the effectiveness of financial systems that they form a part of and may be reluctant to say their department (and manager) has deficiencies.

If the internal audit staff have worked in the department for a long time, possibly in different departments, there may be a familiarity threat as they will be auditing the work of long standing colleagues and friends.

It is therefore difficult for the internal audit function to remain truly objective. However, acceptable levels of independence can be achieved through one, or more, of the following strategies:

- Reporting channels separate from the management of the main financial reporting function.

- Reviews of internal audit work by managers independent of the function under scrutiny.

- Outsourcing the internal audit function to a professional third party.

6 Summary

This chapter has covered:

- the need for internal audit
- the difference between internal and external audit
- the roles of internal audit including:
  - reviewing accounting systems and systems of internal control
  - examining financial operating information
  - special investigations e.g. fraud
  - reviewing compliance with external regulation
  - reviewing value for money (VFM)
  - risk management
- the different types of internal audit work including:
  - financial
  - operation
  - project
  - VFM
  - social and environmental
  - management
- the risks associated with a lack of independence.

Test your understanding answers

Test your understanding 1

1 False.
2 True.
3 True.

Test your understanding 2

Answer (b)

The *external* auditor will express an opinion to the shareholders on whether the financial statements give a true and fair view.

Test your understanding 3

Answer (a) and (c)

Option (b) would not be acceptable as it involves the internal auditor in operational matters.

Test your understanding 4

Internal audit can help management manage risks in relation to fraud and error, and exercise proper stewardship by:

– Commenting on the process used by management to identify and classify the specific fraud and error risks to which the entity is subject.

– Periodically auditing or reviewing systems or operations to determine whether the risks of fraud and error are being effectively managed.

– Where deficiencies which provide opportunity for fraud and error are identified, making recommendations for improvements.

– Monitoring the incidence of fraud and error and investigating serious cases.

In practice, the work of internal audit often focuses on the adequacy and effectiveness of internal control procedures for the prevention, detection and reporting of fraud and error. Routine internal controls (such as the controls over computer systems and the production of routine financial information) and non-routine controls (such as controls over year-end adjustments to the financial statements) are relevant.

It should be recognised however that many significant frauds bypass normal systems of internal control and that in the case of management fraud in particular, much higher level controls (those relating to the high level governance of the entity) need to be reviewed by internal audit in order to establish the nature of the risks, and to manage them effectively.

 Test your understanding 5

Value for money audits – the three 'Es'

(i) Economy – obtaining the best quality of resources for the minimum cost.

(ii) Efficiency – obtaining the maximum departmental/organisational outputs with the minimum use of resources.

(iii) Effectiveness – achievement of goals and targets.

Financial reporting topics

Introduction

This chapter is designed to help you with the key requirements of the accounting standards that are relevant to your AAT Audit and Assurance exam.

IAS 1 Presentation of Financial Statements

This standard provides formats for the statement of profit or loss and other comprehensive income, statement of financial position, and statement of changes in equity.

Accounting policies should be selected so that the financial statements comply with all international standards and interpretations.

Other comprehensive income should be presented in two categories, namely items that:

- will not be reclassified to profit or loss, and
- may be reclassified to profit or loss in future reporting periods.

IAS 2 Inventories

Inventories should be valued 'at the lower of cost and net realisable value' for each separate item or class of product (IAS 2, para 9).

The **cost** of inventory includes:

- Purchase price including import duties, transport and handling costs
- Direct production costs e.g. direct labour
- Direct expenses and subcontracted work
- Production overheads (based on the normal levels of activity)
- Other overheads, if attributable to bringing the product or service to its present location and condition.

Cost excludes:

- Abnormal waste
- Storage costs
- Indirect administrative overheads
- Selling costs.

Some entities can identify individual units of inventory (e.g. vehicles can be identified by a chassis number). Those that cannot should keep track of costs using either the first in, first out (FIFO) or the weighted average cost (AVCO) approach to determining cost.

Some entities may use standard costing for valuing inventory.

Standard costs may be used for convenience if it is a close approximation to actual cost, and is regularly reviewed and revised.

Net realisable value is 'the estimated selling price in the ordinary course of business less the estimated costs of completion and the estimated costs necessary to make the sale' (IAS 2, para 6).

IAS 10 Events after the reporting period

Definitions

Events after the reporting period are **'those events, favourable and unfavourable, that occur between the statement of financial position date and the date when the financial statements are authorised for issue'** (IAS 10, para 3).

Adjusting events after the reporting period are those that **'provide evidence of conditions that existed at the reporting date'** (IAS 10, para 3a).

Non-adjusting events after the reporting period are **'those that are indicative of conditions that arose after the reporting period'** (IAS 10, para 3b).

Accounting treatment

Adjusting events affect the amounts stated in the financial statements so they must be adjusted.

Non-adjusting events do not concern the position as at the reporting date so the financial statements are not adjusted. If the event is material then the nature and its financial effect must be disclosed.

IAS 16 Property, Plant and Equipment

Cost of an asset

Property, plant and equipment is initially recognised at cost.

An asset's cost is its purchase price, less any trade discounts or rebates, plus any further costs directly attributable to bringing it into working condition for its intended use.

Subsequent expenditure on non-current assets is capitalised if it:

- Enhances the economic benefits of the asset e.g. adding a new extension to a building.
- Replaces part of an asset that has been separately depreciated and has been fully depreciated; e.g. a furnace that requires new linings periodically.
- Replaces economic benefits previously consumed, e.g. a major inspection of aircraft.

Depreciation

The aim of depreciation is to spread the cost of the asset over its life in the business.

Important points which should be noted in respect of depreciation are as follows:

(a) Assessment of depreciation, and its allocation to accounting periods, involves the consideration of three factors:

   (i) cost (or valuation when an asset has been revalued in the financial statements)

   (ii) the nature of the asset and the length of its expected useful life to the business having due regard to the incidence of obsolescence

   (iii) estimated residual value of the asset at the end of its useful life in the business.

(b) If the asset's estimated useful life has been revised, the remaining carrying amount should be charged over the new estimated life.

(c) Profit/loss on disposal should be disclosed, if material.

(d) All assets with a finite economic life must be depreciated, even if market value exceeds carrying amount.

(e) Freehold land is not depreciated as it has an indefinite economic life.

(f) Buildings on freehold land should be depreciated if they have a finite life.

(g) The method by which depreciation is calculated for each category of asset should be disclosed in the accounts together with the rates applied to each class of asset.

- The depreciation method and useful life of an asset should be reviewed at the end of each year and revised where necessary. This is not a change in accounting policy, but a change of accounting estimate.

- If an asset has parts with different estimated useful lives, (e.g. a building with a flat roof), the component parts should be capitalised and depreciated separately.

Revaluation of property, plant and equipment

Revaluation of PPE is optional. If one asset is revalued, all assets in that class must be revalued.

Valuations should be kept up to date to ensure that the carrying amount does not differ materially from the fair value at each statement of financial position date.

Revaluation gains are credited to **other comprehensive income** unless the gain reverses a previous revaluation loss of the same asset previously recognised in the statement of profit or loss.

Revaluation losses are debited to the statement of profit or loss unless the loss relates to a previous revaluation surplus, in which case the decrease should first be debited to other comprehensive income to the extent of any credit balance existing in the revaluation surplus relating to that asset.

Depreciation is charged on the revalued amount less residual value (if any) over the **remaining useful life** of the asset.

An entity may choose to make an annual transfer of excess depreciation from revaluation surplus to retained earnings. If this is done, it should be applied consistently each year.

IAS 37 Provisions, Contingent Liabilities and Contingent Assets

- A provision is **'a liability of uncertain timing or amount'** (IAS 37, para 10).
- A contingent liability is a possible obligation arising from past events whose existence will only be confirmed by an uncertain future event outside of the entity's control.
- A contingent asset is a possible asset that arises from past events and whose existence will only be confirmed by an uncertain future event outside of the entity's control.

Provisions

Provisions should be recognised when:

- An entity has a present obligation (legal or constructive) as a result of a past event
- It is probable that an outflow of economic benefits will be required to settle the obligation, and
- A reliable estimate can be made of the amount of the obligation.

Measurement of provisions:

- The provision amount should be the best estimate of the expenditure required to settle the present obligation.
- Where the time value of money is material, the provision should be discounted to present value.

Restructuring provisions:

- Provisions can only be recognised where an entity has a constructive obligation to carry out the restructuring.
- A constructive obligation arises when there is a detailed formal plan which identifies:
    - The business concerned
    - The principal location, function and approximate number of employees being made redundant
    - The expenditures that will be incurred
    - When the plan will be implemented
    - There is a valid expectation that the plan will be carried out by either implementing the plan or announcing it to those affected.

Financial reporting topics: Chapter 17

Specific guidance:

- Future operating losses should not be recognised.
- Onerous contracts should be recognised for the present obligation under the contract.

Contingent liabilities should not be recognised. They should be disclosed unless the possibility of a transfer of economic benefits is remote.

Contingent assets should not be recognised. If the possibility of an inflow of economic benefits is probable they should be disclosed.

IAS 38 Intangible Assets

An intangible asset is **'an identifiable non-monetary asset without physical substance'** (IAS 38, para 8).

Initial recognition

An intangible asset is initially recognised at cost if all of the following criteria are met.

1. It is identifiable – it could be disposed of without disposing of the business at the same time.
2. It is controlled by the entity – the entity has the power to obtain economic benefits from it, for example patents and copyrights give legal rights to future economic benefits.
3. It will generate probable future economic benefits for the entity – this could be by a reduction in costs or increasing revenues.
4. The cost of the intangible asset can be measured reliably.

If an intangible does not meet the recognition criteria, then it should be charged to the statement of profit or loss as the expense is incurred.

Items that do not meet the criteria include internally generated goodwill, brands, mastheads, publishing titles, customer lists, research, advertising, start-up costs and training.

Subsequent treatment

Intangible assets should be amortised over their useful lives.

If it can be demonstrated that the useful life is indefinite, no amortisation should be charged but an annual impairment review must be carried out.

Intangible assets can be revalued but fair values must be determined with reference to an active market. Active markets have homogenous products, willing buyers and sellers at all times and published prices. In practical terms, most intangible assets are likely to be valued using the cost model.

Research and development

The recognition of internally generated intangible assets is split into a research phase and a development phase.

Costs incurred in the research phase must be charged to the statement of profit or loss as they are incurred.

Costs incurred in the development phase should be recognised as an intangible asset if they meet the following criteria:

(a) The project is technically feasible

(b) The asset will be completed then used or sold

(c) The entity is able to use or sell the asset

(d) The asset will generate future economic benefits (either because of internal use or because there is a market for it)

(e) The entity has adequate technical, financial and other resources to complete the project

(f) The expenditure on the project can be reliably measured.

Amortisation of development costs will occur over the period that benefits are expected.

IFRS 15 Revenue from Contracts with Customers

Revenue recognition is a five step process.

1. **Identify the contract**

   A contract is an agreement between two or more parties that creates rights and obligations.

2. **Identify the separate performance obligations within a contract**

   Performance obligations are, essentially, promises made to a customer.

3. **Determine the transaction price**

   The transaction price is the amount the entity expects to be entitled in exchange for satisfying all performance obligations. Amounts collected on behalf of third parties (such as sales tax) are excluded.

4. **Allocate the transaction price to the performance obligations in the contract**

   The total transaction price should be allocated to each performance obligation in proportion to stand-alone selling prices.

5 Recognise revenue when (or as) a performance obligation is satisfied

For each performance obligation an entity must determine whether it satisfies the performance obligation over time or at a point in time.

An entity satisfies a performance obligation over time if one of the following criteria is met:

(a) **'the customer simultaneously receives and consumes the benefits provided by the entity's performance as the entity performs**

(b) **the entity's performance creates or enhances an asset (for example, work in progress) that the customer controls as the asset is created or enhanced, or**

(c) **the entity's performance does not create an asset with an alternative use to the entity and the entity has an enforceable right to payment for performance completed to date'** (IFRS 15, para 35).

For a performance obligation satisfied over time, an entity recognises revenue based on progress towards satisfaction of that performance obligation.

If a performance obligation is not satisfied over time then it is satisfied at a point in time. The entity must determine the point in time at which a customer obtains control of the promised asset.

MOCK ASSESSMENT

AUDIT AND ASSURANCE

1 Mock Assessment Questions – Q2022

The assessment is 2.5 hours long and consists of 6 tasks. You should attempt all of the tasks. Each task is independent and you will not need to refer to previous tasks.

Task 1

This task is about the conceptual and regulatory framework, corporate governance and internal audit. **(10 marks)**

(a) **Identify whether the following statements about the expectations gap are true or false.**

Statement	True ✓	False ✓
An example of the expectations gap is that users of the financial statements may not understand the limitations of the audit process.		
An example of the expectations gap is that users of the financial statements may not understand the concept of reasonable assurance.		

(2 marks)

The shareholders of Jax plc have raised concerns that they have not had reports from the internal audit division, as they believe that they are entitled to see such information.

(b) **Identify to which body the internal audit function primarily reports.**

Body	✓
The external auditors	
The shareholders	
The audit committee	
The government regulator	

(1 mark)

Mock Assessment Questions

(c) **Identify whether the following statements about auditing are true or false.**

Statement	True ✓	False ✓
The external auditor is appointed by the shareholders.		
An internal audit function is required for all UK companies.		
Professional scepticism is a requirement specific to the audit of listed companies.		

(3 marks)

(d) **Complete the following statement:**

The UK Corporate Governance Code is _____GAP 1_____ for UK companies and aims to try and prevent _____GAP 2_____ from abusing their power.

Gap 1	✓
mandatory	
good practice	
irrelevant	

Gap 2	✓
shareholders	
company directors	
the wider community	

(2 marks)

(e) **Identify the type of assurance described in the extracts below.**

Extract	Reasonable ✓	Limited ✓
Nothing has come to our attention to suggest that there are any significant fraud concerns.		
The financial statements for Rey Ltd give a true and fair view.		

(2 marks)

AUDIT AND ASSURANCE

Task 2

This task is about professional ethics. (15 marks)

(a) **Identify whether the following statements about the AAT Code of Ethics are true or false.**

Statement	True ✓	False ✓
The AAT Code of Ethics relates only to members who are undertaking audit work.		
The AAT Code of Ethics is a principles-based approach to ethical dilemmas.		
The AAT Code of Ethics identifies professional honesty as a key ethical principle.		

(3 marks)

You are an Accounting Technician for ASC, an accounting firm which provides a number of accounting services to clients. You have recently been added to the audit team of Wings plc, a national airline listed on the London Stock Exchange.

The audit team is large and many of them have been on the job for a number of years. During the year, the previous audit manager left ASC to work for Wings plc as the Finance Director.

(b) **Identify which TWO of the following threats to objectivity arise from the audit manager leaving ASC to join Wings plc.**

Threat	✓
Self-review	
Intimidation	
Familiarity	
Advocacy	

(2 marks)

Mock Assessment Questions

(c) **Identify which TWO of the following represent appropriate action to take in respect of the audit manager joining Wings plc.**

Action	✓
Select members of the audit team who do not know the manager.	
Reduce the amount of testing on work completed by the new Finance Director, as you are aware of their competence.	
Perform additional file reviews to ensure appropriate levels of audit work is being performed.	
Resign from the client for a minimum of two years.	

(2 marks)

During the course of the audit, you become aware that Wings plc have significant financial difficulties. There is the talk of redundancies for staff, but the directors of Wings plc have come up with some plans to turn the business around. The first option is for them to obtain further bank finance in order to continue with the business and they would like your audit firm to lead negotiations with the bank in order to secure finance on their behalf.

The second option is to sell the company to Fly Inc, a company based in the United States of America. Discussions have taken place with Fly Inc. If the sale were to go ahead, Wings plc would like you to do additional consulting work in relation to the sale. Wings plc is your biggest client and currently makes up 3% of your firm's total practice income.

(d) **For each piece of work identified, select the potential problem and a course of action that ASC could take.**

Piece of work	Problem	Action
Meeting with the bank to secure finance.	Gap 1	Option 1
Gaining additional fees from consultancy work.	Gap 2	Option 2

Gap 1	
Advocacy threat	
Self-review threat	
Intimidation threat	

Option 1	
Reject the work	
Accept with safeguards	
No safeguards needed	

AUDIT AND ASSURANCE

Gap 2	
Self-interest threat	
Familiarity threat	
Advocacy threat	

Option 2	
Reject the work	
Accept with safeguards	
No safeguards needed	

(4 marks)

One of your colleagues at ASC who is not on the Wings plc audit has been in contact with you. They have heard rumours that Wings plc may be struggling financially. Your colleague's parents own shares in Wings plc and they are asking for your advice on what they should do.

(e) **Identify whether the following statements about the situation are true or false.**

Statement	True ✓	False ✓
Speaking to your colleague about this is acceptable as confidentiality does not apply within an audit firm.		
ASC are not allowed to audit Wings plc as an employee's family member has a financial interest in them.		

(2 marks)

Two of the employees of ASC own shares in Fly Inc.

(f) **Identify the appropriate course of action if Fly Inc were to become a client of ASC.**

Employee details	Ensure not on audit of Fly Inc	Employee must sell shares
Frank, an audit manager in ASC		
Sophie, an audit partner in ASC		

(2 marks)

Mock Assessment Questions

Task 3

This task is about the planning process. **(25 marks)**

(a) **Identify whether the following statements about the planning process are true or false.**

Statement	True ✓	False ✓
Materiality must be expressed as a percentage of profit.		
Profit-related pay in an entity will increase the inherent risk in the audit.		
Working papers can be in a variety of forms, both electronic and paper-based.		

(3 marks)

(b) **Identify whether the following situations lead to higher or lower audit risk.**

Situation	Higher risk ✓	Lower risk ✓
The company operates in a complex, technical industry.		
This is the first audit that the audit firm has performed in the industry.		

(2 marks)

You are working on the audit of Spinz Ltd for the year ended 31 December 20X2. Spinz Ltd operates a chain of casino premises and bingo halls. Planning materiality for the audit has been set at £1.2 million.

During the year, Spinz Ltd opened a large new casino. The budget for the set-up of the new venue was originally £3 million, but the final cost exceeded the budgeted amount. The new casino was the fourth casino opened by Spinz Ltd and has been open since 1 October 20X2. The casinos are open 365 days a year and each casino holds the equivalent of 14 days of revenue in cash on its premises.

The margins are relatively consistent across the industry with most casinos having a net profit margin of 20% due to the fixed returns generated by the machines in the premises. These make up the majority of the revenue in each casino other than Casino 3 which generates more revenue from hosting televised poker events with ticketed sales.

Below are some financial details which should help you with the planning of the audit.

	Casino 1	Casino 2	Casino 3	Casino 4 (new)
	£000	£000	£000	£000
Revenue	41,200	21,100	9,200	19,300
Total expenses	(32,960)	(18,300)	(4,700)	(13,200)
Total profit	8,240	2,800	4,500	6,100

In addition to this, Spinz Ltd operate 25 bingo hall premises. There has been criticism of the state of the properties that the bingo halls are run from. As a result, Spinz Ltd undertook some repairs at a number of premises and sold some of the others, reducing the number of bingo halls from 32 to 25.

(c) From the information provided above:

   (i) Discuss the audit risks surrounding property, plant and equipment. **(4 marks)**

   (ii) Explain the audit procedures to be performed over property, plant and equipment. **(6 marks)**

   (iii) Discuss any specific risks identified in the individual casinos and explain the audit procedures to be performed. **(10 marks)**

Mock Assessment Questions

Audit risks surrounding property, plant and equipment

Audit procedures to be performed around property, plant and equipment

Specific risks and procedures on individual casinos

Mock Assessment Questions

Task 4

This task is about procedures for obtaining sufficient and appropriate audit evidence. **(20 marks)**

(a) Identify whether the following situations will lead to an increase or decrease in sample sizes to be chosen.

Situation	Increase in sample size ✓	Decrease in sample size ✓
The detection risk needs to be low.		
Controls are working effectively.		

(2 marks)

(b) Identify which of the financial statement assertions are being tested by each of the substantive audit procedures below.

Audit procedure	Existence ✓	Completeness ✓
Selecting inventory from the warehouse and tracing it to the inventory listing.		
Selecting items from the non-current asset register to physically verify.		
Selecting goods received notes prior to the year-end to confirm they are included in the liabilities balance.		
Selecting inventory from the inventory listing and tracing them to the warehouse location.		

(4 marks)

AUDIT AND ASSURANCE

(c) **For each of the procedures listed below, identify whether it is a test of control or a substantive procedure.**

Procedure	Substantive procedure ✓	Test of control ✓
Observing cash being received from a trade receivable balance post year-end.		
Inspecting a bank reconciliation for evidence of authorisation.		

(2 marks)

You are part of the audit of Shep Ltd for the year ended 31 December 20X1. During the planning of Shep Ltd it was noted that the Financial Controller had left during the year. Shep Ltd took a number of months to find a replacement. During that time, the small accounting department did their best to cover for the absence of a Financial Controller but the absence of anyone in the role led to a lack of regular reconciliations or authorisation control activities being followed.

You have been given the role of auditing the inventory of Shep Ltd. Shep Ltd sells a range of products. The two most popular items are:

Shep Ltd food-to-go: These are ready-meal food items sold via the website and to retailers.

Shep Ltd kitchen equipment: These are high-quality kitchen products, such as casserole dishes and saucepans.

The inventory is held across two sites, evenly spread across both. An inventory count is planned for 31 December 20X1 at both venues.

(d) **From the information provided above:**

　(i)　**Discuss the likely impact that the Financial Controller's absence will have on the audit approach.** **(3 marks)**

　(ii)　**Explain the audit procedures that you will perform over the inventory balance of Shep Ltd. Your tests should specifically cover how you intend to assess the existence, valuation and completeness of inventory.** **(9 marks)**

Mock Assessment Questions

Impact of absence

Approach for testing inventory

Task 5

This task is about procedures for obtaining sufficient and appropriate audit evidence. **(15 marks)**

(a) **Complete the following statement:**

Appropriate evidence is _____GAP 1_____ when it meets one of the financial statement _____GAP 2_____

Gap 1	✓
understood	
correct	
relevant	

Gap 2	✓
assertions	
characteristics	
qualifications	

(2 marks)

(b) **Identify whether the statements about cash and bank are true or false.**

Statement	True ✓	False ✓
Petty cash must be counted on every audit.		
A bank statement is the best form of evidence for a cash balance.		
The auditors should test the bank reconciliation but not produce the bank reconciliation for the client.		

(3 marks)

Mock Assessment Questions

(c) Select the correct category for the following automated tools and techniques.

Technique	Test data ✓	Audit software ✓
Inputting dummy invoices into the client system to see if internal controls are working as intended.		
Extracting information and analysing data.		

(2 marks)

(d) Match the following audit procedures to the type of verification technique it represents, from the picklist below.

Procedure	Verification technique
Contacting a customer to confirm the receivables balance owed to the client.	PICKLIST
Comparing monthly payroll costs to examine any variances.	PICKLIST
Examining an invoice to agree the amount to the figure recorded in the financial statements.	PICKLIST
Reperforming the client's depreciation workings.	PICKLIST

Options
Inspection
Analytical procedures
Observation
Recalculation
External confirmation

(4 marks)

AUDIT AND ASSURANCE

(e) Identify whether the following items represent a misstatement in the account balance.

Item	Misstatement ✓	Not a misstatement ✓
A payment made to a supplier was posted against the wrong supplier.		
Goods received in December 20X1 were not recorded until January 20X2.		

(2 marks)

(f) Identify whether the following tests will be testing primarily for understatement of overstatement of the account balance.

Test	Understatement ✓	Overstatement ✓
A sample of sales have been selected from the receivables ledger and will be traced to see if there are valid goods despatch notes for each of them.		
A sample of physical assets have been selected to see if all items have been correctly recorded on the asset register.		

(2 marks)

Mock Assessment Questions

Task 6

This task is about reviewing and reporting findings and audit opinions. **(15 marks)**

You are part of the audit of Sparx Ltd, a fashion retailer, and you are looking at their purchases controls. You have been given the following information about the purchases system.

Sparx Ltd has 4 retail stores and a central warehouse. Each store can order more goods from the warehouse when they feel that their store is low on an item. There is no set figure for this, but managers tend to order when their quantities are lower than 10. This is done via e-mail from the store manager to the warehouse manager.

Sparx Ltd are always on the lookout for new suppliers and have a wide range of manufacturers that are dealt with. All new suppliers are selected by John Shrat, the purchasing director.

The warehouse inventory system automatically raises a purchase requisition for goods when it hits a set re-order level. This differs per product and is controlled by Julie Jac, the warehouse manager.

Once the purchase requisitions are raised, a purchase order is made with the relevant supplier. Julie can raise purchase orders up to £5,000. Anything over this needs approval from John Shrat.

Each purchase order is generated a unique code incorporating the goods, the supplier and the date. If goods are not received within 10 days of Julie or John raising the order, another order is placed with a different supplier.

(a) From the information provided above:

   (i) Identify and explain FOUR control deficiencies in the purchases system. **(4 marks)**

   (ii) Recommend improvements to the controls in the purchases system. **(6 marks)**

Control deficiencies

AUDIT AND ASSURANCE

Recommended improvements

Mock Assessment Questions

You are looking over some of the audit files from the clients you have worked on, before issuing the audit opinion, and you have found the following information.

Spinz Ltd has an ongoing court case with a customer who is claiming substantial damages. The damages are material but Spinz Ltd have not provided for them as they believe they will win the case. Your legal advisers believe that Spinz Ltd will lose the case.

Shep Ltd had an inventory write-down of £400,000 in January 20X3. This inventory was included in the 31 December 20X2 financial statements. Materiality on the Shep Ltd audit was set at £850,000.

Sparx Ltd has a significant uncertainty over their future funding as a loan is due to be repaid within a year. If this is not extended, Sparx Ltd would not be a going concern. You agree with the way the directors have treated this issue in Sparx Ltd's financial statements and the disclosure they have made in the notes to the accounts.

(b) **Identify whether the above situations will lead to a modified or unmodified audit opinion.**

Audit client	Modified ✓	Unmodified ✓
Spinz Ltd		
Shep Ltd		
Sparx Ltd		

(3 marks)

(c) **Identify TWO items below that are reported by exception in the auditor's report.**

Item	✓
All sections of the annual report are in agreement.	
Proper accounting records have been kept.	
The financial statements are free from material misstatement.	
Accounts agree to the underlying records.	

(2 marks)

AUDIT AND ASSURANCE

2 Mock Assessment Answers – Q2022

Task 1

This task is about the conceptual and regulatory framework, corporate governance and internal audit. **(10 marks)**

(a) Identify whether the following statements about the expectations gap are true or false.

Statement	True ✓	False ✓
An example of the expectations gap is that users of the financial statements may not understand the limitations of the audit process.	✓	
An example of the expectations gap is that users of the financial statements may not understand the concept of reasonable assurance.	✓	

(2 marks)

(b) Identify to which body the internal audit function primarily reports.

Body	✓
The external auditors	
The shareholders	
The audit committee	✓
The government regulator	

(1 mark)

Mock Assessment Answers

(c) Identify whether the following statements about auditing are true or false.

Statement	True ✓	False ✓
The external auditor is appointed by the shareholders.	✓	
An internal audit function is required for all UK companies.		✓
Professional scepticism is a requirement specific to the audit of listed companies.		✓

(3 marks)

(d) Complete the following statement:

The UK Corporate Governance Code is ____GAP 1____ for UK companies and aims to try and prevent ____GAP 2____ from abusing their power.

Gap 1	✓
mandatory	
good practice	✓
irrelevant	

Gap 2	✓
shareholders	
company directors	✓
the wider community	

(2 marks)

(e) Identify the type of assurance described in the extracts below.

Extract	Reasonable ✓	Limited ✓
Nothing has come to our attention to suggest that there are any significant fraud concerns.		✓
The financial statements for Rey Ltd give a true and fair view.	✓	

(2 marks)

AUDIT AND ASSURANCE

Task 2

This task is about professional ethics (15 marks)

(a) Identify whether the following statements about the AAT Code of Ethics are true or false.

Statement	True ✓	False ✓
The AAT Code of Ethics relates only to members who are undertaking audit work.		✓
The AAT Code of Ethics is a principles-based approach to ethical dilemmas.	✓	
The AAT Code of Ethics identifies professional honesty as a key ethical principle.		✓

(3 marks)

(b) Identify which TWO of the following threats to objectivity arise from the audit manager leaving ASC to join Wings plc.

Threat	✓
Self-review	
Intimidation	✓
Familiarity	✓
Advocacy	

(2 marks)

(c) Identify which TWO of the following represent appropriate action to take in respect of the audit manager joining Wings plc.

Action	✓
Select members of the audit team who do not know the manager.	✓
Reduce the amount of testing on work completed by the new Finance Director, as you are aware of their competence.	
Perform additional file reviews to ensure appropriate levels of audit work is still being performed.	✓
Resign from the client for a minimum of two years.	

(2 marks)

Mock Assessment Answers

(d) For each piece of work identified, select the potential problem and a course of action that ASC could take.

Piece of work	Problem	Action
Meeting with the bank to secure finance	Gap 1	Action 1
Gaining additional fees from consultancy work	Gap 2	Action 2

Gap 1	
Advocacy threat	✓
Self-review threat	
Intimidation threat	

Action 1	
Reject the work	✓
Accept with safeguards	
No safeguards needed	

Gap 2	
Self-interest threat	✓
Familiarity threat	
Advocacy threat	

Action 2	
Reject the work	
Accept with safeguards	✓
No safeguards needed	

(4 marks)

(e) Identify whether the following statements about the situation are true or false.

Statement	True	False
Speaking to your colleague about this is acceptable as confidentiality does not apply within an audit firm.		✓
ASC are not allowed to audit Wings plc as an employee's family member has a financial interest in them.		✓

(2 marks)

AUDIT AND ASSURANCE

(f) Identify the appropriate course of action if Fly Inc were to become a client of ASC.

Employee details	Ensure not on audit of Fly Inc	Employee must sell shares
Frank, an audit manager in ASC	✓	
Sophie, an audit partner in ASC		✓

(2 marks)

Task 3

This task is about the planning process. **(25 marks)**

(a) Identify whether the following statements are true or false.

Statement	True	False
Materiality must be expressed as a percentage of profit.		✓
Profit-related pay in an entity will increase the inherent risk in the audit.	✓	
Working papers can be in a variety of forms, both electronic and paper-based.	✓	

(3 marks)

(b) Identify whether the following situations lead to higher or lower audit risk.

Situation	Higher risk	Lower risk
The company operates in a complex, technical industry.	✓	
This is the first audit that the audit firm has performed in the industry.	✓	

(2 marks)

Mock Assessment Answers

(c) (i) Discuss the audit risks surrounding property, plant and equipment. **(4 marks)**

(ii) Explain the audit procedures to be performed over property, plant and equipment. **(6 marks)**

(iii) Discuss any specific risks identified in the individual casinos and explain any audit procedures to be performed. **(10 marks)**

Audit risks surrounding property, plant and equipment
Indicative content (1 mark per point)
• There is a risk that items have been incorrectly capitalised as additions in respect of the new casino.
• As the project is over budget, there is a risk that some of the expenditure was not approved, leading to a potential fraud concern within the business.
• There is a risk that some of the repairs to the bingo halls have been incorrectly capitalised instead of being expensed.
• There is a risk that some of the bingo hall property values may be overstated due to the poor condition of the assets.
• There is a risk that the disposal of the bingo halls have not been correctly dealt with, leading to an incorrect gain or loss on disposal.

Audit procedures to be performed around property, plant and equipment
Indicative content (1 mark per point):
• Obtain a breakdown of the expenditure on casino 4 and examine if all costs meet criteria for capitalisation as property, plant and equipment.
• Investigate the budget overspend and obtain evidence that additional expenditure was authorised at an appropriate level.
• Obtain evidence of the criticism of the bingo hall premises and the results of any inspections which may have been performed during the year.
• Obtain a breakdown of the amounts spent on repairing the bingo halls and ensure any repair costs are expensed rather than capitalised.

AUDIT AND ASSURANCE

- Consider using an external property expert to value the bingo hall properties to determine whether they are overvalued.

- Inspect the sales agreements for the disposed bingo halls and match the proceeds to those recorded in the financial statements.

- Recalculate any gain or loss on disposal using the sales proceeds from the contractual agreements.

- Enquire about the company's depreciation policy and recalculate the depreciation to see if this is in line with expectation.

Specific risks and procedures on individual casinos

Indicative content (1 mark per point, maximum 3 for any one casino)

Casino 1

- Casino 1 has margins in line with the industry, as it has a net profit margin of 20% so there are no obvious concerns over unusual items.

- Casino 1 will have a material cash balance on its premises (41,200 × 14/365 = £1.6m) so there is a risk that this could be misstated.

- A count of the physical cash balance at Casino 1 should be performed at the year-end.

Casino 2

- Casino 2 has a net profit margin of 13.3%, below the industry.

- We should review the costs in Casino 2 to see if it has unusual property costs or staffing costs as these could change depending on the geographical nature of the business.

- The margin generated by the machines in Casino 2 should also be investigated to see if there is a potential error or fraud here.

Casino 3

- Casino 3 has a different business activity so it is expected to have a different margin.

- Obtain a breakdown of the events run in Casino 3 and any contracts which support the TV revenue generated.

- Obtain a list of ticketed sales and confirm a sample of sales through the bank statement.

- For the large events, select a sample of payments made and agree to a supporting invoice, ensuring this is correctly recorded as an expense.

Casino 4

- This seems to have an unusually large margin of 31.6% which suggests a risk that items have not been appropriately accounted for.

- This supports the earlier risk that expenses may have been incorrectly capitalised as part of property, plant and equipment.

- Even though Casino 4 has only generated £19.3m in revenue, it has only been open since 1 October so this represents 92 days. Therefore, the expected cash balance is £2.9m, which is material.

- A count of the cash on site should be performed.

- As this is a new site, a thorough review of controls on the site should be performed, particularly due to the high-risk nature of cash transactions being fraudulent.

AUDIT AND ASSURANCE

Task 4

This task is about procedures for obtaining sufficient and appropriate audit evidence. **(20 marks)**

(a) Identify whether the following situations will lead to an increase or decrease in sample sizes to be chosen.

Situation	Increase in sample size ✓	Decrease in sample size ✓
The detection risk needs to be low.	✓	
Controls are working effectively.		✓

(2 marks)

(b) Identify which of the financial statement assertions are being tested by each of the substantive audit procedures below.

Audit procedure	Existence ✓	Completeness ✓
Selecting inventory from the warehouse and tracing it to the inventory listing.		✓
Selecting items from the non-current asset register to physically verify.	✓	
Selecting goods received notes prior to the year-end to confirm they are included in the liabilities balance.		✓
Selecting inventory from the inventory listing and traces them to the warehouse location.	✓	

(4 marks)

Mock Assessment Answers

(c) For each of the procedures listed below, identify whether it is a test of control or a substantive procedure.

	Substantive procedure ✓	Test of control ✓
Observing cash being received from a trade receivable balance post year-end.	✓	
Inspecting a bank reconciliation for evidence of authorisation.		✓

(2 marks)

(d) (i) Discuss the likely impact that the Financial Controller's absence will have on the audit approach. **(3 marks)**

(ii) Outline the audit procedures that you will perform over the inventory balance of Shep Ltd. Your tests should specifically cover how you intend to assess the existence, valuation and completeness of inventory. **(9 marks)**

Impact of absence
Indicative content (1 mark per point)
• The absence of the Financial Controller will mean that the controls are unlikely to have been operating effectively.
• This means that tests of controls are unlikely to be a good way to test items, due to the lack of authorisation and reviews.
• The best approach will therefore likely be to have a greater focus on substantive audit procedures.
• This means that there will be an increased focus on the detailed testing of the year-end balances, with larger sample sizes being selected.
• It may also mean that audit team members with more experience should be selected due to the increased risk of errors brought about by the lack of controls.

Approach for testing inventory

Indicative content (1 point per procedure)

- It is essential that we attend both inventory counts, as both are likely to involve a material amount of inventory.
- At the inventory counts, we should examine the procedures used to count the inventory to assess their effectiveness.
- As Shep Ltd sell two distinct types of inventory, we should ensure we perform test counts over both inventory lines.

Completeness tests:

- Perform test counts over a sample of items. We should select a sample of goods from the warehouse floor to trace back to the inventory sheets in order to test for the completeness of inventory.
- Enquire with management as to whether any goods were in transit on 31 December. If there are, we should get details of these to ensure they have been taken into account. The risk of misstatement will be higher in the case of larger deliveries.

Existence tests:

- Select a sample of goods from the inventory sheets and trace back to the warehouse floor in order to verify the items exist.

Valuation tests:

- Review a sample of both the food and equipment items and trace the raw materials back to purchase invoices.
- Review the allocation of overheads included within the product to confirm these have been done on a reasonable basis.
- During the count, we should look for signs of food items that have not been stored correctly, as these may need to be written down or written off (i.e. net realisable value lower than cost).
- During the count, we should look for signs of damaged kitchen equipment which could suggest that the net realisable value could be lower than the cost.
- Following the inventory count, we should review the aged listing of inventory to assess if anything needs to be written down. This will be a greater risk in terms of the food products, which are likely to be perishable.
- Inspect a sample of post year-end sales to see if any items are being sold below cost.

Mock Assessment Answers

Task 5

This task is about procedures for obtaining sufficient and appropriate audit evidence. **(15 marks)**

(a) **Complete the following statement:**

Appropriate evidence is _____GAP 1_____ when it meets one of the financial statement _____GAP 2_____

Gap 1	✓
understood	
correct	
relevant	✓

Gap 2	✓
assertions	✓
characteristics	
qualifications	

(2 marks)

(b) **Identify whether the statements about bank and cash are true or false.**

Statement	True	False
Petty cash must be counted on every audit.		✓
A bank statement is the best form of evidence for a cash balance.		✓
The auditors should test the bank reconciliation but not produce the bank reconciliation for the client.	✓	

(3 marks)

(c) **Select the correct category for the following automated tools and techniques.**

Technique	Test data	Audit software
Inputting dummy invoices into the client system to see if internal controls are working as intended.	✓	
Extracting information and analysing data.		✓

(2 marks)

AUDIT AND ASSURANCE

(d) Match the audit procedure below with the type of verification technique it represents.

Procedure	Verification technique
Contacting a trade receivables balance to confirm the balance owed to the client.	External confirmation
Comparing monthly payroll costs to examine any variances.	Analytical procedures
Examining an invoice to agree the amount to the figure recorded in the financial statements.	Inspection
Reperforming the client's depreciation workings.	Recalculation

(4 marks)

(e) Identify whether or not the following items represent a misstatement in the account balance.

Item	Misstatement	Not a misstatement
A payment made to a supplier was posted against the wrong supplier.		✓
Goods received in December 20X1 were not recorded until January 20X2.	✓	

(2 marks)

(f) Identify whether the following tests will be testing primarily for understatement of overstatement of the account balance.

Test	Understatement	Overstatement
A sample of sales have been selected from the receivables ledger and will be traced to see if there are valid goods despatch notes for each of them.		✓
A sample of physical assets have been selected to see if all items have been correctly recorded on the asset register.	✓	

(2 marks)

Mock Assessment Answers

Task 6

This task is about reviewing and reporting findings and audit opinions. **(15 marks)**

(a) (i) Identify and explain FOUR control deficiencies in the purchases system. **(4 marks)**

(ii) Recommend improvements to the controls in the purchases system. **(6 marks)**

Control deficiencies
Indicative content (1 mark per point)
• Managers can order goods via e-mail, which is an informal system. This could lead to stock-outs in the stores or managers ordering goods that are not required.
• All suppliers are selected by John Shrat. This raises the risk of either poor quality supplies or potentially fraud if John uses contacts that he knows. It could also mean Sparx Ltd are not obtaining the best price.
• Each product has a different re-order level, set by Julie. This leads to the possibility that Julie sets inaccurate levels. This could result in over or under ordering.
• All purchase orders are raised by either Julie or John. As no-one else is involved, both parties could raise orders for goods that are not required or even for fictitious goods.
• If goods are not delivered within 10 days, another order is placed from a different supplier. This could lead to duplicate orders being placed and an excess of inventory.

Recommended improvements
Indicative content (1 per improvement)
• Stores could have automatic re-order levels set, linked to the warehouse system.
• All new suppliers to be approved by two individuals, one of which is not John or Julie.
• A list of approved suppliers could be kept and regularly reviewed against deliveries and quality of goods.
• The re-order levels should be reviewed periodically against the demand for products.
• Any change in the re-order level should need a second level of authorisation so it is not all done by Julie.
• Another manager should be given authorisation for purchases under £5,000 and another director needs to authorise purchases over £5,000 to incorporate some segregation of duties from John and Julie.
• The purchase orders should be given sequential numbers so they are easy to trace.
• Outstanding orders should be automatically raised within the system after 10 days for a manager to contact the supplier.
• The existing order should be cancelled before another is placed.

(b) **Identify whether the above situations will lead to a modified or unmodified audit opinion.**

Audit client	Modified ✓	Unmodified ✓
Spinz Ltd	✓	
Shep Ltd		✓
Sparx Ltd		✓

(3 marks)

Mock Assessment Answers

(c) Identify TWO items below that are reported by exception in the auditor's report.

Item	✓
All sections of the annual report are in agreement.	
Proper accounting records have been kept.	✓
The financial statements are free from material misstatement.	
Accounts agree to the underlying records.	✓

(2 marks)

References

The Board (2023) *IAS 1 Presentation of Financial Statements*. London: IFRS Foundation.

The Board (2023) *IAS 2 Inventories*. London: IFRS Foundation.

The Board (2023) *IAS 16 Property, Plant and Equipment*. London: IFRS Foundation.

The Board (2023) *IAS 37 Provisions, Contingent Liabilities and Contingent Assets*. London: IFRS Foundation.

The Board (2023) *IAS 38 Intangible Assets*. London: IFRS Foundation.

The Board (2023) *IAS 40 Investment Property*. London: IFRS Foundation.

The Board (2023) *IFRS 3 Business Combinations*. London: IFRS Foundation.

References

INDEX

A

Accounting
  estimates, 212
  systems, 15, 45

Accruals, 205, 207

Accuracy, 94, 124

Adverse opinion, 250, 262, 263

Analytical procedures, 47, 69, 70, 91, 98, 110, 111, 113, 115, 117, 123, 172, 173

Appointment of auditors, 271, 275

Artificial intelligence, 81

Assurance, 2, 3, 9, 292

Audit
  approach, 47, 52, 56, 61, 70, 72, 87
  committees, 286, 309, 314, 315
  evidence, 91, 92, 94, 96, 97, 117
  objectives, 95, 101
  planning memorandum, 47, 55
  programme, 129, 143, 144
  quality, 80
  risk, 47, 56, 58, 61, 62, 63, 65, 69, 71
  sampling, 91, 99, 100, 101, 102, 103, 117
  software, 33, 46
  trail, 31

Auditor's
  removal, 277
  report, 2, 3, 4, 11, 234, 237, 243, 248

Automated tools and techniques, 32

B

Bank
  confirmation letter, 189
  reconciliation, 188, 193, 200

Big data, 78

Block sampling, 107

Blockchain technology, 82

C

Capital reserve, 222

Cash and bank, 170, 196

Circularisation procedures, 169

Classification, 158, 204
  and understandability, 94, 124

Cloud computing, 83

Cold review, 313

Companies Act 2006, 3, 6, 16, 238, 239, 240, 243, 244, 258, 260, 261, 264, 272, 279, 280, 308, 310

Companies Act, 6, 51, 57, 66, 219, 220, 221, 271, 272, 273

Completeness, 93, 124, 158, 159

Completion, 233, 234, 236, 237, 251

Comply or explain principle, 283

Computation, 98, 122

Computer environment, 29

Conclusions Relating to Going Concern, 246

Confidentiality, 57, 295, 296

Continuous stocktaking, 132, 151

Control
  account, 171
  environment, 16, 26, 28
  procedures, 27, 28
  risk, 62, 63, 64, 71, 72, 102

Corporate governance, 282

Credit transactions, 240

Current
  assets, 153, 154, 155, 156, 157, 161, 162, 163, 167
  audit file, 75

Cut-off, 94, 124, 137, 138, 144, 146

Cyber security, 84

Index

D

Data analytics, 78
Debenture loans, 205, 209
Depreciation, 156, 157
Detection risk, 63, 103
Difference between internal and external audit, 324
Direct circularisation, 174
Directional testing, 94
Directors'
 loans, 239
 remuneration, 239
Disclaimer, 251, 255, 264
 of opinion, 262, 264

E

Emphasis of Matter, 265, 266
Engagement letter, 11, 50, 51
Enquiry, 98, 122
Estimates, 212
Evaluation of misstatements, 257
Existence, 94, 124, 157, 158, 159, 160, 162, 165
Expected error, 102, 103, 105
Expenses, 228
External confirmation, 98, 123

F

Financial
 audit, 328
 statement assertions, 93, 95, 111, 113, 114, 123, 125, 127
 statements, 2, 4, 233, 234, 238, 239, 240, 242, 243, 244, 245, 246, 248, 249, 250, 251, 261
Flowcharts, 17, 18, 24
Fraud, 307, 315, 316

G

Going concern, 233, 246, 247, 248, 249, 250, 251

H

Haphazard selection, 107
Hot review, 313

I

IAASB, 9
IAS 1 Presentation of Financial Statements, 335, 336, 337, 339, 340
ICQ, 36, 40
IESBA Code, 308
 of Ethics, 295
IFAC, 298, 299, 300, 301, 302
Income statement, 156, 157, 159, 160, 165, 222, 238
Independence, 292, 321
Independent auditor's report, 258
Information
 processing controls, 30
 technology controls, 31
Inherent risk, 62, 63, 100, 102
Inspection, 97, 122
Intangible non-current assets, 153, 164
Internal
 and external audit, 323
 audit, 15, 321, 322
 audit and corporate governance, 287
 audit function, 328
 control evaluations, 40
 control questionnaires, 17, 35
 control(s), 15, 26, 34, 43
International
 Accounting Standards, 238
 Ethics Standards Board for Accountants' Code of Ethics for Professional Accountants (IESBA Code), 5
 Standards on Auditing, 3, 5, 9
Inventory, 7, 32, 37, 39, 55, 56, 57, 58, 62, 64, 65, 67, 75, 76, 92, 94, 97, 112, 113, 115, 116, 122, 124, 129, 130, 131, 132, 133, 134, 135, 136, 137, 138, 139, 140, 141, 142, 143, 144, 145, 146, 147, 148, 149, 150, 151, 160, 182, 196, 207, 213, 215, 245

L

Letter of representation, 212

Loans, 208

Long-term loans, 208

M

Management
 audit, 330
 letter, 235, 237
 representation letter, 237, 243
 representations, 233, 241

Manual controls, 30

Material
 deficiency, 254
 misstatement, 92, 114
 uncertainty related to going concern, 250

Materiality, 6, 47, 56, 58, 66, 67, 68, 87, 93, 99, 100, 105, 257

Modified, 260, 262, 265, 269
 opinion(s), 62, 253, 262

N

Narrative notes, 17

Negative circularisations, 175

Net realisable value, 131, 142, 336

Non current assets, 115, 116, 124, 153, 154, 155, 158, 163, 182, 220, 222, 263

Non-sampling risk, 105

Non-satistical sampling, 110

O

Objectivity, 293, 294

Observation, 97, 122

Occurrence, 94, 124

Operational audit, 328

Other matter paragraph, 266, 267

Other matters, 255

Overheads, 141

Ownership, 158, 160, 162

P

Patents, 164

Payables, 101, 176, 203, 205, 206, 207, 213, 214, 215, 216, 217, 224, 278, 318

Payroll, 229

Peer review, 314

Performance materiality, 66

Periodic stocktaking, 133, 151

Permanent audit file, 74

Physical or logical controls, 29

Planning, 16, 47, 48, 52

Population, 101, 103

Positive circularisations, 175

Presentation, 158

Professional
 Indemnity Insurance (PII), 309
 scepticism, 44, 45

Project auditing, 328

Provisions, 203, 210

Q

Qualified opinion, 262, 263

Quality control, 307, 309, 310

Quasi-loans, 240

R

Random selection, 106

Reasonable assurance, 5, 7

Receivables, 31, 36, 37, 75, 94, 98, 101, 107, 108, 110, 113, 114, 115, 123, 124, 169, 170, 171, 172, 173, 174, 176, 178, 179, 181, 182, 183, 184, 185, 186, 187, 200, 206, 218
 circularisations, 169

Recognised Supervisory Bod(ies), 274, 309

Representation letter, 235, 237, 241, 243, 244

Research and development, 165

Reserves, 220

Index

Retained earnings, 222

Revaluation reserve, 221

Revenue, 228

Review procedures, 312

Rights and obligations, 94, 124

Risk
   map, 27
   matrix, 27

Roles of internal audit, 326

S

Sample size, 102, 104

Sampling
   risk, 102, 103, 104, 105, 109, 110
   units, 101

Segregation of duties, 29

Share
   capital, 203, 218, 219, 220, 221, 223
   premium, 221

Social and environment audit, 329

Statement of
   financial position, 4, 54, 62, 75, 130, 151, 154, 156, 159, 160, 163, 175, 187, 218, 238, 279, 281
   profit or loss, 279, 281

Statistical sampling, 109

Stocktake, 129, 130, 132, 135, 144, 146, 151

Stratification, 103

Stratified sampling, 107

Subsequent events, 212, 213

Substantive
   procedures, 72, 92, 93, 95, 96, 101, 102, 104, 105, 106, 109, 111, 113, 114, 116, 135, 206, 228, 229
   tests, 71

System of internal control, 26, 34

Systematic selection, 106

T

Tangible non-current assets, 153, 154, 155, 158, 160, 161

Technology, 80

Test data, 33, 46

Tests of control, 16, 42, 43, 71, 72, 92, 93, 96, 101, 102, 104, 105, 106

The engagement letter, 47, 50, 51

The expectation gap, 8

Tolerable error, 102, 103, 105

Tort, 307, 308

Trade
   marks, 164
   payables, 205, 206, 213, 214, 215, 216, 217

True and fair view, 2, 3, 5, 6, 13, 260, 261, 263, 264

U

Uncertainties, 265, 266, 268

Unmodified, 263, 266, 268
   opinion, 62, 258, 253

V

Valuation, 94, 124, 130, 155, 156, 158, 159, 160, 163, 337

Value for money audit, 329

W

Walk-through test, 25

Working papers, 73, 74, 76, 233, 234, 235, 236

Work-in-progress, 130, 140

Written representation, 244